Nathaniel Marshman Williams

Commentary on the epistles of Peter

Nathaniel Marshman Williams

Commentary on the epistles of Peter

ISBN/EAN: 9783337729189

Printed in Europe, USA, Canada, Australia, Japan

Cover: Foto ©Lupo / pixelio.de

More available books at **www.hansebooks.com**

COMMENTARY

ON THE

EPISTLES OF PETER.

BY

NATHANIEL MARSHMAN WILLIAMS, D. D.

PHILADELPHIA:
AMERICAN BAPTIST PUBLICATION SOCIETY
1420 Chestnut Street.

PREFACE.

This attempt to expound the Epistles of Peter and the Epistle of Jude is the attempt of one who has spent life chiefly in the work of a preacher and pastor, not in the work of a professional exegete. Such a mode of life ought, perhaps, to have deterred from the attempt. But, however that may be, the writer may be permitted to say that, while aiming to adapt the work to the wants of the people, he is not without hope that some of his brethren in the ministry, who, though not exegetes by profession, have been more or less accustomed to the study of the Greek, may find at least something to aid, even them, in the better understanding of these remarkable Epistles. In his treatment of the very difficult, and, as he cannot but think, greatly misunderstood passage concerning the preaching of Christ to the spirits in prison, he acknowledges his indebtedness to S. C. Bartlett, D. D., President of Dartmouth College, for what manifestly is the true view of the Greek. Owing to what has been denominated "the new movement" in theology—so far as that movement pertains to the subject of a second probation—this part of Peter's First Epistle (3 : 18-20) is worthy of very careful study. Another topic now commanding much interest is the relation of wives to their husbands, and upon this the writer has ventured to express some general thoughts, besides endeavoring to educe the meaning of the verses bearing upon the subject. It is an interesting fact, that of the two apostles who have given practical precepts concerning the relation of husband and wife, the one was married and the other was unmarried. Sarcastic allusions to Paul's bachelorship are, therefore, less worthy of the source from which they flow. Here Paul the unmarried and Peter the married are one. In the Introduction to the Second Epistle of Peter will be found a brief consideration of the question recently sprung upon the attention of Christian scholars by Rev. Edwin A. Abbott, D. D., of England. It is claimed that a comparison of the Second Epistle with the writings of Josephus yields a new and unanswerable argument against the authority of the Epistle. It is a question of much importance, and will undoubtedly receive a yet more thorough examination.

The conditions upon which this work was to be prepared included preparation, if deemed needful by the writer, of Critical Notes, "as a vindication of the view presented." The writer has conformed to the condition, but, in doing so, has felt that such additional attempts are quite unworthy of being classed under a designation which appropriately means something so much higher.

As this part of "An American Commentary," a work so wisely under the general supervision of President Hovey, goes forth from the hand of the writer, it is his desire that it may not prove to be harmful, even if it fail to be helpful.

N. W. WILLIAMS.

Marshfield, Mass.

INTRODUCTION TO THE FIRST EPISTLE OF PETER.

I. PETER.

PETER, whose original name was Simon (see on 2 Pet. 1 : 1), though a native of Bethsaida, became a resident of Capernaum. His father bore the name of Jonas, or, according to some Greek manuscripts, John. See John 21 : 15, 16, 17, where, in the thrice-repeated question, the Revisers have, in accordance with the Greek of Westcott and Hort, *Simon, son of John*. In Matt. 16 : 17 are the names Simon Bar-jona (Bar-Jonah, in the Revision). Some would translate the Greek, Simon *son* of Jonah. Others take Bar-Jonah as a patronymic, like Bar Abbas, and Bar Timaeus. According to Dr. Schaff, Bar-Jona is a contraction for Bar-Joanna (Chaldaic)—*i. e.*, son of John. As to the name *Peter*, see on the first verse of the First Epistle. Our apostle had a brother who was called Andrew, and that he married is clear from Matt. 8 : 14, where it is said that his *wife's* mother was sick. His wife must have been then living; for in 1 Cor. 9 : 5 Paul makes distinct allusion to her as traveling with Peter. This was as late as A. D. 57, long after the sickness reported by Matthew.

Peter, in company with his father and brother, followed the business of fishing. He was not rich, yet he seems not to have been poor. He was not versed in Greek learning, nor in the learning of Rabbinic schools; yet there is no reason to doubt that he had a respectable share of such knowledge as prevailed among the people. Illiteracy, as known in the United States, in this year of grace, 1888, was not known in Palestine in the times of Christ and the apostles. In Acts he is indeed spoken of—and John not less—as *unlearned and ignorant*, "illiterate and obscure." This is what the rulers and elders and scribes "perceived." These having been educated in Rabbinic schools, were so far superior to Peter; but *unlearned* must not be so explained as to imply that the apostle had enjoyed none of the common opportunities of education. His social position, unlike, for example, that of Nicodemus, or that of Joseph of Arimathæa, was not among the aristocracy of Palestine; he was a plebeian. Amid the perils and toils of his daily life, he inclined to the service of God; for no sooner had John the Baptist made his public appearance, than Peter became interested in his mission, and this prepared him to take a step forward. He became a disciple of him of whom John was but the forerunner. ONE OF THE TWELVE, he was ONE OF THE THREE; for with James and John he shared the special confidence of Christ, and received special instruction. The "close companionship" of men so unlike as John and Peter in natural qualities is worthy of notice. See Mark 9 : 2; Luke 22 : 8; John 18 : 15; 20 : 2-8; Acts 3 : 1; 4 : 13. Each of the apostles had a distinctive temperament, and a distinctive cast of mind; but not one of them stands out in the Gospels with such clearness of outline, and such fullness of detail as does Peter; and, till Paul appears in Acts, no one even in that book is so prominent. It is impossible to mistake him for any other. But his prominence is not that of rank, or of office, but that of spiritual activity. Though he introduced the first Gentile into

INTRODUCTION TO THE FIRST EPISTLE OF PETER.

the Christian Church, and may have been the means of introducing others, yet, acting with Paul upon the principle of a division of labor, he wrought, chiefly, for the spiritual good of Jews.

Of the latter part of Peter's life little is known. He disappears from the history in Acts after the Council in Jerusalem (15 : 7-11) A. D. 50 or 51. Thus, if we reckon from Pentecost, A. D. 33, he is kept before us seventeen years. Paul appears A. D. 36, fourteen or fifteen years before the disappearance of Peter, and remains before us till A. D. 63 or 64, the historian abruptly closing with the report of his activity in preaching while a prisoner in Rome. While, then, it is approximately correct that the former half of Acts is chiefly a record of Peter's labors, and the latter half a record of Paul's, it is an interesting fact that the two apostles, as is clear in the history itself, came into intimate Christian relations, and, contrary to what some have affirmed, lovingly wrought for the same spiritual end. Though Peter is seen no more in Acts after the Council, yet we catch glimpses of him in Paul's Epistle to the Galatians, and in his First Epistle to the Corinthians; and though, as Farrar says, "From his own epistles we learn almost nothing about his biography," we do learn much of his innermost spirit. Tradition makes him to have gone very early to Rome, and to have founded the Roman Church; but, if well sifted, the tradition is found to be chaff. That he went to Rome near the close of life, after the Roman Church was founded, and after the death of Paul, is strongly attested. He suffered martyrdom, and probably about A. D. 67.

The natural and spiritual characteristics of Peter are not less worthy of study than Paul's. His temperament, though not like Paul's, the best, was such as to make him capable of great activity and endurance. It was not the best, for it was such as to expose him to sudden and needless, sometimes very sinful, flashes of feeling; and these reported themselves in explosives of startling force. He was not given to logical thinking, and was therefore not accustomed to draw conclusions. A blow hastily originated, and as hastily aimed, was his common way; yet in most cases he meant well. His Divine Master was sincerely and warmly loved; but failure to see the higher nature of his Master's mission caused him to speak sometimes in words which were more unseemly than the spirit which lay behind them. Of one terrible exception no one needs to be reminded. What may charitably be considered as only faults growing out of his temperament, culminated at last in—

> . . . "the deep disgrace
> Of weakness."

As Longfellow continues—

> "We shall be sifted till the strength
> Of self-conceit be changed at length
> To meekness."

The flashy nature of the apostle became a miracle of continuous energy and boldness, clothed, as shown in his First Epistle, in tenderness and persuasiveness scarcely inferior to John's. After the ascension, one instance of inconsistency with his own principles, and only one, occurred; and, what must be considered as a striking interposition on behalf of the new faith, that did not occur till God had brought into the church one who was quick to see, and bold to resist Peter's vacillation. See Gal. 2: 11-14. In view of our apostle's natural characteristics, it must be said that his spiritual life became such, under the teachings of Christ, followed by the baptism of the Holy Spirit, as to afford

INTRODUCTION TO THE FIRST EPISTLE OF PETER. 7

scarcely less proof of his supernatural endowment than is given of Paul's by Paul's conversion and life.

This sketch of Peter's life would be incomplete without allusion to the apostle's influence in the writing of the Gospel of Mark. The belief that he had something to do in the preparation of that gospel is well founded; but precisely what he did is uncertain, and probably can never be determined. See a discussion of the question in Dr. W. N. Clarke's Commentary on Mark, belonging to the present series—Introduction, "The relation of Peter to this Gospel," pp. 10-12. What proportion of the remarkable vivacity of the gospel is due to Mark, and what proportion to Peter, it would be equally impossible to decide. Little, however, is hazarded in saying that the gospel, compared with the two epistles, and viewed in the light of Peter's characteristics, bears in a marked degree the imprint of Peter's mind.

II. THE OBJECT OF THE EPISTLE.

This is given in 5:12. It was both hortatory and confirmatory. If persecution by the civil power had not yet fallen upon the Churches of Asia Minor, yet there was reason to believe that the danger was not far off; and it is clear that the Christians of that region were suffering from the tongues of those among whom they lived. They needed patience to bear the revilings of the wicked, and faith to meet the coming storm of governmental power. They also needed new assurance that the religion of Christ was divine. The exhortations are enforced by the fact that they had been called by the grace of God, by the fact of the sufferings of Christ, by the nearness of Christ's coming, and by the glory which awaits them in heaven.

III. THE PLAN OF THE EPISTLE.

The plan is not obvious, and therefore is not easily given. The thought advances, but not so consecutively as in some of Paul's epistles. This is less surprising, as doctrinal teaching, which requires argument, and therefore more orderly and condensed thinking, was not a part of the apostle's design. The introduction may be considered as embraced in the first twelve verses, and the conclusion in the last five. Between these parts occur three series of exhortations: the first, pertaining to their own individual life (1:13-2:10); the second, to their relations to others—servants in their relations to masters, wives in their relations to husbands, husbands in their relations to wives, and all in their relations to people of the world (2:11-4:6); the third, to their own individual life again (4:7-5:9). In the last is a commingling of the consolatory. In concluding, the apostle expresses the divine purpose in the form of a promise (see upon 5:10), gives utterance to a doxology, expresses the object of writing the Epistle, sends greetings, and pronounces the customary benediction.

IV. THE CHARACTERISTICS OF THE EPISTLE.

These are not in accordance with the characteristics of Paul or of John. Peter's traits of character and peculiarities of mind are everywhere visible. It is not impossible that such an epistle could have been written by Peter, even if Peter's experience during the Lord's ministry had been different; but it is certain that the Epistle is colored by his experience as it actually was. Illustrations of this will be cited in the Notes.[1] Yet

---

[1] *Horæ Petrinæ*, by Dean Howson, though, as the writer himself remarks, fragmentary, and its subject-matter capable of fuller treatment, is an interesting view of the point referred to.

it is a striking proof of his present greater breadth of religious views and stronger faith in the unseen and eternal. It is characterized by little less originality than the epistles of Paul. Some of the thoughts are found in no other part of the Scriptures, and some are as "hard to be understood" (2 Pet. 3: 16) as anything in the writings of that profoundest of all the inspired writers. While distinctly evangelical, and so far in union with the teachings of Christ and Paul, it is permeated, like the Gospel of Matthew, with the spirit of the Old Testament, as seen in its very numerous quotations. In no respect does it teach views opposed to those taught by Paul. While there were some in that early age of Christianity who said "I am of Paul," and some who said "I am of Peter," neither the one apostle nor the other allowed himself to be the head of a party. The doctrines which Paul taught directly and fully Peter taught indirectly and in part. The exhortations of the Epistle imply all the great doctrines of the Christian faith. The Epistle contains not a trace of assumption of rank over the other apostles. It is simply the Epistle of Peter an apostle, and he seems almost to foretell the bold assumption of the papal power; for, in addressing the elders, he calls himself a co-elder. See on 5: 1. Too much has been made of the admitted similarity existing between some parts of this Epistle and some parts of the Epistle to the Romans, and of that to the Ephesians. Similarities between our Epistle and that of James have also been noticed. The early Christians, not excepting the apostles themselves, would as naturally fall into similar forms of language in expressing the more common thoughts as Christians of our own times. There is nothing improbable, however, in the supposition that Peter had become so familiar with some of Paul's forms of expression as either purposely or unconsciously to use them. Such imitations, conscious or unconscious, may be seen by comparing Mic. 4: 1-3 with Isa. 2: 2-4, and Ezek. 31: 14-18; 32: 18-32 with Isa. 14: 9-19. See the article "Isaiah," in Smith's "Dictionary of the Bible," pp. 1151, 1164. Isaiah and Micah were contemporaneous, and may have heard each other.

V. THE AUTHENTICITY OF THE EPISTLE.

That Peter was the author is undoubted. Many of the writers who followed the apostles, as Polycarp, a disciple of John; Papias, who wrote about A. D. 140–150; the Shepherd of Hermas, second century; the Peshito Version, before A. D. 150; the Old Latin Version, before A. D. 170; Basilides, a heretic of the earlier part of the second century; the churches in Vienne and Lyons in a letter written about A. D. 177; Tertullian, born in the latter half of the second century; Origen, A. D. 186–253; and Eusebius, A. D. 270–340—all awaken the belief, and some give positive proof by quotations, that they were acquainted with the Epistle, and knew it to be the work of Peter.

VI. THE READERS, TIME, AND PLACE.

The persons to whom the Epistle was sent are believed by some to have been Gentile Christians, but it contains strong evidence that they were chiefly Jewish Christians. That some were Gentiles is not improbable. The time, as judged by many, was A. D. 66. It might have been a little earlier. The place in which it was written was Babylon in Chaldea.

THE FIRST EPISTLE OF PETER.

CHAPTER I.

PETER, an apostle of Jesus Christ, to the strangers scattered throughout Pontus, Galatia, Cappadocia, Asia, and Bithynia,

1 Peter, an apostle of Jesus Christ, to the elect who are sojourners of the Dispersion in Pontus,

Ch. 1: 1-12. INTRODUCTION, 1, 2; INSCRIPTION AND SALUTATION.

By an Epistle General is meant one directed not to any given church, but to Christians at large, though not necessarily to all Christians even of the same period. Those here addressed must be presumed to be members of churches. The Greek word for general is *katholike* (catholic). But in the best Greek Testament (Westcott and Hort) is a much shorter title—PETROU A, that is, "First of Peter." Revision: THE FIRST EPISTLE OF PETER.

1. Peter. Instead of standing last, as in modern times, the name of the writer stands first. He uses the name given him by Christ. (Matt. 16: 18.) *Petros* (Peter) is Greek, and means *rock*. In many places *Cephas* is used, which is a Syro-Chaldaic word, also meaning *rock*, and this may have been the name by which the other apostles and Christ were accustomed to address the writer of our Epistle. That Simon *was to be* "called Cephas (which is, by interpretation, Peter)," was declared by our Lord when Andrew brought him unto Jesus. (John 1: 42.) "Thou *art* Peter" was declared by Christ, when at a later period Simon made the ever-memorable confession, "Thou art the Christ, the Son of the living God." The new name expresses both the natural energy and the spiritual firmness for which this apostle was distinguished. But it was applied to him also, because before the conversion of Paul he was to be the chief agent in laying the foundation of Christianity. "Upon this rock I will build my church" refers therefore to Peter, not to Christ, not to Peter's confession. The other apostles, however, though less prominent in zeal and labor, are also the foundation upon which "the saints" are built. (Eph. 2: 20.)

An apostle of Jesus Christ. In mentioning his apostleship, he uses no such confirmatory expressions as are used by Paul in nearly all his epistles—e. g., *called* (Rom. 1: 1); *through the will of God* (1 Cor. 1: 1; 2 Cor. 1: 1; Eph. 1: 1; Col. 1: 1); *not from men* (Gal. 1: 1); *according to the commandment of God* (1 Tim. 1: 1). Reason: Paul's apostleship was called in question; Peter's was not. **To the strangers . . . elect.** In the Greek, 'elect' stands before the word translated 'strangers,' and the Revision has *the elect who are sojourners.* The persons addressed are described as *chosen.* Election is the loving purpose of God to save men. See Matt. 24: 31; Luke 18: 7; Rom. 8: 33. In these passages the adjective is used. The verb is used in the same sense. (Mark 13: 20; John 13: 18; Eph. 1: 4.) The noun *election* is so used. (Rom. 11: 5; 1 Thess. 1: 4; 2 Pet. 1: 10.) Here, as in many other places, it is the election, not of communities, but of individuals. Election should be considered, not so much as a dogma to be believed, as a fact to be felt and rejoiced in. The point of the harmonious meeting of God's in-working and man's out-working (Phil. 2: 12, 13) is as difficult for man to detect in the spiritual world as in the natural, *and no more so.* "It does not follow," says Luther, "that because individuals are elected all will attain the end for which God elected them," and we are referred to 2 Pet. 1: 10. But that passage and the very important words in Heb. 6: 4-6, with others of similar import, teach only the *possibility* of final apostasy; and the warning, for such it is, is to be regarded as a means by which the salvation of the elect is secured. **To the strangers scattered**—more exactly, *sojourners of the Dispersion.* In the time of Christ and the apostles, Jews were widely dispersed in lands more or less remote from Palestine, and this scattered body of Jews was called "The Dispersion." But there were several bodies of the Dispersion; as the Babylonian, the Egyptian, the Roman, the Syrian. See John 7: 35; James 1: 1. Allusions to the Dispersion are found in Acts 2: 9-11. Most of those who heard the gospel on the Day of Pentecost, Parthians and Medes, dwellers in Pontus and Asia, etc., belonged to the Dispersion. It is probable that many of those whom Peter now addresses by letter had heard his stirring words in Jeru-

2 Elect according to the foreknowledge of God the Father, through sanctification of the Spirit, unto obedience and sprinkling of the blood of Jesus Christ: Grace unto you, and peace, be multiplied.

2 Galatia, Cappadocia, Asia, and Bithynia, according to the foreknowledge of God the Father, in sanctification of the Spirit, unto obedience and sprinkling of the blood of Jesus Christ: Grace to you and peace be multiplied.

salem. 'Sojourners,' because dwelling in a country not their own. Jews felt that they were not at home when not in Palestine. In 2: 11 and in Heb. 11: 13, the word is used figuratively, for all Christians are only sojourners in this world; but here the word must be taken in the literal or national sense. **Pontus,** bordering on the Black Sea, was the northeastern province of Asia Minor. On the western side of Pontus was **Galatia,** and on the southern, **Cappadocia. Asia** was the maritime part of Asia Minor, bordering on the Ægean Sea, and included, at least, Mysia, Lydia, and Caria, with Ephesus as the chief city. **Bithynia** was in the northwestern corner of Asia Minor, and was bounded on the north by the Black Sea. As Pontus was nearest Babylon, and Asia the farthest, it was natural for the writer to mention Pontus first and Asia last, if he wrote from Babylon; but if he wrote from Rome, it would not have been natural. These are geographical terms, but "each is the name of a province." (Dean Howson, Smith's "Dict. of Bible.")

2. According to the foreknowledge—in consequence of it as a divine rule. Foreknowledge is not the same as predestination or purpose. "Him being delivered by the determinate counsel and foreknowledge of God.' (Acts 2: 23; compare Rom. 8: 29.) Though, strictly, foreknowledge and election, or foreordination, are each eternal, yet, in our conception, foreknowledge precedes foreordination, or the divine counsel. That is the conception which the apostle here expresses. That they were foreknown only as repenting and believing is neither affirmed or implied. What Peter teaches is that the election was based upon the foreknowledge. God foreknew; and whom he foreknew he elected. God could not be ignorant of his own purpose. (Eph. 1: 4, 5, 11; Rom. 8: 29, 30.) If the men to whom the apostle wrote were saints, they either made themselves saints, or they were made saints by God; and as the change was wrought by God, and as God does nothing without a purpose, he made them saints because he purposed to make them such; and as his purposes can have no beginning, his purpose to make them saints was an eternal purpose. Love was the source of all. Without the love, and the foreknowledge, and the purpose, the salvation of any would have been impossible. Election has too often been preached as mere doctrine: it should be preached as an expression of infinite love. **Through sanctification**—not *through sanctifying.* It expresses a state, not an act; not, 'through,' but *in.* The Greek preposition seldom expresses instrumentality. The meaning is, that they came into and continue in that state of sanctification or holiness of which the Holy Spirit is the ground or source. The Holy Spirit makes those holy whom the Father elects. No holiness without election; no election without holiness. **Unto obedience.** 'Unto' expresses result. The election led to this result: they became obedient. But is not faith the result of election, and obedience the fruit of faith? or, to say the least, is there not "obedience of" (or *to*) faith? See Rom. 1: 5. Peter, as well as Paul, held faith in the highest estimation. (Ver. 5, 8, 21; 2: 6.) It was to him the foundation of all Christian conduct; yet he could sometimes speak freely of obedience without first reminding the readers that faith is the root, and obedience only the fruit. Some think that 'obedience' is here used in so wide a sense as to include faith—faith being supposed to precede all other acts of obedience. The true explanation of the next clause makes this view probably correct. **And sprinkling of the blood**—sprinkling *with* the blood. Notice Peter's familiarity with the Old Testament. His escape, not less complete than Paul's, from Pharisaic bondage to the letter of the Mosaic Economy, is seen in the very use that here and elsewhere he makes of facts which occurred under that economy. Peter saw the spiritual import of the rites instituted by Moses. (The inconsistency which he showed at Antioch, and for which Paul reproved him, was exceptional.) Many things were sprinkled with the blood of animals (Lev. 4: 6; 16: 15, 19), and the people themselves (Ex. 24: 8); and as the blood of Christ was shed for sinners (Heb. 9: 11, 12; Col. 1: 14),

3 Blessed *be* the God and Father of our Lord Jesus Christ, which according to his abundant mercy hath

3 Blessed *be* ¹the God and Father of our Lord Jesus Christ, who according to his great mercy begat us

Or, God and the Father.

Peter addresses the elect as having obtained the precious boon of being sprinkled with the blood of Jesus. The apostle does not deem it necessary to express very clearly the distinction between the atonement and its application through faith; but as he is expressing the results of their election, he must have had in his conception the latter rather than the former. The sprinkling is the application of the atonement made by the shedding of Christ's blood on the cross. In his early Christian life, how unable was Peter to see that Christ must die! (Matt. 16: 22; Mark 9: 9, 10; 14: 47.) This inability led to some of his most unseemly utterances. The accurate and elevated views of the Epistle respecting the Messiah's death show the greatness of the change through which he passed. The evidence of the change is seen as early as the Day of Pentecost. (Acts 2: 23, 24.) **The Father.** The reference to the Father, to Jesus Christ, and the Holy Spirit, though not proving the equality of the three, reminds us of it as taught elsewhere, and shows us the deep interest which Peter was persuaded each had in the salvation of men. **Grace and peace.** Both are gifts; but the latter is the fruit of the former. Grace is the love of God shown toward the undeserving. A being morally endowed who has never sinned, needs no grace. Peace comes from the consciousness of being justified before God. (Rom. 5: 1.) **Be multiplied.** God's grace may more and more abound, as also the peace which flows from it. Whether the salutations and benedictions of the epistles are only expressions of a wish, or are a kind of prophetic declaration, is not in every case easily determined. In Rom. 1: 7, and in some other places, no verb is used; and it is chiefly that which awakens the doubt. Here a verb is used, and in that mood which expresses a wish.

An epistle in the mere salutation of which the writer takes his flight, poised upon the eternal and electing love of God, and quickly sees men rising up new in the Holy Spirit and rejoicing in the atoning blood of Christ, cannot but be worthy of our profoundest and devoutest study.

3. Here begins the introduction proper, which extends through ver. 12. It is pervaded by the most elevated views of God's mercy, the Christian's inheritance, the benefit of afflictions, and the absorbing interest manifested in the work of Christ alike by prophets and angels. **Blessed be.** The Greek has no verb, and an omission of this kind "is very common," Buttmann says, "in all parts of the New Testament." What verb is to be supplied is in question. Some would supply a word which would make the formula expressive of a *desire* that God *may be* praised, including actual, conscious praise by the writer. Others (Buttmann) would supply the indicative (*is*), in which case we should have, *Blessed is the God and Father.* In support of this view is the fact that the Greek of this very verb is found in Rom. 1: 25 ("who *is* blessed for evermore"); and particularly 1 Pet. 4: 11 ("to whom *is* [Common Version *be*] praise and dominion"). The indicative seems to be preferable, though it is a question not easily decided. 'Blessed'—worthy of all praise. Compare Eph. 1: 3-14, between which and this is a deep undertone of inspired harmony, with characteristic variations. **Our Lord**—often applied to the Father as the Supreme Sovereign—is here and elsewhere applied to Christ as the Head of the New Dispensation. He is not here conceived as the Word (*Logos*, John 1: 1), but as the Messiah, in which character he is ever, as here, represented as subordinate to the Father. (Col. 1: 3; Rom. 15: 6; 1 Cor. 15: 24, 28.) Yet we may speak of Christ, even in his Messianic character, as the Word that became flesh. (John 1: 14.) *Our Lord!* is the exultant cry of the elect. **According to his abundant mercy**—in consequence of it. The elect are not begotten in consequence of anything which they themselves do. The preposition indicates that the ground of God's begetting was his mercy. 'Abundant'—God's mercy, viewed as a quiescent attribute, is great; showing it is greater than creating ten thousand worlds. It is the greatest act which God can do. It is an attribute for the exercise of which there is no call, except toward the sinful, and

begotten us again unto a lively hope by the resurrection of Jesus Christ from the dead,
4 To an inheritance incorruptible, and undefiled, and that fadeth not away, reserved in heaven for you,

without this the sinful would remain sinful. **Hath begotten us**—better, *begat us*. It was a single and finished act in the past, which the Greek language was able to express by what is called the Aorist tense. We shall meet with many such instances, which in most cases the Revised Version recognizes, but which the Common Version very often overlooks. Making the sinful spiritually new is one act, quickly wrought, by which the depraved nature is so changed that the subject thenceforth loves the Creator and all that the Creator loves. **Again** puts this spiritual act in contrast with the act by which the readers began their natural life. '**Begat**'—figurative and very expressive. (John 3: 3.) But they were no more begotten into fully developed Christians than they were begotten into fully developed intellectual and bodily life. Regeneration is only the beginning of spiritual life; but if, from the time when it is supposed to take place, there is no growth, nothing can be admitted as evidence that it occurred at all. **Unto a lively hope.** Says Paul to the Ephesians, "Having no hope." This was the sad state of even the most cultivated Gentiles at the birth of Christ. From some of the sepulchral inscriptions came affecting evidence of the hopelessness of man, and from the lips of modern skepticism fall words which echo the inscriptions.

> The weariest and most loathed worldly life,
> That age, ache, penury, and imprisonment
> Can lay on nature, is a paradise
> To what we fear of death.

Blessed with a written revelation, the Jews were the only people who can be said to have had hope of a future happy existence; and their hope had firmness of foundation only so far as it rested on the promise of a coming Saviour. **Lively**—*living, life-producing, and abiding*. It refers, not merely to eternal life as an object of hope, but to the life which accompanies the hope; and this life is blissful even here. A hope with no life would leave us where the Romans were, without a written revelation, and where the Jews were with a revelation while trusting in the traditions which they added to it. **By the resurrection.** Connect this not with '*living*' (living

again unto a living hope by the resurrection of 4 Jesus Christ from the dead, unto an inheritance incorruptible, and undefiled, and that fadeth not 5 away, reserved in heaven for you, who by the power

in consequence of Christ's resurrection), nor with 'begotten,' but with 'living hope.' The living hope into which they were begotten had its ground in the resurrection of Christ. (1 Cor. 15: 13, 20.) The true view of a blissful life for the saints includes the view of a resurrection of the body. The disembodied state, in the comparatively brief period between death and the resurrection, was regarded by the apostles as exceptional and unnatural. The resurrection of Jesus Christ settled the great question of a future re-embodying, blissful state. The hope will not disappoint. (Rom. 5: 5.) Christians are now showing far too little interest in the general resurrection, and too seldom does this crowning fact of Christianity find place in the pulpit.

4. To an inheritance—some say *patrimony*—that is, something the possession of which passed over legally from father to son; and so the kingdom of God may be viewed as a patrimony which fell to the readers as sons of God, as heirs. It is probable, however, that the word is here used in the more general sense of *possession*, chiefly in its completed form in heaven. It is so used in both the Old Testament and the New. (Acts 7: 5; Heb. 11: 8.) The land of Canaan was called the possession of the Jews. These saints of Asia Minor were begotten to a possession—the kingdom of God. How rich were they! Three well-chosen adjectives describe it. **Incorruptible**—God is said to be incorruptible (Rom. 1: 23); the raised body also (1 Cor. 15: 53, 54), while the buried body is called corruptible. The incorruptible possession to which men are begotten is one which is secure from perishing through any essential defect of its own. **Undefiled**—*free from impurity; a holy possession*. **Fadeth not away**—suggested, perhaps, by the fading nature of all earthly beauty. Of the possession, therefore, viewed as beautiful, we may exclaim, as Milton sings of the imaginary flower of the earthly paradise: "Immortal amaranth!" **Reserved**—*kept in store*, not merely stored up, but kept, watched over, so that it may not be lost to us. By this possession is not meant heaven; for it is kept for us in heaven, the latter being viewed not as a state, but as the place in

5 Who are kept by the power of God through faith unto salvation ready to be revealed in the last time.
6 Wherein ye greatly rejoice, though now for a sea- of God are guarded through faith unto a salvation
6 ready to be revealed in the last time. Wherein ye greatly rejoice, though now for a little while, if need

which. In respect to security, the possession is infinitely superior to those earthly treasures which rust can corrupt, and thieves steal; and to gold, which is ever losing weight, and, therefore, value. The value of the saints' possession will forever increase.

5. Are kept—*are guarded*. Though Peter does not here use the same word for "kept" (reserved) as in ver. 4, yet the idea is nearly the same. The possession is kept for those begotten, and those begotten are guarded for the possession—double security. The saints not kept, the possession would go unpossessed; the possession not kept, the saints would find themselves begotten to eternal poverty. See a military use of the word "kept" in 2 Cor. 11: 32. God watches over us and guards, and so keeps us. **By the power of God.** The Greek preposition for *by* is used here also (*εν, in*). We are kept *in* the power of God, in that the power of God is the element in which we are kept. God, as the God of power, is the cause of the keeping, and the cause becomes effective by our being in it. But we are not kept irrespective of a given mental constitution. God honors his creative wisdom by requiring the use of our free will. (Phil. 2: 12.) **Through faith**—*by means of* faith. Faith is twofold—the assent of the intellect and the trust of the heart; more briefly, assent and trust. One may have the former (James 2: 19.) without the latter; one cannot have the latter without the former. For many instructive illustrations of faith, see the Old Testament; and see Heb. 11 for the same facts grouped and condensed. Faith in God comprehends faith concerning all that he has revealed to us, whether in matter or in mind; all that he has promised, and all that he has required; and therefore it includes, as of surpassing importance, faith in his Son, Jesus Christ, as the infallible Teacher, the Almighty Worker, the propitiating Redeemer. He who desires to be saved should not be unwilling to believe; and he who is unwilling to believe gives little evidence of sincerity in desiring to be saved. See on the word "believe," ver. 8. **Unto salvation.** Connect this neither with 'begotten,' in ver. 3, nor with 'faith,' but with 'kept.' We are kept unto salvation.

Salvation is the end, God's great mercy (ver. 3) the ground, and faith the means. Salvation is here used in a broad sense, including deliverance from sin and punishment, and the attainment of holiness and bliss. It may be synonymous with 'inheritance' in ver. 4; only there the apostle's heart glows with the *nature* of the possession, as is clear from the adjectives he employs. From the first word to the word 'salvation,' this verse is a clear echo of Peter's experience; and many such echoes shall we hear as we advance through the Epistle. See Luke 22: 31, 32. Peter himself was kept in the early part of his Christian life through faith, his faith being the fruit of his Master's prayers. "When once thou hast turned again, confirm thy brethren." (Luke 22: 32, Rev. Ver.) This Peter is now faithfully doing, and will continue to do throughout the Epistle. **Ready**—in the plan and purpose of God. **To be revealed**—to be brought out yet more distinctly to their apprehension, and especially to become their actual and conscious possession. "A *present* salvation" is a form of words quite current among some, and expresses a Scriptural fact; but salvation in its completed form does not become the believer's till 'the last time.' **The last time.** Much difference of opinion has been awakened concerning this phrase. See "the last day" (John 6: 39, 40, 44, 54; 11: 24; 12: 48); "the last days" (Acts 2: 17; 2 Tim. 3: 1; James 5: 3); "these last days" (Heb. 1: 2); "these last times" (1 Pet. 1: 20); "the last time" (1 John 2: 18); "the end" (1 Cor. 15: 24). *"The last days"* (in Peter's Pentecostal address) undoubtedly covers the entire Christian Era. The days of that period are called "the last," because the period was "the world's last great moral epoch." (Dr. H. B. Hackett, "Commentary on the Acts," belonging to the present series.) The words before us cannot refer to the entire period of the Christian Economy, but to the end of it. How soon the last day was to come is not affirmed. Huther says: "The entire manner of expression indicates that he hoped it was near." (4: 7.) But concerning the question, see more on 4: 7.

6. Greatly rejoice—not, *will* rejoice, for the verb is not used in a future sense.

son, if need be, ye are in heaviness through manifold temptations:

7 That the trial of your faith, being much more precious than of gold that perisheth, though it be tried with fire, might be found unto praise and honour and glory at the appearing of Jesus Christ:

7 be, ye have been put to grief in manifold trials, that the proof of your faith, *being* more precious than gold that perisheth though it is proved by fire, might be found unto praise and glory and honour at the

Wherein refers not to "the last time," but to the fact of being kept. The writer may also have in his eye the fact mentioned in ver. 4. 'Greatly rejoice' is the translation of one word in the Greek, and that expressive of joy very intense. A milder word could have been used; but it was not like Peter to express himself weakly, and notwithstanding their trials the readers' state of mind required the stronger word. Here is no exaggeration (Peter had long ago thrown off that habit), though some find it difficult to see how Christians can justly be described as exultant when "put to grief in manifold trials." (Revised Version.) But see the yet stronger representation in ver. 8. The face of the statue of a distinguished American of the last century was at first thought by some imaginative minds to smile on the one side, and to wear a serious aspect on the other. It is certain that Paul and his companions were sorrowful, yet were always rejoicing. (2 Cor. 6: 10. See 3: 14; 4: 13.) Sorrow under trials and joy under conscious divine support, and in the certainty of final salvation, are not only possible, but have, even in our own times, many signal illustrations. **Now for a season**—*for a little time.* Great as it is, the joy is accompanied by, or occasionally intermitted by, sorrow. 'Now' cannot refer to the entire life, though even that compared with eternity would be 'a little time'; but it refers to the brief period of trials through which they are passing. The apostle here also would confirm his brethren by speaking of the brevity of their sorrow. **If need be.** This modifies 'ye are in heaviness.' God may see it to be *necessary* that ye sorrow. **Temptations**—*trials*, chiefly oppositions by the wicked, whether persecutions by the civil power or slander (2: 12), and the difficulties to which these led, as poverty, or disarrangement of business. **Manifold**—*of various kinds.* They are called 'temptations,' not in the special sense of enticements to sin (James 1: 13), but in the sense of proofs or tests. A word signifying temptation, instead of a word meaning test, was preferable, because the afflictions were really permitted for the purpose of putting their faith to a sufficient strain to prove its genuineness, and to make it stronger. See the instructive language, 4: 12. Complaining under trials is proof that the complainer needed them, and that a few more might not be amiss. **Through** —*in* is better, as in the Revised Version.

7. The end or object of their trials. **Trial** here indicates not the means or the process, but the result, thus: that the tried or proved excellence of your faith. The excellence was to be proved such by the tests applied. See Rom. 5: 3-5. Strong tests, great faith. Temptation, therefore, in the sense of test, ought not to expose to criticism, as it often does, those to whom it is applied. It may prove them to be objects of special love (Job 42: 10, 12; Heb. 12: 6. 7), while their critics may deserve to be visited with special displeasure. (Job 42: 7.) **Much more precious.** Faith? or faith as proved to be excellent? The latter. The end of their trials is, that the proved excellence of their faith may be found more precious than gold—not '*of* gold,' as in the Common Version. See Job 23: 10; Jer. 9: 7. **That perisheth.** Tested faith is contrasted with gold. The latter is perishable. Its nature is such that it will perish. The former is imperishable (Luke 22: 32), and so we have another echo of Peter's experience—a "reminiscence," Dean Howson might have called it. See his "Horæ Petrinæ," Chap. X., Reminiscences in the First Epistle. **Though it be tried with fire**—*though it is proved by fire*—another quality of that gold with which faith is compared. Gold as well as faith is declared to be tried—*i. e.*, proved, tested. Faith is proved by afflictions; gold by fire. But tested faith is more precious than tested gold. **Might be found**—a significant expression. It is not equivalent to *might be.* It indicates the result of searching; may be found after the searching investigations of the Judgment Day. See 2: 22: "Neither was guile *found* in his mouth." **Praise** and **honor** and **glory**—though *their own*, will be the result of divine working. Contempt and slander were the coin with which the world

8 Whom having not seen, ye love; in whom, though now ye see *him* not, yet believing, ye rejoice with joy unspeakable and full of glory:

8 revelation of Jesus Christ: whom not having seen ye love; on whom, though now ye see him not, yet believing, ye rejoice greatly with joy unspeakable, 9 and ¹full of glory: receiving the end of your faith,

1 Gr. *glorified*.

paid off the elect of Asia Minor; but in the balance of the Last Judgment something will be found on the other side. **At the appearing**—*revelation* or *manifestation*. See ver. 13; 4:13; 2 Thess. 1:7; 1 Cor. 1:7, where the word is used, as here, relative to the second coming of Christ; but when that will occur is not here said. See on 4:7.

8. The apostle's reference to Christ's second coming easily suggests a connecting link between that and the leading thought of the verse—their rejoicing. The link is this: that these Christians of Asia Minor, living far from the scene of Christ's labors, had had no personal acquaintance with Christ. **Whom having not seen**—better, as in the Revision, *not having seen*. Sight is supposed by many to be necessary to the awakening of love. Peter had seen Christ; but he does not teach that love is conditioned upon sight. What the character of Christ was they had learned by the preaching of Paul and others. They loved him, therefore. Personal acquaintance with Christ as a condition of loving him is as needless for men now as it was then. The verse should be carefully compared with John 20:29. **In whom** may be connected with **believing**, or with **rejoice**; the former is to be preferred. **Now** belongs only to **see not**. As implied in the first clause, they do not see him; but in this clause the fact is emphasized that they do not see him **now**. Thus it is implied that they will see him at his revelation. By the conjunctions **though** and **yet** too much contrast is made between not seeing and believing. Some contrast is intended, but not as great as in John 20:20, where a blessing is pronounced upon those who become believers without first seeing. The literal translation is, *in whom, now not seeing, but believing*. The readers having never had an opportunity to see Christ according to the flesh, Peter reminds them that their state is one not of seeing, but of believing. Such has been the state of nearly all who have become believers—that is, nearly all who have believed, have believed by means of testimony. **In whom believing.** In the New Testament sense, *to believe* is much more than *to give credit to*, which was the sense as used by common Greek writers. When Christ came, the Greek word took on a new meaning. To believe on (*in*) Christ is to rely on him as being, being to us, all that he professes to be. It is *to resign one's self unto Christ*. **Ye rejoice**—*ye exult*. The same intense word that is used in ver. 6 is here made by the translators, in consequence of the words which follow, unnecessarily weaker. Some, thinking that these afflicted Christians could not so rejoice, insist that the verb, though in the present tense, must be taken as a future; but as in ver. 6 so here the apostle describes present joy. See on ver. 6. **Unspeakable**—joy which cannot be expressed, or, perhaps, cannot be exhausted, in words. **Full of glory**—literally, *glorified*. In its completed degree, it is to be referred to heaven, but foregleams of it are often to be seen here. The joy of the world is anything but glorious. How often is the joy of the world assumed for the purpose of hiding sorrow! The joy of irrational animals is never assumed.

REMARKS.

No English reader should be surprised to learn that, like the manuscripts of all other books which have descended from antiquity, those of the Bible, made by hand before printing was invented, contain *variations of reading*, so called. That is to say, one manuscript *varies* from another in the spelling, or the omission, or the place, of a word. Most of these variations are very slight, as a long vowel in one manuscript, and a short one in another; one kind of accent in one, and another kind of accent in another; an adjective preceding its noun in one, and following it in another. A word, and even many words, may be found in one manuscript which are wanting in all the others. The Greek and Roman classics contain far greater variations than the Bible. Shakespeare's plays give evidence, in the notes of editors and commentators, of much more serious variations of reading than the New Testament, though the former were written less than three hundred

9 Receiving the end of your faith, *even* the salvation of *your* souls.
10 Of which salvation the prophets have inquired and

10 *even* the salvation of *your* souls. Concerning which salvation the prophets sought and searched dili-

years ago. The folio edition of Othello (1623), for example, "contains one hundred and sixty-three lines which are not found in the quarto" (1622), and "there is a quarto edition of 1630 which differs in some readings from both of the previous editions." Speaking of Lear, an editor says: "Large passages which are found in the quartos are omitted in the folio; and some lines are found in the folios which are not in the quartos; and these are, for the most part, essential to the progress of the action, or to the development of character." There are no less than four different readings of the eighth line of Macbeth. It must be attributed to the ever-watchful providence of God that the principal manuscripts of the New Testament, so many hundred years older than the writings of Shakespeare, vary so little that not a doctrine taught by Christ or his apostles has been put in jeopardy. Learned and pious men have done a work for which all men should be grateful, in examining and comparing them, that the correct reading may be ascertained. It may be added that many of the most valuable manuscripts, including the four oldest, were "entirely unknown" to King James' translators.[1] Now that they are known, the importance of thoroughly examining and comparing them, that a more correct Greek text, and from that a more correct English Bible, may be obtained, is obvious. (See Crit. Notes.)

9. Receiving—receiving as a prize. Those who make the rejoicing future make the receiving future. But the **end,** the consequence or result, of their faith is received in this life. The participle in the Greek is the present. Yet doubtless Peter intends to remind them that they receive the completed end, the *end ended,* and that can be realized only at the second coming of Christ. (ver. 5.) **Faith ... salvation.** So divine a beginning "must needs" have so divine an end—'Salvation.' See on ver. 5. The frequency with which Peter refers to the result of all trials and all joys shows the strength of his conviction and the intensity of his feelings concerning that particular point. Let us in this respect be like him. **Your souls**—literally, *souls.* There is no Greek for 'your.' Not to the exclusion of the deliverance of the body from imperfection (Rom. 8: 23), but only the soul is specified because it is the chief part of that which is benefited by the work of Christ.

10-12. The swift but untired wing of the apostle, bearing the spirit forward to the glorious end, is not thereby unfitted to fall back to the earth, and to touch once more the soil of Israel. For the very purpose of throwing a brighter halo around the future, the writer takes us back to the past, as if even from the ministration of death some rays of glory might be gathered which will brighten the ministration of the Spirit. (2 Cor. 3: 7, 8.) This closing part of the Introduction contains three chief thoughts: That prophets showed the deepest interest in the salvation mentioned (ver. 10); that their interest centred around the question of the time when the Messiah's sufferings and glories were to occur (ver. 11); that they were informed by revelation that the great things upon which they were engaged were not for themselves, but for men of future times (ver. 12). These points are presented, especially in the original, with an energy of style characteristic of our apostle.

10. Of which—*in respect to which.* The **prophets**—rather, *prophets.* He refers to prophets as a class. In striking accord is this representation by Peter with what he had heard, "privately," with other disciples, from his Divine Teacher. See the very interesting passage in Luke 10: 23, 24, of which the words before us are an echo—a "reminiscence." It need not be said that the apostle refers only to *good* prophets, for it is clear that Peter proceeds upon the assumption that prophets were good men. A bad man, as Balaam (2 Pet. 2: 15). might give utterance occasionally to a prophecy concerning some one thing (John 11: 51, 52); but those who were prophets by profession were called to their work by divine prompting and were good men. A prophet, in the Old Testament sense, was one who received communications from God and declared them to others. This might or might not be in the form of prediction.

---

[1] *Revisers;* for the Common Version was in no proper sense a translation.

searched diligently, who prophesied of the grace *that should come* unto you:

11 Searching what, or what manner of time the Spirit of Christ which was in them did signify, when it testified beforehand the sufferings of Christ, and the glory that should follow.

12 Unto whom it was revealed, that not unto themselves, but unto us they did minister the things, which are now reported unto you by them that have preached the gospel unto you with the Holy Ghost sent down gently, who prophesied of the grace that *should*
11 *come* unto you: searching what *time* or what manner of time the Spirit of Christ which was in them did point unto, when it testified beforehand the sufferings ¹ of Christ, and the glories that should follow
12 them. To whom it was revealed, that not unto themselves, but unto you, did they minister these things, which now have been announced unto you through those who preached the gospel unto you ² by the Holy Spirit sent forth from heaven; which things angels desire to look into.

1 Gr. *unto*.......2 Gr. *in*.

One of the functions of the prophets was teaching; but predicting future events was one of the chief characteristics of ancient prophecy. The coming, the sufferings, and death of the Messiah, with the spreading glories of his kingdom, even to victory over all foes, were the most important of all the prophecies. See especially the remarkable fifty-third chapter of Isaiah. **Have inquired and searched diligently**—literally, *sought diligently and searched diligently*. In the Greek both verbs express very earnest investigation of the question before them. Successive generations of prophets concentrating their powers upon any point involved in the work of saving men, is a picture in remarkable contrast with that of men searching for perishable gold. The second clause of the verse may be read thus: *Who prophesied of the grace for you*—i. e., *appointed for* you. It hints at the divine intention. **Grace.** See on ver. 2.

11. **What, or what manner of time**—*unto what*—i. e., unto *what time* (definite future time); or, unto *what kind* of time—time marked by what kind of condition or circumstances. They earnestly sought to know both the exact time and the nature of the time. These two points involved desire to know more of him who was to suffer. They wanted to know more than they wrote, and to understand better what they did write. **The Spirit of Christ.** The Being who was known among the Jews as Jesus the Son of Mary is here clearly assumed to have had existence in the several periods of prophetic inquiry. His Spirit, either his own spirit or the Holy Spirit, was in the prophets. In either case the effect was the same. It was by *the Spirit* that the things were revealed to prophets, and declared to them beforehand. The two facts, that the coming Deliverer was to suffer, and that his sufferings were to be followed by **glory**—rather, *glories*—were not the result of the investigation which prophets made, but of teaching by the Spirit of Christ, and that Spirit is not to be conceived in this case as external to them, and so as merely suggesting the facts to their minds, but as in them. Their entire spiritual being was pervaded by that Spirit, and therefore they knew of the sufferings and the glories. See Rev. 22: 6. "And the Lord God of the holy prophets sent his angel," etc.; or, according to the correct Greek, "The Lord God of the spirits of the prophets"; and see in the Commentary of this series Dr. J. A. Smith's interpretation. **Sufferings of Christ**—sufferings *for* Christ, appointed for Christ. 'Glories.' The glory "of the resurrection, of the ascension, the present session at the right hand of God, of the second advent, and the new creation, and Israel restored, and the church perfected, and the everlasting kingdom." (Dr. John Lillie, "Lectures on Peter.") What prophets longed to know was the more particular fact concerning *the time when*. We are longing to know when Christ's second advent will come; prophets longed to know when the final glory will come; but, like them, we have not the means of deciding.

12. While they prophesied, it was at the same time **revealed** unto them that **not unto themselves**, not for their own good, **but unto us** (*you* is the approved reading), for the good of Christians in Peter's time, and all times following, they **did minister** by *announcing* or *declaring*. Peter speaks from his own standpoint. *He* can see that prophets ministered to the elect of his own time: prophets themselves knew by revelation the general fact that they ministered to persons who were to live in some future unknown time. **The things**—*these things*, as in the Revised Version; the same things which preachers of the gospel have declared, the sufferings and glories of Christ, and whatever particulars are embraced under these general divisions. **With the Holy Ghost—**

from heaven; which things the angels desire to look into.
13 Wherefore gird up the loins of your mind, be sober, and hope to the end for the grace that is to be brought unto you at the revelation of Jesus Christ;

13 Wherefore girding up the loins of your mind, be sober and set your hope perfectly on the grace that [1] is to be brought unto you at the revelation

[1] Gr. *is being brought*.

in the Holy Spirit, that is, by the aid of whose in-dwelling power the gospel was preached to you. **Sent down**—*sent forth.* "Nowhere else," says Lillie, "out of more than one hundred and thirty instances, does the English version add *down* to the meaning of ἀποστελλω," the Greek verb here used. Preaching without the Holy Spirit is "forced work." **Which things.** Again the apostle rises from earth to heaven. **The angels** (omit the article), 'angels,' as well as prophets, though having no personal need of redemption (Heb. 2: 16) **desire**—*earnestly desire.* **To look into.** If the original meaning of the word were allowed to govern the meaning here, the angels are represented as stooping down and looking intently at something. To say the least, they are represented as earnestly desiring *to know* the things referred to in ver. 11. It does not imply that angels are very ignorant of what has been done to save men (Luke 2: 11, 14; 21: 41); but it expresses their strong desire to know all that is possible relative to this most wonderful work of divine love. See the very interesting words of Christ Luke 10: 24. Notice the present tense, 'desire.' They desire now, and they have desired ever since Peter wrote. They are still longing to know more, and are ever learning something new concerning the salvation of men. Why should men themselves be indifferent? In these two verses (11, 12) is striking proof of the *inspiration* of the prophets. See 2 Pet. 1: 21.

Ch. 1: 13-2: 10. First Series of Exhortations.

The introduction is ended, and now begins the first series of exhortations. The former is the doctrinal basis of the latter. In Paul's Epistle to the Romans, the doctrinal basis constitutes the larger part, while here it is the smaller part. Peter and Paul are so far alike that their exhortations spring from doctrine; but they differ in the degree of prominence given to the two parts. While the Holy Spirit was indeed their guide, it is also true that Paul, by his mental constitution, was more given to doctrinal reasoning than Peter. The example of each apostle is a reproof to ministers, so far as they allow their preaching to be wanting in a groundwork of doctrine, and to Christians generally, so far as that kind of preaching fails to awaken their interest.

13. The First Exhortation. **Wherefore**—in consequence of all that has been said. **Gird up**, etc.—*having girded up.* As all who in ancient times were accustomed to wear long, flowing garments would of course tuck them up under their girdles when about to put forth extra effort, as running, so ought the readers—all others as well—to **gird up the loins of** their **mind**—that is, to be ever in a *state of preparation* for the future. **Be sober**—be in that state of circumspection and self-control which will keep you from falling under enticements to sin, to whatever part of your nature they may be addressed. The word was much used relative to wine drinking, but here it has a wider meaning. See 4: 7; 1 Thess. 5: 6. **And hope.** The Common Version conveys the impression that 'gird up,' 'be sober,' 'hope,' are co-ordinate, or equally emphatic. But the first two, in the Greek, are participles: *having girded, and being sober, hope.* In 'hope,' therefore, lies the main thought. Peter has been called the apostle of hope, and Paul the apostle of faith; but neither Peter's view of faith was deficient (1: 5, 21; 2: 7), nor Paul's view of hope (Rom. 8: 24; 5: 4, 5). **To the end**—an erroneous rendering. It should be, *perfectly*—i. e., strongly and constantly, without intermittent doubting. **For the grace**—*upon the grace;* set your hope upon the grace, rest upon it—not upon the grace already given, but upon that ample and richer grace yet to be bestowed. Westcott and Hort, in their Greek Testament, connect 'perfectly' with 'be sober,' but the Revised Version connects it with 'hope.' The latter seems to be preferable; for 'hope' admits of degree more easily than 'sobriety.' **To be brought.** This does not refer merely to the future. The original participle is in the present tense; it is, *even now being brought.* Yet, as is often the case with

Ch. I.] I. PETER. 19

14 As obedient children, not fashioning yourselves according to the former lusts in your ignorance:
15 But as he which hath called you is holy, so be ye holy In all manner of conversation;
16 Because it is written, Be ye holy; for I am holy.
17 And if ye call on the Father, who without respect

14 of Jesus Christ; as children of obedience, not fashioning yourselves according to your former 15 lusts in *the time of* your ignorance: but 1 like as he who called you is holy, be ye yourselves also holy 16 in all manner of living; because it is written, Ye 17 shall be holy; for I am holy. And if ye call on him as Father, who without respect of persons

1 Or, *like the Holy One who called you.*

the Greek present participle, the idea of the future is included. **Revelation of Jesus Christ**—the second coming of Christ. That the words imply belief that the second coming was near is held by a large number of expositors. See on 4: 7.

14-16. THE SECOND EXHORTATION; an exhortation to holiness.

14. As begins a new sentence. The ancient Hebrews sometimes expressed character, not by an adjective, as we are accustomed to do (a cursed man, an enlightened man, etc.), but by a noun, connecting with it another noun meaning *son* or *child*, thus: "children of transgression" (Isa. 57: 4); "children of iniquity" (Hos. 10: 9). This form is found in the Greek of the New Testament, and is called a Hebraism—*e. g.*, "children of light" (Eph. 5: 8); "children of wrath" (Eph. 2: 3); "children of curse"—*cursed children* (2 Pet. 2: 14); "children of disobedience" (Eph. 2: 2). So instead of **obedient children** (ver. 14) we have *children of obedience*. It is a more significant form of expression; for, as was natural in the Oriental imagination, those who are obedient are conceived as having obedience for their mother. (Winer ¿ 34.) This poetic peculiarity is found in the Greek Classics, as well as in the New Testament. '**As**' means, *as becomes*. **The former lusts** —not merely lascivious desires, but sinful desires of whatever kind. **Not fashioning yourselves.** Their former desires were the models according to which they fashioned (*formed*) themselves. **In your ignorance**— in the time of it, and in consequence of it. It was "ignorance of divine things" (Acts 17: 30; Eph. 4: 18; 1 Tim. 1: 13; Rom. 10: 3), and was held to be criminal. So far as the readers were Gentiles, they showed their ignorance through worship of idols; so far as they were Jews, they showed it by overlooking the exalted nature of him whom they professed to worship. According to the model of their former desires, they were not to fashion themselves. The Greek noun (σχῆμα—*scheme*) from which

the verb is derived, expresses "the changing and transitory *fashion* of this world." (Dr. Schaff.)

15. A different translation of this is as follows: *But* [fashioning yourselves] *according to the Holy One who called you, be ye also holy,* etc. **Holy**—morally clean, separate from all moral impurity. It is a source of inexpressible joy that there is one Being in the universe who is not only infinitely holy, but is infinitely above the possibility of ever becoming unholy. The Holy One called them with "an effectual calling"—a powerful motive for being holy themselves. Conforming themselves to the Holy One is not only an outward act; it is also, and chiefly, an inward state. Holiness as a state of heart manifests itself in the external life. **Manner of conversation**— *manner of living*. **All.** No sinful form of life should be indulged.

16. Because—conclusive, and no reasoning can be more conclusive than that which is based upon the divine formula. **It is written.** See our Lord's use of it in Matt. 4: 4, 7, 10. Written in Lev. 11: 44; 19: 2, and many other places in the Old Testament. **Be ye holy**—ye *shall* be holy, according to another and approved reading. Neither the most exact conformity to moral law, nor the most scrupulous attention to the rites of Christianity, will answer in the place of holiness.

17-21. THE THIRD EXHORTATION, not the second expanded.

17. In fear—reverential sense of accountability, allied to holiness (vs. 15. 16), not precisely the same (2 Cor. 7: 1). See also 1 John 4: 18; Phil. 2: 12. **If**—not expressive of doubt, but a significant way of affirming. **Call on the Father.** The Revised Version has, *If ye call on him as Father*. If ye call on him in prayer, say some; but the meaning seems to be this: *If ye call him Father*—that is, If ye surname God Father. (See Crit. Notes.) *God* is the more comprehensive name of the Supreme Being; 'Father' is the less comprehensive; for, strictly, it can be used only

of persons judgeth according to every man's work, pass the time of your sojourning *here* in fear:
18 Forasmuch as ye know that ye were not redeemed with corruptible things, *as* silver and gold, from your vain conversation *received* by tradition from your fathers;
19 But with the precious blood of Christ, as of a lamb without blemish and without spot:

judgeth according to each man's work, pass the
18 time of your sojourning in fear: knowing that ye were redeemed, not with corruptible things, with silver or gold, from your vain manner of life
19 handed down from your fathers; but with precious blood, as of a lamb without blemish and
20 without spot, *even the blood* of Christ: who was

---

by those who become God's children by the begetting power of God's Spirit (1:3). By a very simple figure, therefore, 'Father' may be considered as God's *surname*, a name added to the more comprehensive name. Matt. 10:25 well illustrates the language used by our apostle: "If they have called the master of the house Beelzebub, how much more them of his household?" In the true reading, the Greek verb is the same, and it is evident that Jesus is saying nothing about *invoking* either himself, or his disciples, or Beelzebub. If they *surnamed* (when his enemies did so we are not told, and it is of no importance) Jesus Beelzebub, how much more will they *surname* those who belong to him Beelzebub! If the Christians of Asia Minor call God Father, they ought to reverence him. That God is their Father is a reason why they should reverence him. Though a Father in his nature, he can be an impartial Judge. See Acts 17:31. Yet even in this life God is ever judging. **Work**—the inward, as well as the outward, life. **Pass the time of your sojourning in fear.** The readers are exhorted to a life of fear, not merely to a few distinct acts of fear.

18, 19. The exhortation is enforced by reference to the redemption effected by Christ. **Forasmuch as ye know**—*knowing*, assigns a reason, and the reason should act as a motive. **That ye were not redeemed**, etc. —therefore lead a life of fear—divine logic. **Silver and gold**—the second time Peter has alluded to gold. In ver. 7, it is "gold that perisheth"; here it is **corruptible**. "Silver and gold have I none," he said to the lame man. (Acts 3:6.) See also Acts 8:20: "May thy silver perish with thee." Farrar ("Early Days of Christianity") speaks too strongly, however, in asking his readers to "notice the Petrine *contempt* for dross." Translation according to the order of the Greek: *Knowing that not with perishable things, silver or gold, ye were redeemed from your empty* (fruitless) *manner of life derived from ancestors, but with precious blood, as of a lamb faultless and*

without blemish, Christ. 'Redeemed'—not merely delivered, but delivered by the payment of something, a ransom. 'Derived from ancestors.' The basis was hereditary transmission of depravity, but probably the only reference here is to instruction and example. Such a manner of life was self-perpetuating. But they chose it and loved it. 'The precious blood'—not merely his death, but his blood. This is the ransom by which they were redeemed. (Heb. 9:22.) Christ's *life* is a ransom (Matt. 20:28); Christ himself is a ransom (Tit. 2:14). This the readers *know*. Their conviction of the fact is perfect, and such should be the conviction of the elect in all times. Christ is not the Saviour of men, unless men receive him as a ransom. **As of a lamb.** 'As' is not a comparison of Christ with a lamb. The translation given above shows that *Christ* is in apposition with *lamb*. Lamb designates Christ, not an animal. But why is Christ here called a lamb? Only or chiefly because he bore his sufferings with patience? Only because of his freedom from sin? ("Without blemish and without spot?") He is likened to a lamb by Isaiah (53:7), and apparently for no other reason than that he was patient under suffering. But notice the connection in Isaiah: "The Lord hath laid on him the iniquity of us all." (Ver. 6.) See also Ex. 12, relative to the paschal lamb, and John 1:29. Peter was so familiar with the idea of *sacrifice*, as illustrated in the death of the paschal lamb, that he must have used this word *lamb* to express not only innocence but substitution. See 2:24. **Without blemish and without spot**—*blameless and spotless*, suggested by Ex. 12:5. See our Epistle 2:22; Heb. 7:26. Few persons have the hardihood to deny that Jesus was sinless. In what harmony are Peter and Paul relative to the way of salvation! They are alike in agreeing that men can be saved only by the blood of Christ offered as a ransom. Compare Rom. 3:24, 25.

20. Still keeping his eye upon the duty of living in holy fear (ver. 17), the apostle reverts,

20 Who verily was foreordained before the foundation of the world, but was manifest in these last times for you,
21 Who by him do believe in God, that raised him up from the dead, and gave him glory; that your faith and hope might be in God.
22 Seeing ye have purified your souls in obeying the truth through the Spirit unto unfeigned love of the brethren, *see that ye* love one another with a pure heart fervently:

foreknown indeed before the foundation of the world, but was manifested at the end of the
21 times for your sake, who through him are believers in God, who raised him from the dead, and gave him glory; so that your faith and hope
22 might be in God. Seeing ye have purified your souls in your obedience to the truth unto unfeigned love of the brethren, love one another ¹ from the

---

¹ Many ancient authorities read *from a clean heart.*

---

as in ver. 2, to the eternity past. Redemption was not the result of a change in the mind of God. **Foreordained.** The Greek means *foreknown,* as in ver. 2. Not merely as preexistent was Christ foreknown, but as the Redeemer to come, and that before the **foundation,** or *creation,* of the world. (Eph. 1:4.) **Verily, indeed . . . but.** Notice the contrast. **Manifest**—*was manifested.* **In these last times**—more correctly, after the approved reading, *in the last of the times;* from the first advent to the second. (Heb. 1:2.) See on ver. 5, where "the last time" has a narrower sense. **For you**—*on your account, for your sake.*

21. Like Paul, Peter makes his thoughts roll on in successive clauses, like waves, sometimes seeming to repeat himself, but seldom doing so. Some say that he here gives the *aim for* which Christ was manifested—namely, to awaken within them faith in God; but perhaps he rather intended to *describe* those for whom he was manifested. **Who by him do believe in God.** Not that they believed *before* he came; but for those who believe not, believe not that God raised Christ from the dead and gave him glory, and persist in believing not, Christ cannot be said to have been manifested. In the general sense he appeared in the world for the good of all men; but with *efficacious, eternal results* only for those who believe. 'In God.' They are represented as believing in God, not as Creator, but as the Raiser of Christ from the dead, and as the Crowner of Christ with glory, which is substantially the same as to say that they believe in Christ. The latter is often represented as the *direct* object of faith (ver. 8; John 3: 16; 6: 40; yet see John 5: 24; 14: 1.) **Glory**—by bringing him to his right hand, and there making him the object of worship by angels and saints. (John 17: 5, 22; Eph. 1: 20-22.) **That your faith and hope,** etc. The clause expresses result, not design,

thus: so that your faith and hope are *in (on)* God. Another translation is, So that your faith *is* (has become) also hope in God, which is probably incorrect. Peter's favorite idea, *hope,* is expressed the third time.

22. THE FOURTH EXHORTATION.

22. The first (ver. 13), *hope;* the second (ver. 15), *be holy;* the third (ver. 17), *fear;* the fourth (ver. 22), *love one another.* **Seeing ye have**—*having.* It is not a reason for loving one another, or a way of accounting for the obligation to do so. It expresses, not merely one past act of purifying, but a continuous act ever running parallel with that of loving one another. **Your souls.** The purifying is not external, a sense which the word sometimes has (John 11: 55; Acts 21: 24), but internal. **In obeying the truth**—*in obedience to the truth,* the truth being viewed as the element in which they are continually to purify their souls, not as the instrument by which. 'Truth' is the revelation made in the gospel. Faith, then, is not here overlooked by the apostle. 'In obeying'—*in your obedience.* See on the same word in ver. 2. Faith receives the truth and appropriates it; hence, obedience. **Through the Spirit.** As these words are not well supported by manuscript authority, they are rejected from the text. **Unto unfeigned love.** The preposition indicates the tendency. Inward purifying ever tends to create love toward the children of God. 'Unfeigned'—not manifested for a selfish end. (1 John 3: 18.) The hand and the tongue do not love, but neither do they fail to execute the heart's love. **See that ye**—not in the Greek, and unnecessarily inserted in the Common Version. **Love one another.** Peter is like John in spirit. "Let us love one another," says the latter in his First Epistle. This sweet word of exhortation may perhaps imply greater proportionate growth in Peter than in John. **With a pure heart**—with a heart morally clean. But the Greek word for pure,

23 Being born again, not of corruptible seed, but of incorruptible, by the word of God, which liveth and abideth for ever.

23 heart fervently: having been begotten again, not of corruptible seed, but of incorruptible, through the 24 word of ¹God, which liveth and abideth. For,

1 Or, *God who liveth.*

καθαράς, is wanting in so many manuscripts that it is rejected by many of the best critics. 'From the heart' is more correct. **Fervently.** The word means stretching toward, directed intensely toward the object—an important exhortation, lest they become cold and selfish.
23. Mutual love enforced. **Being born again**—or, better, *having been begotten again.* See ver. 3, where occurs the same Greek word, and where the Common Version is more correct than here. **Not of corruptible seed**—not according to natural law. (John 1: 13; 3:4-6.) **But of incorruptible**—according to a supernatural law, begotten not by man, but by the Spirit of God, or by God himself. (John 1:13; 3:4-6.) **By the word of God.** Some wrongly regard 'the word of God' as the incorruptible seed. But they were begotten *of God*, 'of' indicating *the source* of their new life; but were begotten *by* (by means of) the *word* of God (James 1:18), the truths of the Bible, the gospel. (1 Cor. 4:15.) **Which liveth and abideth forever.** For the last word there is no corresponding Greek in the four oldest manuscripts. More literally, *by God's living and abiding word.* See Acts 7: 38, where 'life-giving oracles' refers to the commands, chiefly the moral law, given on Mount Sinai. But according to Paul (Rom. 8:3; Gal. 3:21), the law was weak, and could not give life. Yet the gospel may be strong and life-giving, even if the law is not so. Besides, the law is called *life-giving*, 'with reference not to its effect, but to its nature or design.' (Hackett on Acts 7: 38, "lively oracles.") But Peter speaks of the *effect* of the word. Paul and Peter, then, are still one, notwithstanding the effort of some to set them at variance. 'Liveth'—not inoperative, not unadapted to serve as means of bringing life to dead souls. The reasonings and exhortations of Plato's "Dialogue Against Atheism" and of his "Dialogue on the Soul's Immortality," though remarkable as productions of a Greek who had no knowledge of the Bible, might be preached in every possible variety of language, and not a human soul probably would thereby be regenerated. Abideth—not transient, but intended for all periods of time, never to be superseded by human philosophy. If the present *form* of the word—*i. e.*, as expressing the special intellectual traits of the several writers—will pass away at "the end," yet *the word of God* will remain. Compare Luke 21: 33. Thus even in heaven it will be our study, with whatever additional word God may there give us. In this life the *form* in which God's truth is enshrined must not be rejected under the pretense of retaining the truth in its spirit. A well-known lexicographer represents a *vase* as "rather for show than for use"; and this expresses the estimate which some put upon the written word. But the vase broken, the contents are lost—for him who breaks it.

A different explanation of 'the word of God which liveth and abideth,' has been given. Some connect 'liveth and abideth,' not with 'word,' but with 'God.' This requires the change of *which* into *who*, and we have, 'Of God who liveth and endureth.' The American Revisers suggested this rendering, and though it was not adopted, 'who liveth' stands in the margin of the English editions of the Revised Testament. In some other passages, prominence is given to the living and enduring nature of the *word*. Compare Heb. 4: 12; Acts 7: 38; Ps. 119: 89; Luke 21: 33. See also ver. 25: "The word of the Lord endureth forever." But there the original word is not the same, and strictly means *saying*.

24. This verse illustrates the nature of God's word by contrasting it with man. For assigns a reason: they have not been begotten by man, 'for' all flesh (*every man*), As **grass**—is so transitory, therefore so weak, that he has no power to impart spiritual life. The words are quoted, with a little variation, from Isa. 40: 6, 8. Isaiah says, "All flesh is grass"; Peter says, 'as grass.' Isaiah says, "Our God"; Peter, 'the Lord.' The New Testament writers did not feel under obligation to make all their quotations with verbal exactness. They seem to quote sometimes from the Greek translation of the Hebrew, called the Septuagint, and sometimes they seem to quote from memory, and

24 For all flesh *is* as grass, and all the glory of man as the flower of grass. The grass withereth, and the flower thereof falleth away:
25 But the word of the Lord endureth for ever. And this is the word which by the gospel is preached unto you.

All flesh is as grass,
And all the glory thereof as the flower of grass.
The grass withereth, and the flower falleth:
25 But the ¹ word of the Lord abideth for ever.
And this is the ¹ word of good tidings which was preached unto you.

¹ Gr. *saying*.

when quoting from memory, they may have in mind the Septuagint, or the Hebrew itself. Their variations from the Hebrew need not cause difficulty; and the student of the Bible should reverentially abstain from acting as censor of the evangelists, and apostles, and of Christ for the variations in question, till he understands much better than any man has yet understood the relation of the free working of the human mind to the free working of the Divine Spirit. **All the glory**—whatever man, in his unrenewed state, regards as specially adapted to promote his own honor, as wisdom, power, riches. (Jer. 9: 23; James 1: 11.) **Withereth and falleth.** The original form of the verb expresses *habitualness*. The grass is accustomed to wither, and the flower is accustomed to fall. Or it may express the necessity and universality of the fact. Grass necessarily or universally withereth, etc. Compare Matt. 6: 29, 30. See Crit. Notes.

25. The word which by the gospel—better, as in the Revised Version, *the word of good tidings which was preached*. The Being referred to in John 1: 1 (the Word, the Logos) is not meant here. Peter alludes much to the Old Testament, but only as it sheds its light upon the coming of the Messiah. He and the other apostles used it, not for Jewish, but for Christian ends. **Preached unto you**—by Paul and others, so that you heard it, and by means of it were begotten to the new life. Thus is enforced the duty of mutual love.

CRITICAL NOTES.—CHAPTER I.

8. *Knowing* (εἰδότες) is rejected from the Greek for *seeing* (ἰδόντες). (Lachmann, Tischendorf, Tregelles, and Westcott and Hort.) Huther, however, in Meyer, says that both words give a suitable meaning; and that as both are sustained by weighty authorities, it cannot be decided which is the original. Bengel and Huther prefer 'knowing' (εἰδότες). On rhetorical ground (variety) one might prefer the former; for then in the first clause the readers would be spoken of as not *knowing* Christ (personally), and in the second as not *seeing* him; but the result is the same in either case. The evidence has increased in favor of the word expressive of sight.

17. If ye *call on* (*invoke, pray to*) the Father. ἐπικαλεῖσθε is held by some as having this sense; this is its meaning in Acts 7: 59; Rom. 10: 12, 13, 14, and many other places. ἐκάλεσαν (*have called*), the same verb without the preposition ἐπί (*on*) in Matt. 10: 25, is rejected by the best critics for ἐπεκάλεσαν, which cannot there mean to *call on*—that is, to invoke or pray to, but *to call* a name *upon*. The preposition both there and here implies the addition of a name to another name. It need not be translated "surname," but that word very well expresses the thought. The Son of Mary bore the name of Jesus, and his enemies added the name Beelzebub. So to the name *God* is *added* the name *Father*. On the passage in Matthew, see Meyer, and especially Buttmann, p. 151, *note*. Trench ("Authorized Version"): "Here, too, it must be confessed that we have left a better, and chosen a worse, rendering. The Geneva had it, 'And if ye call him Father, who,' etc.; and this, and this only, is the meaning which the words of the original . . . will bear." Hackett on Acts 15: 17: *Upon whom my name has been called*—i. e., given, applied to them as a sign of their relationship to God. See James 2: 7. (Do they not blaspheme *that worthy name by the which ye are called* ἐπικληθέν)?

24. ἐξηράνθη (*withereth*) and ἐξέπεσε (*falleth*) are indeed aorists, a tense which, in itself, generally expresses a past, completed act. Winer insists that even here this sense should be adhered to (*withered, fell*), but Buttmann says that the aorist sometimes expresses what is habitual, and "just as well and still more frequently the necessity or universality of an action or state." The gnomic aorist, as it is called, has the sense of the present. See Thayer's edition, p. 201, 1876.

In our study of the chapter, it has been seen that, after an argumentative, doctrinal introduction, ver. 13 begins a series of exhort-

CHAPTER II.

WHEREFORE laying aside all malice, and all guile, and hypocrisies, and envies, and all evil speakings, 2 As newborn babes, desire the sincere milk of the word, that ye may grow thereby:

1 Putting away therefore all ¹wickedness, and all guile, and hypocrisies, and envies, and all evil speakings, as newborn babes, long for the ²spiritual milk which is without guile, that ye may grow thereby

---

1 Or, *malice*........2 Gr. *belonging to the reason*.

---

ations. Of these four have been given. The chapter is one of exceeding richness, and its doctrines and exhortations are as well adapted to Christians of the present time as to those of the apostolic age. The student should not fail to see it as a striking and beautiful portrait of Peter, not merely as "converted" (*turned*) after his terrible denial of Christ, but as one who had grown much "in the grace and knowledge of our Lord and Saviour Jesus Christ." (2 Pet. 3: 18, Rev. Ver.)

Ch. II: 1-10. FIFTH EXHORTATION: *Desire the sincere milk of the word.*

1. Wherefore points to the ground on which the exhortation rests. You have been born by means of the word (1:23); therefore desire the word. You have been exhorted to mutual love (1:22), the child of that new birth which was effected by means of the word, and this implies obligation to lay aside all malice, etc.; therefore desire the word. Laying aside malice, etc., is to run continually parallel with desiring the word. **Laying aside—** *putting off.* It was at first applied to putting off something external, as a crown or a garment, and therefore this is a figurative use of the word. The use of the figure was not intended to teach that the sins mentioned are only external. **Evil speaking**—speaking against a person, backbiting (2 Cor. 12: 20), and so far as they take on words, all other sins are but molds into which the hot passions of the heart are poured. (Matt. 15: 18, 19.) **Malice** (*wickedness* in the Revised Version), **guile, hypocrisies,** and **envies**—too far from being strangers in the hearts of most men to make explanation necessary. So common were these forms of sin in the ancient world, both Jewish and Gentile, that Christ and the apostles gave them no quarter, whatever mercy they showed to the penitent who had been guilty of them. See Matt. 5: 22, 44; 12: 36; 15: 19, 20; Rom. 1: 28-30; Gal. 5: 19-21. To 'lay aside' is the duty of Christians, which implies repentance; to repent is the duty of others, which implies laying aside. The former, addressed to men while impenitent, might lead to a course of self-righteousness.

2, 3. As—as new-born babes are wont to do. **New-born babes.** 'Babes' is here not used in contrast with adults (full age), as in Heb. 5: 13, 14; it is not expressive of special weakness of character, as in 1 Cor. 3: 1; Heb. 5: 13; does not necessarily refer to "those just entering on the Christian life." (Robinson.) The Epistle contains no evidence that the readers had but recently been born again; it contains proof to the contrary. Not 'new-born babes,' but 'desire,' etc., is expressive of Christian character as it should be maintained to the end of life. **Desire**—*long for.* **The sincere milk of the word**—much quoted, but a poor representative of the original. The Greek for 'word,' instead of being a noun, is an adjective, the same as is found in Rom. 12: 1, and there rendered *reasonable*—that is, pertaining to your rational or spiritual part. So here the milk for which the readers are to long is such milk as pertains to their spiritual nature—spiritual milk. 'Sincere' is not a fitting word to describe the quality of *milk;* rather, *without guile, pure, unadulterated.* Long for the spiritual, pure milk; by milk is meant *the word of God.* That word, pure, unmixed with error, spiritual, is the proper nourishment for regenerate souls. For that nourishment we are exhorted to long. As the new-born babe turns with instinctive earnestness to its mother for nourishment, so should all Christians most earnestly desire the word of God. In respect to this longing for God's word, we are to be babes, however old we may be. **Thereby**—not *by means of,* but *in* (ἐν) it; grow in the power of it, grow in the spiritual power which it will minister. **That ye may grow**—the *end* for which they should receive into their souls the word of God. The word may be desired as a means of usefulness, but it is right that one's own growth be the chief end. Not "work and grow," but "study and grow," is the divine direction. Nourish

CH. II.] I. PETER. 25

3 If so be ye have tasted that the Lord is gracious.
4 To whom coming, as unto a living stone, disallowed indeed of men, but chosen of God, and precious,

3 unto salvation; if ye have tasted that the Lord is
4 gracious: unto whom coming, a living stone, rejected indeed of men, but with God elect, [1] precious,

[1] Or, honorable.

your new life with the truth of God's word, or your working will be the child of self-conceit. A blustering and egotistic working shows that the worker needs more milk of the word. "Work and grow" is one of those maxims which has some truth, but much error. See Crit. Notes. **If so be**—'if,' but, as in 1: 17, not a sign of doubt. **Ye have tasted**—*ye tasted*—namely, at your conversion. If ye tasted, as I doubt not you did, that the Lord is *gracious (good)*, long for the spiritual, pure milk of the word. "Taste and see that the Lord is good." (Ps. 34: 8.) In the Hebrew, *Lord* is *Jehovah*, yet Peter does not hesitate to apply it to Christ. 'Tasted.' Compare Heb. 6: 4: "And have *tasted of* the heavenly gift." It is not merely *sipped*, as understood by many Christian people, but it expresses inward experience or enjoyment, very full, possibly. In the New Testament the verb is found in connection with death (Matt. 16: 28; Mark 9: 1), and, of course, cannot mean that the experience of death was slight. Tasting death is full experience of death. So here, to 'taste,' etc., is to have inward experience of the Lord's graciousness. Sipping is quite too common; it makes one weak and thin.

4. The new exhortation (*desire*) and the end (*growth*), lead the apostle to a vivid description of the gracious Lord, and of themselves, as subjects of the new birth. This will quicken their desire and promote their growth. **To whom**—the Lord—*i. e.*, Christ. **Coming**—by faith—*i. e.*, *believing*. Not, *having first come*, and after that *built up a spiritual house* (ver. 5); but the two are to run on together during the earthly life; ever coming and ever built up. Some came to Christ only with the feet; some come only with the head. The coming must be that of the heart; and such coming implies the coming of the entire man. **A living stone.** That the figure was suggested to Peter by his own name (Petros, *rock*) is improbable. He comes to the use of the figure more directly; he comes to it through his familiarity with the Old Testament. The verse is tinged with language drawn from Ps. 118: 22; Isa. 28:

16, yet the words are not a quotation. The severest taste need not be offended at the application of the term 'living' to 'stone.' Christ is life—is the Giver of life. As bread he is the same. (John 6: 51.) Not even while held by the "great stone" of Joseph's tomb (Matt. 27: 60), was he other than a living stone. Living—a little key for unlocking great treasures—a living *hope* (1: 3); the living *word* (1: 23); and now a living *stone*. **Disallowed indeed of men**—*rejected* after being tried. **Chosen.** See on 'elect' (1: 2), and compare 2: 9. Christ was chosen as the Messiah—chosen to his redeeming work and to all its blessed results. (Isa. 42.) Contrast Peter's quiet positiveness of conviction with the exasperated infidelity of the rulers expressed too weakly in that skeptical and semi-hypocritical *if*: "If he be Christ, the chosen of God." (Luke 23: 35.) **Precious**—*honorable*, and honorable because precious; costly. (Matt. 3: 17; Heb. 1: 3, 6. 9; Col. 1: 19.) How the golden music of Peter's word revives the spirit when fainting under earthly fatigues, or when longing for some new consciousness of spiritual life! **Chosen of God**—*elect with God*. It is infinite capacity which so appreciates the excellence of the living stone. How marked the contrast which the apostle makes between God's estimate and man's! Rejected by men! The rejection was foretold by Christ himself (Mark 8: 31); and the severest rebuke of himself which ever fell upon the ear of Peter from the lips of Christ, "Get thee behind me, Satan!" was administered because of his hasty and unseemly "rebuke" of his Master, when the latter announced the certainty of the very event of which Peter now speaks. "The Son of man must be rejected." Peter sees with the utmost clearness that this was to be; and in the blessed consequences resulting, he rejoices. It was indeed love, but love with blurred vision, which prompted the original utterance. His sight was long ago made clear. At a later period of his ministry, Christ spoke of himself as rejected *by this generation* (Luke 17: 25). Isaiah says, Rejected *of men*; and this was the great and fearful fact, that so far as it

5 Ye also, as lively stones, are built up a spiritual house, a holy priesthood, to offer up spiritual sacrifices, acceptable to God by Jesus Christ.
6 Wherefore also it is contained in the Scripture,

5 ye also, as living stones, are built up, ¹a spiritual house, to be a holy priesthood, to offer up spiritual sacrifices, acceptable to God through Jesus Christ.
6 Because it is contained in ²scripture,

1 Or, a spiritual house for a holy priesthood........2 Or, a scripture.

---

knew him the human *race* rejected him—the exceptions were very few. Among the saddest representations of art is that of "Christ Rejected."

5. Ye . . . are built up. Many take the verb as imperative, instead of indicative: Be ye yourselves also built up. The apostle is still filled with the thought of their growth. Not, Be living stones, but be built up **as living stones.** He thinks of them both as individuals, and as individuals connected with each other. He is not thinking of them as organized bodies; for there were many churches there, and he represents them as growing into *one* building. The picture is exceedingly graphic. "Look unto the rock whence ye are hewn." (Isa. 51:1.) Once dead stones in the quarry, now living stones! But the building of which they form a part has this peculiarity, that it is capable of indefinite growth. He does not yet say that the living stone, Christ, is a corner-stone, and that it is that upon which they are to be built. Perhaps the conception is in his mind; for he soon gives utterance to the thought. **A spiritual house**—not the foundation, or even a part of it. See on corner-stone in the next verse. To be built up as a mere house, however large and elaborate—as the Roman Catholic Church, for example, and even some Protestant (National) Churches, is foreign to Peter's view. **Spiritual**—because, being begotten by God (1:3), they may ever become more like the children of God—*i. e.*, more holy. (1: 15, 16.) **A holy priesthood.** In many valuable manuscripts, a preposition (εἰς *into*) stands before these words. Be built up a spiritual house *into*—i. e., for the purpose of becoming a holy priesthood. If 'house' is used for *temple*, the transition to *priesthood* was easy. Becoming a body of holy priests was *the end* to which becoming a temple looked. They were to be not only stones, but living stones; not only living stones constituting a temple, but, with greater boldness of view, this temple itself was to become a community of priests, and that community was to be a *holy* one. The Jewish priest was accustomed to draw especially near to God to offer sacrifice and incense for others, as well as for himself; and thus he was supposed to be set apart from others. (Num. 16:5; Exod. 19:22.) So these Christians are all alike to be holy, and all alike to draw near to God. No one is to be a priest in any higher sense than another. *Priest*—applied officially under the Christian economy to ministers of the gospel, as has been done many centuries by several ecclesiastical bodies, is not in harmony with the spirit of this passage. *Altar* has been applied, unscripturally, to a given part of a *Christian* house of worship, and even *sacrifice* to the ministration of the Lord's Supper. Bad seed—bad fruit. Jewish terms with a Jewish meaning, instead of Jewish terms with a Christian meaning, well nigh ruined Christendom. All Christians are now priests, and ought to be as holy as the priests of ancient Israel were supposed to be.

But this great community of priests is made such, in order to **offer up spiritual sacrifices.** The Jewish sacrifices ought always to have been offered with spiritual feeling, but not often were they so offered; and had they been so offered, they were in themselves material, animal. (Heb. 9: 10, 13, 22.) 'Spiritual'—offered with the spirit, and not of a material nature. Offering one's self (Rom. 12:1), praise (Heb. 13:15), and doing good, almsgiving (Rom. 15: 16), are included in spiritual sacrifices. **Acceptable to God.** See Rom. 15: 16; 12: 1; 14: 18. Such sacrifices, and the offering of them, are well pleasing to God. **By Jesus Christ.** Some say, well pleasing *through Christ*; others, *to offer up through Christ*. The former seems preferable. Thrilling to every child of God is the efficacy of that mediation by which sacrifices, so worthless in themselves, are made pleasing to Him who is infinitely pure.

6. Wherefore—*for*, or *because*. **Also** has little manuscript authority. The apostle proves what he has said by quoting from Isa. 28: 16. But parts of Isaiah's description are left out. Compare the two. **In Sion.** 'Sion' (*Zion*) was the southwestern hill on which

Behold, I lay in Sion a chief corner stone, elect, precious: and he that believeth on him shall not be confounded.

7 Unto you therefore which believe *he is precious:* but unto them which be disobedient, the stone which the builders disallowed, the same is made the head of the corner,

Behold, I lay in Zion a chief corner stone, elect, ¹ precious:
And he that believeth on ² him shall not be put to shame.

7 ³ For you therefore who believe is the ⁴ preciousness: but for such as disbelieve,
The stone which the builders rejected,
The same was made the head of the corner;

---

1 Or, *honorable*........2 Or, *it*........3 Or, *In your sight*........4 Or, *honour.*

Jerusalem was built, and was sometimes used for the entire city. Being the residence of the kings, and (Ps. 132: 13) the "habitation" of Jehovah, it was the seat of divine and of human government. There God laid the chief corner-stone of the Jewish theocracy, or of the house of David. The words express, therefore, stability of Jewish government; but reference to the Messiah is clear, in which nearly all expositors are agreed. A **chief corner-stone**—not a *chief* corner-stone, but a stone laid at the *extreme angle*—that is, a *corner-stone.* The context shows that it was to be a *foundation* corner-stone, and this is distinctly said by Isaiah. Such a stone supports all that is above it. It binds together the two sides; but this idea, on which some like to linger, is not expressed either here, or in Isaiah. Hence the pleasing and Scriptural fact that Jews and Gentiles are bound together by a common union with Christ is put into Peter's words, not drawn out of them. See Eph. 2: 20, where the readers are said to be built on the apostles and prophets, as well as on Christ. Christians in general are not a part of the foundation; and this is a fact of very great importance. That they are a part of it is a conception foreign to the New Testament, and is a fruitful source of error. The words in 1 Tim. 3: 15 do not teach the contrary. That the apostles, in connection with Christ, are a part of the foundation, Christ as the corner-stone, "the first and chief part," indeed, shows that their teachings are authoritative, and authoritative because they are the voice of Christ in them. Christ and the apostles deliver truth; we receive it. See Bernard's "Progress of Doctrine in the New Testament," p. 125, and elsewhere. **Elect, precious.** See on the same words in ver. 4. **Believeth on him.** The preposition implies *resting upon him.* See on 1: 8. **Shall not be confounded**—*be put to shame* (Rom. 5: 5); that is, shall receive the end for which his faith is placed upon Christ—*final glory.*

7. Unto you therefore which believe he is precious. To millions of the elect, accustomed to read only the English, this is one of the richest things in the Epistle, and to reject it as not the true expression of the mind of the Spirit will seem like the ruthless crushing of a diamond. Yet it is the duty of all to sit reverently at the feet of the Divine Teacher, and to receive all that may there be taught. To the believer, the preciousness of Christ will not be lost, or in the least diminished, even if it is not taught directly in the words before us. **Therefore**—in view of what I have said relative to the living stone. Therefore to you who *believe,* who rely upon the stone as the true foundation, is '*the honour.*' See margin of Revised Version. The word *honour* stands in contrast with the idea implied in *shall not be put to shame.* (Ver. 6.) See Crit. Notes. It is there implied that he who believeth not shall be *dishonored.* It also stands in contrast with what follows. Thus the contrast is twofold: (*a*) He that believes not shall be dishonored; to you, on the contrary, who believe, is the honor. (*b*) To you who believe is the honor; they, on the other hand, who believe not, stumble against the stone, and so are dishonored. The apostle speaks of the *reward* which is conferred upon believers, not of what Christ is to them; though precious he most certainly is.

Them which be disobedient—better, both in style and thought, as in the Revised Version, *such as disbelieve.* The critics adopt the Greek word for *disbelieving* (ἀπιστοῦσιν), instead of that for *the disobedient* (ἀπειθοῦσι). The unbelief is active, and more or less hostile. Thus are contrasted the faith of Christians and the disbelief of others. **Which the builders disallowed** (or *rejected*)—which the working religionists, the Scribes and Pharisees, who were very busy, and thought themselves very skillful in building a spiritual house, *rejected.* Their own Scriptures (ver. 6) proved that the building would be useless, unless God's stone were used; but they not only did not want it—they rejected it. The

8 And a stone of stumbling, and a rock of offence, *even to them* which stumble at the word, being disobedient: whereunto also they were appointed.

9 But ye *are* a chosen generation, a royal priesthood,

8 and,
A stone of stumbling, and a rock of offence;
[1] for they [2] stumble at the word, being disobedient:
9 whereunto also they were appointed. But ye are an elect race, a royal priesthood, a holy nation, a

1 Gr. who........2 Or. stumble, being disobedient to the word

same—*this*. It is a case not of mere repetition (*the stone . . . the same*), but of emphasis, *this very* stone which the builders rejected. To a consciously condemned builder the use of the word was like thrusting the blade to the hilt. Peter quotes from Ps. 118: 22. Of what egregious folly and sin were the builders guilty! Compare Matt. 7: 24-27, and note especially our Lord's own solemn citation of the passage, in presence of the very men to whom it was applicable. (Matt. 21: 42.) **Is made** —*has become*, implying that he continues to be the head of the corner. What the builders rejected as a *stone* unfit to be used in the building at all, God caused to become, by the resurrection and glorification, the *cornerstone*. See Crit. Notes.

8. And . . . offence. 'Offence' recalls the solemn application of the same word (σκάνδαλον) to Peter himself, when he rebuked his Master. (Matt. 16: 23.) He came to the right view by severity, administered in wonderful love. The Greek word is originally "a *trap-stick*—a bent stick on which the bait is fastened, which the animal strikes against, and so springs the trap." (Robinson.) Hence, it came to mean a *trap*, and was at length easily applied to whatever was the cause of one's falling morally. Peter quotes from Isa. 8: 14. Christ rejected became ruin to the rejecters. The rejecters brought ruin on themselves; but in that ruin must not be overlooked the active and just pleasure of God. See Luke 10: 21; 2: 34; 20: 18. Even **to them** was unnecessarily supplied, and even the Revisers supply 'for.' Literally, *who stumble at the word, being disobedient;* or (as in the margin of the Revised Version), *stumble, being disobedient to the word*. They are not represented as stumbling both at Christ and the word. They stumble at that word which has respect to redemption by Christ as the only ground of salvation. See 1 Cor. 1: 18, and especially 1: 23, of the same Epistle. Preaching Christ as less than the corner-stone of all durable human hopes is perilous work. It saves none, and ruins all who like it. **Whereunto**—*to which* stum-bling, not to which disobedience. In the original, 'stumble' is a verb, and 'being disobedient' is a participle. The main thought is expressed in the verb, and it is the main thought to which 'whereunto' should be referred. **Appointed**. The Greek is the same as is found in 1 Thess. 5: 9: "For God hath not *appointed* us to wrath." They are unbelieving, which is a sin; they stumble, and though that also is a sin, yet it is here viewed as a punishment of the unbelief, and in this respect God appointed them to it. That one who persistently refuses to believe in Jesus Christ may be appointed by God, after "much long-suffering," to the ruin which is implied in stumbling, is an obvious principle of his moral government, and is recognized as such with remarkable calmness and independence by the sacred writers. See the very important words in Rom. 9: 22. The appointing was before the stumbling, for the verb is in a past tense. There is a power back of the devil's.

9. Another description of the readers and equally of all the regenerate, the more striking in contrast with that of the unbelieving just given. It is an additional evidence of Peter's knowledge of the Old Testament, for nearly every item is Scriptural in language as well as in thought. **A chosen generation,** *an elect race*. (Isa. 43: 20; Deut. 7: 6; Isa. 45: 4.) The original for *chosen* is here used the fourth time since the Epistle opened. The word bristles with no such difficulties that one need fear to use it often. Applied at first to Israel as a race chosen by God from all other nations, it is here applied to all Christians. These have been chosen out of the world to eternal life. **A royal priesthood.** See Ex. 19: 6, where it is "a kingdom of priests." Peter's form is according to the Septuagint. The delicate pencil of John has given us a similar picture (Rev. 1: 6; 5: 10) in a different form; "kings and priests" in the Common Version, which Keil and Delitzsch ("Pentateuch") affirm to be in the Greek the correct reading. But the correct reading gives us *a kingdom*, *priests*. See the "Commentary on the Revela-

Ch. II.] I. PETER. 29

a holy nation, a peculiar people; that ye should shew forth the praises of him who hath called you out of darkness into his marvellous light:
10 Which in time past *were* not a people, but *are* now

people for God's own possession, that ye may shew forth the excellencies of him who called you out of
10 darkness into his marvellous light: who in time past were no people, but now are the people of

tion" (this series), by Justin A. Smith, D. D. On 1: 6, Dr. Smith says: "The correct rendering of the Greek in the word we here distinguish is important. A less ambiguous translation would be, *made us to be a kingdom*—that is, made a kingdom *of* us, not *for* us. Believers are spoken of collectively as a 'kingdom,' in the sense in which that word is so often used in the New Testament, not individually as 'kings.' The word 'priests' applies to them individually, as well as collectively, and has reference to the abolishing of that ancient ritual, in which approach to God must be always with priestly intervention." All Christians are priests. They are a kingdom. Their priesthood has royalty. **A holy nation.** (Ex. 19: 6.) See on 1: 15, 16. **A peculiar people.** (Deut. 7: 6; 14: 2.) 'Peculiar' is not here equivalent to *odd* (*oddity* may be a blotch on character), but *to owned as property, belonging to;* and this is doubtless the sense in which King James' Revisers used the word, *peculiar* being derived from the Latin word *peculium* (property). The Greek is, literally, *a people for a possession*—that is, *designed for* a possession. For *special* possession (Farrar, "Early Days"); for *God's own* possession. (Revised Version.) Israel was acquired by Jehovah for his possession; in no such exalted sense was any other nation his property. So the readers of the Epistle, so all Christians, are God's possession, acquired through the redeeming work of Christ (Tit. 2: 14), and in this sense the unregenerate are not God's possession. See Eph. 1: 14; Acts 20: 28; Isa. 43: 21.

This vivid description must not be weakened by the supposition that it is merely ideal. It describes what Christians are now, not what they will be either in the millennium or in heaven. So far as men are not what this description makes them, they are without evidence that they have been born again. Introduction of persons into Christian churches in infancy has done much to make the description inapplicable; so also has hasty reception of adults professing to believe. The character of Christians as here given is so exalted that, if it is not realized in a community which rejects infant church-membership,

superficiality in preaching and method of working may justly be presumed. That (denoting design) **ye should shew forth,** etc., by publishing wide. **The praises**—*virtues* (the meaning of the Greek), as applied to God, is very uncommon. The singular is used in 2 Pet. 1: 3, and that also is applied to God. Though *holiness* is the term almost always used in the Scriptures for the purpose of expressing God's moral nature, and though *virtus* (virtue) was used by the Romans to express, chiefly, mere natural bravery, yet we need not be so surprised as some are (Farrar and Dr. Edwin A. Abbott) at the application of the word, either singular or plural, to the Divine Being. Here it may be rendered, as in the Revised Version, *excellencies.* See Isa. 43: 21. **Who hath called**—*who called you* is more exact; called at the time of your conversion. It was God's effective calling through the Holy Spirit. **Out of darkness**—darkness of sin and ignorance, leading always to misery. (Col. 1: 13.) Nothing in the material universe more expressively symbolizes the state of the unrenewed mind. 'Out of.' Yet the darkness is not external. **His light.** The natural light represents the ineffable light of God's life. Compare John 1: 4. **Marvellous**—in itself, and to angels and saints. Darkness! light! Out of! into! The greatest change expressed in the smallest words.

10. Which (*who*) **in time past,** etc. See Hos. 1: 9, 10; 2: 23. Speaking of the state of Israel at the time when he was writing, the prophet says substantially this: They are not God's people; God has no mercy for them, so thoroughly have they forsaken the Lord; but the time will come, the time of the Messiah, when they will become God's people, and will be the object of God's compassion. Peter applied this to the readers. They, too, were once not a people. He does not say, not the people *of God;* but he says, **not a people.** See Crit. Notes. They were not even a people, so wanting were they in oneness of characteristics. Sin disunites and scatters. As several interpreters express it, they were a *not-people;* humiliating, but true. He speaks of them as individuals, and as a community. But the disunited and scattered ones, brought together

the people of God: which had not obtained mercy, but now have obtained mercy.

11 Dearly beloved, I beseech you as strangers and pilgrims, abstain from fleshly lusts, which war against the soul;

12 Having your conversation honest among the Gen-

God: who had not obtained mercy, but now have obtained mercy.

11 Beloved, I beseech you as sojourners and pilgrims, to abstain from fleshly lusts, which war against the
12 soul; having your behaviour seemly among the Gen-

by the spiritual change which each has received through the ransom paid by Christ, are now a people, and more—they are God's people. It is equally true that once they "were in the condition of those that have received no mercy; but now ye did receive mercy." (Lillie.) The public prayers of the German missionary, Dr. J. G. Oncken, offered during his visit to this country, were characterized by the outpouring of fervent praise for the amazing change which grace had wrought upon the Christians present. Peter is here virtually exhorting the saints of Asia Minor to extol the grace which wrought a similar change upon themselves.

Ch. 2: 11—4: 6. SECOND SERIES OF EXHORTATIONS.

This series, speaking generally, pertains to relations to the world without; embracing particularly, relation to (*a*) rulers; (*b*) masters; (*c*) husbands; (*d*) wives; (*e*) persecutors—a classification which must be taken as only in part correct, for the thoughts of the several divisions are not a little intermingled; and in the exhortations to husbands, both the husbands and the wives are supposed to be members of the church.

11, 12. PRELIMINARY GENERAL EXHORTATIONS. Dearly beloved. *Beloved* is more correct; and such everywhere else in Peter's Epistles is the rendering. Very tender is the address, more like the nature of John than of Peter; but Peter's nature has been overmatched by grace. **I beseech** (*you*); tenderness still, not prelatical lordliness; real, not assumed for effect, which is possible along with great arrogance of power. **As strangers and pilgrims**—*as being* such, *as those who know* that they are such. As to the former word, see on 1: 1. The two Greek words, which here have a figurative meaning, are used in nearly the same sense—that of *sojourners* in the world, having no right of citizenship, not permanent residents. **Fleshly lusts.** Compare the exhortation in 1: 14; 2: 1, and see similar forms of expression in Gal. 5: 16; Eph. 2: 3; 2 Pet.

2: 18. '**Lusts**'—sinful desires in general, including, doubtless, *uncleanness* or *impurity*, then so painfully common in all classes of society, from the lowest to the highest (so painfully common now), that the pure, in the sense to which Peter refers, were, probably, exceptions. '**Fleshly**'—*carnal;* so called because they proceed from our corrupt nature. It is a figurative use of the word. The flesh was indeed conceived as in some sense the occasion of wrong desires, but strictly the desires are desires of the soul, not of the material nature; and fleshly desires are desires of the soul viewed as unregenerate. The readers are a holy nation (ver. 9), but they have not become superior to the necessity of exhortation. **Abstain**—literally, *hold yourselves off from.* This I exhort you to do as persons who are not citizens of this world, who belong to a commonwealth which is in heaven (Phil. 3: 20); a motive the strength of which can be *felt* only by those who are *sojourners.* **Which war.** This military term is used also by James (4: 1), and by Paul (Rom. 7: 23), *warring against.* Sinful desires are not a besieging army waiting for surrender, but are foes of merciless activity. **Against the soul.** If sinful desires are desires of the soul, how can they be said to war against the soul? They are viewed by the apostle as having their seat outside the soul—that is, in the flesh; and the soul is viewed as the immortal, spiritual part of man. It was possible for the readers to relapse, and the apostle's exhortation is to be a means of keeping them. Several hundred years before Peter's time, a Greek philosopher, who had no written revelation, wrote of an *immortal battle* between right and wrong.[1] The "grandeur" of the conception is second only to that of the Scripture.

Verse 12 enforces the exhortation of ver. 11 by the consideration that God may come to be glorified by the Gentiles, who shall have been converted through the influence of their holy walk. **Conversation**—*course o' life.* (1:15, 18.) **Honest**—literally, *beautiful.* It is not. *beautiful course of life*, which might, perhaps,

---

[1] Plato, "Against the Atheists." See Lewis' ed., 1845, p. 68, line 12.

tiles: that, whereas they speak against you as evil doers, they may by your good works, which they shall behold, glorify God in the day of visitation.

13 Submit yourselves to every ordinance of man for the Lord's sake: whether it be to the king, as supreme;

tiles: that, wherein they speak against you as evildoers, they may by your good works, which they behold, glorify God in the day of visitation.

13 Be subject to every ¹ordinance of man for the

---

¹ Gr. *creation*.

---

refer only to a *day's* course of life, or a week's, but it is, having *your course of life* beautiful, which can mean nothing less than that their entire course of life must be beautiful. The Revised Version renders *seemly*, but it renders the same word in the latter part of the verse, *good*. A life may be beautiful in the sense in which the word was used by ancient Greek philosophy, without being morally good. The life enjoined by Peter is far better than the beautiful life extolled by the Greeks. **Gentiles**, living under the Roman government, were the most numerous of the inhabitants living in the region to which the Epistle was sent. The form of the allusion to Gentiles is one of the grounds for supposing that the majority of the readers were Jews. Christianity raises no impenetrable barrier between the regenerate and the men of the world (consider the necessary relations of the two classes in business and social life), but it is justly inexorable in its demand that the lives of the former shall in no degree be modeled by the principles of the latter. The principles which underlie the business, politics, and pleasures of the world, are too corrupt to be used by men of heavenly birth. Spiritual alliance with God, and acting upon such principles, are as impossible as for "the fountain" to "send forth from the same opening sweet water and bitter." (James 3: 11. Rev. Ver.) Professions of such alliance, while acting upon such principles, are worthless, and the sooner either the principles or the professions are renounced, the better. **That whereas**, etc. *So that, in what they speak against you as evildoers, they, when beholding, may,* etc. **As as being, evil doers**. The Christians were slandered by the unconverted Gentiles. They were misunderstood. "If in hot climates the long absence of rain brought on a drought; if in Egypt the Nile failed to irrigate the fields; if in Rome the Tiber overflowed its banks; if a contagious disease was raging; if an earthquake, a famine, or any other public calamity occurred, the popular rage was easily turned against the Christians." (Neander.) According to the same historian, Augustine reports that it became a proverb in North Africa, "If there is no rain, tax it on the Christians." Though referring to a later time, the proverb throws light upon the words of Peter. If the readers lead a life of holiness ("good works") before their slanderers, these will be so changed that in the very same things in which they misunderstand and malign them, they will at length be led to praise God. **Behold**—a strong word, one which implies sharp observation and contemplation; not mere seeing, for which the Greek has another word. **Day of visitation**. In Job 10: 12, and Luke 19: 44, these words are used to express God's favor; in Isa. 10: 3, and many other places, God's displeasure. Should God have mercy upon their slanderers, they will praise him for that in you of which they now speak so unjustly. If the words are used in the latter sense, the slanderers are represented as the unwilling means of glorifying God when the day of punishment comes.

13, 14. First Exhortation (*particular*). The general exhortation of ver. 11, enforced in ver. 12, is now resolved into particulars. First: *Submission to the civil power*. **Submit yourselves**—so some translate; others, *be subject*. The submission must be voluntary, not yielded with reluctance. See Crit. Notes. **To every ordinance of man**—*to every human institution*—that is, every institution originating with men; a comprehensive direction applicable to the citizen, the servant (ver. 18), and to the wife (3: 1). Applied to the citizen, it requires him to render obedience to the civil power. It was possible that some of the Christians might be "contentiously conscientious." They might refuse to do what it would not be sinful to do. Such instances are known to have occurred. See Neander, "Church History." Such superfluity of conscientiousness it was important to prevent, lest the charge of being evildoers should be just. It was not necessary for Peter's purpose to remind them of the possible existence of such civil requirements as it would be sinful to obey. His opinion concerning that point may be seen in Acts 4: 18-20. His present silence is

14 Or unto governors, as unto them that are sent by him for the punishment of evil doers, and for the praise of them that do well.
15 For so is the will of God, that with well doing ye may put to silence the ignorance of foolish men:
16 As free, and not using *your* liberty for a cloak of maliciousness, but as the servants of God.

Lord's sake: whether it be to the king, as supreme;
14 or unto governors, as sent ¹by him for vengeance on evil-doers and for praise to them that do well.
15 For so is the will of God, that by well-doing ye should put to silence the ignorance of foolish men:
16 as free, and not ²using your freedom for a cloak of
17 ³wickedness, but as bondservants of God. Honour

1 Gr. *through*........2 Gr. *having*........3 Or, *malice*.

not the result of greater conservatism. He is older, indeed, but he has as much natural courage as ever, and a good deal more grace. If by submitting to every ordinance of man he meant submitting even if it involved commission of sin, why did he not save himself from martyrdom? Compare Paul's view in the very important passages, Rom. 13: 1–5. The relation of Christians to civil government involves questions of the highest importance. **For the Lord's sake**—the best of motives. 'Lord,' 'Christ'; for both by Peter and Paul the word is almost always used in reference to Christ. **Whether,** etc. The king in this case is the Roman emperor. **As supreme**—as one *who is* supreme. His superiority in rank, etc., is a motive (*as*) why you should submit. It implies sovereignty over all other rulers of the Roman empire, as well as over the people. Whether the government is a monarchy or a republic is not the question. "The powers that be are ordained of God." (Rom. 13: 1.) Government, not necessarily the form of it, is a divine ordinance. **Governors**—rulers who presided over Roman provinces. Representatives of the king, they, too, should be obeyed. They are sent to maintain the government, and that can be done only by punishing (*vengeance*) those who refuse allegiance, and by commending (*praise*) those who are loyal. While the method of dealing with criminals should not be unnecessarily harsh, it ought not to be so mild as to lose the character of punishment. The fiendishness of secret attempts to take the life of rulers, and to demolish public buildings, deserves something much severer than is meted out to common criminals.

15. **For** introduces a reason why they should submit (ver. 13) to the ordinances of men—namely, that the slanderers, even if not led to glorify God, may at least be made to stop their slandering. **For so is**—for the will of God *is such*. *What* is the will of God? Neither *the well-doing, nor the putting to silence the ignorance of foolish men*, but both combined into one—*i. e., putting to silence by well-doing.* God's will should be sufficient to determine their course. No false views of freedom must be permitted to make them disloyal. Modern communism was not spawned from such words as these. **Well-doing**—in their general mode of life, but especially by obedience to rulers. **Put to silence**—primary meaning, "to muzzle, as oxen treading out grain." (1 Tim. 5: 18.) "But when the Pharisees had heard that he had put the Sadducees to silence"; *muzzled* them. (Matt. 22: 34.) The plain meaning is, *stop the mouth,* so that the objector finds himself unable to reply. **The ignorance**—ignorance begotten of culpable prejudice against the truth, as illustrated in the life of the Christians. **Of foolish men**—of *the* foolish men. The article points out the slandering Gentiles of ver. 12. Fools of this sort have not all died off.

16. Still anxious to keep them loyal to rulers, that the religion which they profess may not be dishonored. Whether the connection is with ver. 13, or with ver. 14, or with ver. 17, is not easily decided; with the first is most probable. Submit (ver. 13) **as free.** Free, though required to submit. Freedom and loyalty to rulers may co-exist. Only when, in its submission to rulers, the soul disobeys God, is it in bondage. And besides, in submitting to government they are free because they recognize government as appointed by God. **Your liberty**—the freedom implied in the word 'free.' Both the Common and the Revised Versions supply 'your' without necessity. *As free, and not using the freedom*—a needful caution. **For a cloak**—*as* a cloak, though some consider that *as* should be connected with *using*—as free, and not as using the freedom, etc. They must not use the freedom for a *covering* of *wickedness*. See Gal. 5: 13; 2 Pet. 2: 19. **As the servants of God**—as being, as knowing that you are God's servants. This is the positive, and of course the stronger, representation.

17 Honour all *men.* Love the brotherhood. Fear God. Honour the king.
18 Servants, *be* subject to *your* masters with all fear; not only to the good and gentle, but also to the froward.

all men. Love the brotherhood. Fear God. Honour the king.
18 ¹Servants, *be* in subjection to your masters with all fear; not only to the good and gentle, but also

1 Gr. *Household servants.*

They must not only (negatively) not attempt to hide wickedness by boasting of their freedom (Huther), but they must be as God's *servants.* No word in the Greek tongue (δοῦλοι, *slaves*) could have more strongly expressed the duty of being entirely subject to God. If the application of the term to Christians is not pleasant, it is because the word, as applied to those held in bondage to men, so often suggests degradation and injustice. Used in reference to Christians, it implies neither, but expresses only, or chiefly, *the rendering of absolute, unconditional service.* The Revised Version uses the strong word *bondservants.* Elsewhere we learn that the service as required is just, and as rendered, is cordial; but these are not expressed by the word itself.

17. Closing the section which began at ver. 11. It is a fine specimen of rapid, condensed thinking. It is like a quick, powerful closing of orchestral music. The apostle ascends from men in general to men of spiritual relationship; from these he ascends to God himself, and ends by dropping to the key-note: 'Honor the king.' **Honour all men**—not humanity, but *men,* and men without exception are to be honored. Wealth, office, and learning may deserve respect, especially the last; but Peter has no thought of them here. Men are the work of God—that is the chief reason why they are to be honored. Honor the lowest of them, which can be done by helping them up. **Love the brotherhood** —the entire Christian body—that is, all Christians. These are supposed to be members of Christian churches; yet, as this is not universally the case, the love must not be restricted to such; and therefore it need not, it must not, be restricted to denominational lines. True Christian love for the universal brotherhood of Christians should be conscientiously cultivated, which is possible in connection with inflexible adherence to the truths and ordinances of Christianity. Christian love is not inconsistent with vigorous defense of truth, nor even with sharp invective against bold and persistent teachers of fatal error. See Matt. 23; 2 Pet. 2: 1-3, 17, 18; Jude 4,

8, 11-13. Compare Rom. 10: 1 with Rom. 16: 17, 18. But controversy among those who were alike begotten to the living hope should be conducted with delicate respect for one another's conscientious, though perhaps unfounded, convictions. Christ says, "Love your enemies" (Matt. 5: 44); Peter says nothing to the contrary. **Fear God**—reverence him. It includes love; but in contrast with honoring men and the king, the apostle enjoins awe in view of God's superiority over all. It implies humility. **Honour the king.** See on ver. 13.

18. SECOND EXHORTATION *(particular).* This is included under the general exhortation of ver. 13. In that, all are exhorted to submit to every human institution; here is enjoined upon servants submission to their masters. **Servants**—*house-servants* (οἰκέται, pertaining to the house; not the stronger term δοῦλοι, bondservants, *slaves,* used in ver. 16). Both words, however, were applied to persons held in involuntary servitude. Yet some house-servants may have been freemen. Slavery existed in the times of the apostles, and had long existed. It was allowed by the Roman government; and whatever may have been the conviction of individuals relative to its wrongfulness, no general and active combination against it had arisen. It was prevailing in the region to which this Epistle was sent. Yet *slave* is used but once in the Common Version (New Testament), and but once in the Common Version (Old Testament); *servant,* as in the passage before us, being preferred. The Revised Version uses for the same Greek word (δοῦλος) *servant* in Matt. 8: 9, but *bondservant* in 2: 16, of our Epistle. That all these servants were slaves cannot be proved; that none of them were slaves is entirely improbable; that a large majority of them were slaves is almost certain. See the context, and Eph. 6: 5-9; Col. 3: 22; 4: 1; 1 Tim. 6: 1, 2; Tit. 2: 9, 10; and the Epistle to Philemon. That Onesimus had been a slave would be conceded by all interpreters. See Hackett on the Epistle. **With all fear**—in fear of offending their masters, yet not with slavish fear,

C

34   I. PETER.   [Ch. II.

19 For this *is* thankworthy, if a man for conscience toward God endure grief, suffering wrongfully.
20 For what glory *is it*, if, when ye be buffeted for

19 to the froward. For this is [1] acceptable, if for conscience [2] toward God a man endureth griefs, suffering
20 ing wrongfully. For what glory is it, if, when ye sin, and are buffeted *for it*, ye shall take it patiently?

1 Gr. *grace*........2 Gr. *of.*

---

slaves though they were—for they are Christians; but with fear pervaded by fear of God. (1:17.) 'All fear'; fear at every point where it would be necessary, in order to secure what the apostle here requires them to do. **The good**—*the kind.* **The froward**—*the crooked,* that is, the perverse, fretful, easily angered. "Untoward" is the translation in Acts 2: 40, and "crooked" in Phil. 2: 15 (Common Version); more consistently in the Revised Version, *crooked* in both places, but inconsistently with the rendering here. The character of the master, whether marked by kindness, or by severity, is not to be the standard by which the conduct of the servants is to be governed. They are to submit to their masters for the sake of One who is far above their masters, yet took upon him the form of a *bond-servant.* (δοῦλος. Phil. 2: 7.) They are to regard themselves as submitting to God rather than to men. We shall fail to appreciate the spirit of this inspired direction unless this is borne in mind. See Eph. 6: 5-7; Col. 3: 22-24; Tit. 2: 10.

This exhortation to servants no more implies approval of slavery than the command to submit to the king implies approval of monarchy in distinction from republicanism. The direction to submit was eminently wise, as the state of society was at that time. But while such were the directions for the time being, Christianity contemplated, by the equality in Christ which it taught (1 Cor. 12: 13; Gal. 3: 28; Philemon 16; Col. 4: 1), the final removal of slavery from the world. To Christianity is due the removal thus far. In his translation of Paul's Epistle to Philemon, Dr. Hackett uses *servant* instead of *slave;* yet he has no doubt that Onesimus was a fugitive from slavery.[1]

19, 20. From ver. 19 to the close of the chapter, the apostle enforces the duty expressed in ver. 18, chiefly by the duty of submission to masters whose treatment of them is severe. It is enforced by two considerations: 1. God's approval; 2. Christ's example. The former is taught in the verses before us. **For this is thankworthy**—what follows in the same verse. The original of 'thankworthy' is a noun, and is often rendered *grace,* as in the margin of the Revised Version. But some insist that it here means *praise.* For this is praise—that is, an object of praise. The meaning may be as follows: *For if a man for conscience toward God endure grief, suffering wrongfully*—*this is grace*—that is, it shows God's grace toward him; or, it conciliates the favor of God toward him. **If a man**—*if any one.* **For conscience toward God.** Some say: "The knowledge of God concerning us," because God knows your sufferings; but the better view is that which makes it refer to one's knowledge of God. The sense, then, is this: If through one's knowledge of God, as the Being who takes cognizance of all one's sufferings, one **endures,** *bears up under,* instead of sinking. **Grief**—*grievances.* **Suffering wrongfully;** allusion to such masters as might indulge in severity. It was the possible severity which would lead to the grievances.

Heaven me such uses send,
Not to pick bad from bad; but, by bad mend.

20. For what glory—a strong denial that there is any glory at all in so doing. **Buffeted.** The related noun means *a box on the*

---

[1] "Slave," he says in a note, "(softened from sklave, and originally a national appellation, sklavonic, or sclavonic), is comparatively a modern word in our language, and altogether too restricted to represent the Greek δοῦλος." Dr. T. J. Conant says on Matt. 8: 9: "The word *servant* has, in English, the same extent of application as the Greek word δοῦλος. The latter (properly a bondman, a slave, from δέω, to bind), is often employed where the English word *bondman* or *slave* would be inappropriate. It is used, for example, as an expression of unlimited devotion to another's will; and this of his own free choice, and in the most honorable relations. . . . It is necessary in translating to employ a term that has the same comprehension as the Greek term. Compare, e. g.," [Luke] "17: 7-10.... ver. 10: *Say we are unprofitable servants;* unprofitable *bondmen* or *slaves* would not express the meaning." In his "Authorized Version," Trench has a paragraph upon the meaning of δοῦλοι (servants), from which it is clear that his view is substantially the same as that of Hackett and Conant.

Ch. II.] I. PETER. 35

your faults, ye shall take it patiently? but if, when ye do well, and suffer *for it,* ye take it patiently, this *is* acceptable with God.

21 For even hereunto were ye called: because Christ also suffered for us, leaving us an example, that ye should follow his steps:

22 Who did no sin, neither was guile found in his mouth:

but if when ye do well and suffer *for it,* ye shall 21 take it patiently, this is ¹ acceptable with God. For hereunto were ye called: because Christ also suffered for you, leaving you an example, that ye 22 should follow his steps: who did no sin, neither

---

1 Gr. *grace.*

---

ear, and so the verb means *to give a box on the ear.* Sometimes the smiting was done with the fist. Many of these Christian servants were doubtless made to feel, practically, the etymological meaning of the word; but the term was sometimes used to express a wider range of abuse. For your faults—the entire clause, more exactly, *if doing wrong and being buffeted;* yet the abusive treatment is supposed to be caused by the wrong doing. 'Doing wrong' is here, literally, *missing the mark*—a significant way of expressing the act of committing sin. Take patiently—*bear up under.* It has essentially the same meaning as *endure,* in ver. 19. Acceptable with God. In the Greek it is the word for grace, as ver. 19 (*"thankworthy"*); this is *grace,* and the word must have the same meaning as there. Notice the addition, 'with God.' Bearing up under abuse may be the result of natural heroism, or of philosophic pride. As enjoined by Peter, it is a virtue of heavenly birth.

21. This enforces the duty (ver. 18) by the example of Christ. They should bear up under the sufferings inflicted by masters, inasmuch as Christ suffered for them; and he suffered for them *without sin, patiently,* and *as their substitute.* See Crit. Notes. Even —unnecessarily inserted. Hereunto—not unto slavery; not, exclusively, unto suffering, but *unto patience under suffering.* Called. See Acts 14: 22; Rom. 8: 28-30; 1 Thess. 3: 3. It is only servants to whom he refers, yet the spirit of the words is applicable to all to whom the Epistle was sent. (3: 8. 9.) The calling implies divine purpose, but divine purpose relative to the patience enjoined, and not also relative to the sufferings inflicted, would have been poor comfort. The Christian who believes suffering to be only the result of natural law, or man's wickedness, or the devil's malignity, surrenders himself so far, however ignorantly, to one of the most pestiferous principles of Paganism. "God has nothing to do with it"— a very common saying—is not the teaching of Christianity. See what this same apostle taught on the Day of Pentecost concerning God's purpose relative to Christ's crucifixion. (Acts 2: 23.) Man's wickedness, always committed freely, is part of the good man's schooling. The point of harmony between man's freedom in wrong doing and God's purpose eludes us. Here every man is an agnostic. Denying the existence of such a point is easy, but the difficulty is not thereby removed. To the sharper sight of the next life that may be one of the things brought within its angle; it may not be. It may not be visible in the brightest light of eternity. Because. This assigns the reason why these Christian servants are called to suffer—namely, Christ also suffered. It is conceivable that Christ might have passed through the world without suffering, but he *suffered.* Peter sends the argument home by adding, *for you*—for us, in Common Version, but in Revised Version after the more approved Greek—for your good, or in your stead. Concerning the meaning of the preposition—that is, whether it implies substitution —see Crit. Note. Leaving us. Here, also, a better reading requires *you;* leaving *behind,* a clear allusion to the Lord's ascension. An example. The word means literally a copy to be followed in writing. As a child learns to write by imitating the copy at the head of the page, so we must imitate the suffering Christ by suffering ourselves, not complaining because we are not allowed to choose the kind, but accepting the kind which God gives. Follow his steps—a change of figure which rhetorical precision would condemn. They are to imitate the copy that they may follow *upon* his footsteps. See the same figure in Rom. 4: 12. Both figures being dropped, the simple form is, leaving an example for you to follow.

22. Who did no sin—the first fact in the suffering Redeemer's case. Jesus suffered, not as a wrong doer, but as a sinless one, which makes appeal to servants yet stronger. Though

23 Who, when he was reviled, reviled not again; when he suffered, he threatened not; but committed *himself* to him that judgeth righteously:

23 was guile found in his mouth: who, when he was reviled, reviled not again; when he suffered, threatened not; but committed ¹*himself* to him who judg-

¹ Or, *his cause.*

Peter supposed them to be innocent under suffering, yet in this representation of Christ's sinlessness, there is an indirect allusion to their own want of sinlessness. The words are still another evidence that Peter had made the Old Testament a study. They are quoted, as also the remaining words of the verse, from Isa. 53: 9, not according to the Hebrew, but according to the Septuagint, which is believed to have been much used by the Jews in our Lord's time.

No sin—though born of a daughter of Eve, Jesus had no taint of the depravity of Eve. He lived among great sinners, yet took no harm from their character. He had human appetites, but not one of them became his master. He was capable of ambition, but no such vice found place in his heart. No man ever had greater reasons, greater opportunities, and greater power to indulge in revenge; yet he forgave the greatest personal insults, and loved the wrong doer even unto death. Wise above all the men of his time, he neither treasured up wisdom in self-gratification, nor, when disclosing it, disclosed it in vanity. With capacity for a life of study and meditation superior to that of any of his contemporaries, he gave himself to active toil for the good of others, seeking solitude only that by renewing his exhausted strength, and obtaining fresh supplies of spiritual power, he might continue his labors for the selfish and rebellious. He sought honor neither from the bad nor from the good; and, with bold consistency, cried in the ears of men, "How can ye believe which (*who*) receive honour one of another, and seek not the honour which cometh from God only?" In suffering, not less than in doing; in death, not less than in life, he was distinctly conscious of the spirit of obedience to the will of God, instead of being blindly impelled by the divinity within him. His virtues were not those of an angel or of God, but of man. They were thoroughly human; yet they were so united with the divine that the divine and the human were scarcely distinguishable. So in this God-man dwelt infinite excellence. (Heb. 7: 26; 2 Cor. 5: 21.) **Neither was guile found.** Though freedom from guile (*deceit*) is included in freedom from sin, yet Christ's freedom from that particular form of evil, so characteristic of fallen man, seemed to Peter to require, for the sake of servants, special mention. Nathanael was not sinless, but he had no guile, even according to Christ himself. (John 1: 47.) Such Nathanaels are rare. '*Was found*'—more expressive than *was*. No guile *could be detected* in his words. (Rev. 14: 5.) See Winer. Neither his enemies, nor his friends, with the latter of whom he held the most intimate relations, could ever see in him the least deceit, though the former called him while his body lay in Joseph's tomb (Matt. 27: 63), "that deceiver." See more on 1: 7 concerning 'might be found.' Deceit in the mouth has bad parentage—deceit in the heart. (Mark 7: 22.) "Naught, naught, saith the buyer; but when he is gone his way then he boasteth" (Prov. 20: 14); the full-blown deception of not a few buyers in the present time. Elymas, the sorcerer (Acts 13: 8-10), "full of all subtilty"—the deceit of opposers of the gospel. Expose one such deceiver, and another springs up. Simon Magus (Acts 8: 23, 24), the deceit of a hypocrite, the worst kind. Nothing did the guileless Saviour so severely denounce as the last. Deceit in conducting religious affairs is sure to rebound upon those who practice it.

23. The second fact: *He suffered patiently.* The chain of argument enforcing the duty of servants to bear up under their sufferings, must not be defective; this link is therefore added. **Reviled.** Christ was the object of criticism during his entire public life, and this at times broke forth into such malignant accusations as that of being in league with Satan; being a glutton and a wine-bibber; a companion of persons loose in character; a boaster (Matt. 26: 61); a pretender (claiming to be the Messiah and King of Israel), and a blasphemer. But under no form of reviling did Christ revile in return. **He threatened not.** He denounced hypocrites with severity never equaled, but he never threatened in revenge for what he suffered. **But committed.** In the original the verb has no object. We may supply *himself*, or *his affairs*, or *it* (the reviling and suffering). Perhaps *his judg-*

| 24 Who his own self bare our sins in his own body on the tree, that we, being dead to sins, should live unto righteousness: by whose stripes ye were healed. | 24 eth righteously: who his own self ¹ bare our sins in his body upon the tree, that we, having died unto |

1 Or, carried up . . . to the tree.

ment—that is, judgment of himself, may express the thought which lay in the mind of the writer. The Revised Version supplies *himself*, and puts *his cause* in the margin. **Judgeth rightcously.** What confidence that he should be vindicated! Compare Job 19: 25-27. Nineteen centuries have passed, and evidence of his blamelessness, not stronger indeed than at first, is still spreading, and is destined to spread till "he shall have put down all rule, and all authority and power." (1 Cor. 15: 24.) In the patience of Christ under suffering, his followers have a lesson of infinite persuasiveness.

24. The third fact: *He bare our sins.* This point applies to others than servants. Yet he returns to those who were suffering in servitude. The verse is one of inexpressible importance and preciousness. It answers the question: How *are we saved ?* The meaning of a preposition (*for*, ver. 21) is not here the point. **Who his own self**—*who himself.* Whatever is here affirmed as having been done was done by Christ himself. Not an angel aided him in bearing man's sin. The strength ministered by an angel in Gethsemane (Luke 22: 43) was ministered that he might be able to bear it alone. **Bare our sins**—evidently suggested by Isa. 53, especially ver. 11, 12. In what sense did Christ bear our sins? By *taking them* away through the influence of his love in suffering? Then his sufferings were not a substitute for those which we deserve; he did not suffer *in our place*. Three ways of getting an answer are open to us: 1. We may show what Isaiah meant, assuming that Peter's meaning must be the same. 2. Without seeking Isaiah's meaning, we may inquire for Peter's meaning in the light of the New Testament. 3. We may combine both methods. The twofold method will bring us to the conclusion that Christ bore our sins upon the cross in the sense of suffering what God accepted in place of the penalty deserved by ourselves. This is the very least that can be said. Some think that he bore our sins in the sense of suffering the penalty itself—the penalty due to all the sins of all human beings. As the sufferer was God-man; as his sufferings were intense beyond all human conception; as they were chiefly the sufferings of the soul; and as there was an unfathomable depth of mystery in them, we cannot limit them by any known standard; and yet, strictly speaking, penalty (punishment) implies guilt. But that guilt cannot be ascribed to Christ is clear from ver. 22. If it be said that guilt may be ascribed to him figuratively, that is conceding that guilt cannot be ascribed to him in the sense in which it is ascribed to an actual sinner. For the sake of precision of language, therefore, it seems better to restrict the term *penalty* to punishment inflicted for one's own sin. In John 1: 29, a different Greek word is used for *taketh away;* but as Meyer and others say, that word may mean either *take away,* or *take upon himself* in order to bear. Substitution is the meaning expressed there, as well as in the passage before us. See Crit. Notes.

Alas! alas!
Why all the souls that were, were forfeit once;
And he that might the vantage best have took
Found out the remedy: How would you be,
If he, which is the top of judgment, should
But judge as you are ? Oh, think on that;
And mercy then will breathe within your lips,
Like man new made.

In his own body—*in his body.* Compare "present *your bodies* a living sacrifice." (Rom. 12: 1.) No contrast between the body and the soul is intended. Christ bore our sins in his soul as truly as in his body. Compare Matt. 26: 38. But as it was the body which was nailed to the cross, it was natural to make it prominent in the tragic representation. Yet 'body' may be used here, as in Romans, for the entire person. **On the tree.** Primary meaning, *on the wood,* or on a *beam of wood.* The use of the original word for *cross* was borrowed from the Hebrew language, and is therefore called a Hebraism. The chief baker was to be hanged on a *tree.* (Gen. 40: 19.) A body was not to remain all night on a *tree.* (Deut. 21: 23.) Joshua hanged five kings on five *trees.* (Josh. 10: 26.) "Tree, like *treow* in Anglo Saxon, was often used in early English in the sense of 'wood' in general, as 'vessels of tre'

25 For ye were as sheep going astray; but are now returned unto the Shepherd and Bishop of your souls.

sins, might live unto righteousness; by whose 25 ¹stripes ye were healed. For ye were going astray like sheep; but are now returned unto the Shepherd and ²Bishop of your souls.

1 Gr. *bruise*........2 Or, *Overseer*.

(Chaucer), 'cuppe of tre'; and also specifically to denote something made of wood, particularly a bar or beam; a meaning still preserved in the compounds *axle-tree, cross-tree, whipple-tree*.... The cross in early English poetry is often called 'Christos tre' (Chaucer)."—Ezra Abbott in "Smith's Bib. Dict.," p. 3321. There were modes of putting criminals to death in our Lord's day to which such deep disgrace would not have been affixed. The final object of Christ's death, in the case of men themselves, was to make them "dead to sins and alive unto righteousness." See Rom. 6: 11, and consider the relation of this great inward change, wrought by the Saviour's substituted sufferings, to baptism. (Rom. 6: 3-6.) Dead *to* sins, not dead in sins. (Eph. 7: 1.) In the latter case sins are viewed as the "efficient cause" of the state of death. **By whose stripes**—not scourging, but the effect of it. The Greek word is in the singular number, and may refer, therefore, not merely to scourging, but to his entire course of suffering —death as the culmination of all. **Were healed.** Sin is a fearful disease; regeneration is restoration to health. Sinlessness, to which the regenerate are to attain, is life in the form of perfect health; and this life is attributed to the death inflicted upon Christ. Self-healing is impossible, for the tendency of man is ever toward a worse state; and great care should be taken by those who use means to heal others, that the means be not such as to heal slightly. (Jer. 6: 14.) Bodily disease may need change of treatment; for diseases of the soul the apostolic method is still good, and in revivals of religion departure from that method shows how little reliance is placed upon God to do the needed work. Giving the wrong medicine shows ignorance of the disease. On the "Satisfaction of Christ," as treated by Grotius against Socinius, see in "Bib. Sac.," 1879, a translation of the Latin treatise by Rev. F. H. Foster. Grotius' view, that the sufferings of Christ were a penalty or punishment inflicted upon Christ himself— that is, the penalty which is deserved by us, would now find few advocates; but the treatise as a whole, it is quite superfluous to say, is one of great power against those errors of Socinians which are more or less distinctly reproduced in Unitarianism.

25. The writer has said that we should live unto righteousness, and that they have been healed. This easily suggests their former state, and all the more easily the figure by which it is represented, because in the very chapter (Isa. 53) which has supplied him with the main thought, men are represented as going astray like sheep. (Ver. 6.) **As sheep going astray**—by the more approved Greek, *Ye were straying as sheep*. In most affecting terms it expresses the fact of their former separation from God. Plato represents men as God's sheep, but not for the purpose of showing that they have strayed. The remarkable thirty-fourth chapter of Ezekiel, in which the metaphor greatly expanded, is applied to Israel, should be read in connection with the description by Peter. See also John 10 and Ps. 23. Not as slaves, but as sinners, they were once straying, yet their state of servitude before conversion adds to the effect of the description. Straying sheep encounter want and wolves, and straying men are fearfully exposed to teachers of error (*thieves, robbers, hirelings, wolves*, John 10: 8, 12). False teachers are both straying sheep and prowlers. **Are now returned**—*have now turned*, but this is not an implication that divinely ministered strength to turn was not needed and given. **Bishop**—*overseer*. The Common Version and the Revised Version are alike unfortunate; for *bishop* does not necessarily imply oversight, which is precisely what is implied in the Greek. A bishop, in the sense used not long after the apostles died, was unknown. **The Shepherd and Bishop** (*overseer*)—Christ, not God, though in 5: 2 Peter calls the elect the flock of God. That Christ is meant is clear from Ezek. 34: 23, 24. He is *the chief Shepherd.* (5: 4.) **Your souls** —connected with 'Shepherd' as well as with 'Bishop.'

Thus is the duty of bearing up under their sufferings enjoined upon the servants by the example of Christ as a sufferer; more particularly by the three facts that his sufferings were borne without sin, with patience, and as a substitute. The appeal is adapted to all Christian sufferers of all times. This chapter is even richer than the first. Like that, it is chiefly hortatory, but here also the practical is not without strong support in doctrine. While the exhortations of the first are radiant with electing love, shining indeed, also, with that glory of Christ which was to come after his sufferings, the exhortations of this chapter glow with ineffable brightness; for Christ's death appears in its mightiest efficacy. Verses 24, 25 give additional evidence (compare 1: 18, 19) of Peter's attainment of correct views concerning the necessity and object of Christ's death.

CRITICAL NOTES.—CHAPTER II.

3. εἰς σωτηρίαν (*unto salvation*) is found after αὐξηθῆτε (*may grow*) in so many valuable manuscripts, that it is judged to have been originally a part of the Epistle. It is accepted as genuine by Lachmann, Tischendorf, Tregelles, Westcott and Hort, and the Revisers. "It indicates," says Huther, "the aim of all Christian growth."

The Greek word for honour (τιμή) occurs in Peter, in not one case with the meaning *preciousness*, unless it has it here. It occurs in 1: 7; 3: 7; 2 Peter 1: 17, and in the Common Version is translated *honor*. The Revised Testament of the Bible Union translates *honor* in the case before us. The English and American Revision translates *preciousness*, but puts *honor* in the margin. It translates in all the other passages *honor*. Translating differently here is one of the few inconsistencies of the Revised Version. Not only the context, but the *usus loquendi* (customary way of speaking), shows that *honor* is the true meaning. The old interpreter Bengel, born in 1687, understood it as the Revisers of 1611 did, but in the American translation of his Notes he is corrected by the editor, who says that the rendering of the English is quite out of the question. In the German, Luther's translation, is the same as that of the Common English Version. On the other hand, the view which is here taken is that of Wiesinger, Gerhard, De Wette, Brückner, Weiss, Schott (all from Huther), of Huther himself, Fronmuller, and Alford. Lillie seems to prefer *preciousness*, and applies it to the Saviour, but afterwards in a note admits that *honor* would be rather more agreeable to current Greek usage. The before *honor* points to ἔντιμον (*honored*, "precious") in ver. 6. The stone is *honored;* and he that believeth in him shall not be *dishonored*. You believe; therefore to you is not dishonor, but *the honor*. This view is held by Dr. Robinson also, who defines τιμή as a state of honor conferred in reward. The position of πιστεύουσιν (*who believe*) is worthy of notice: *Unto (for) you, therefore, is the honor, for you who believe*, so that even if τιμή should be translated *preciousness*, and should be applied to Christ, not that but πιστεύουσιν (*believe*) would be the emphatic word.

7. εἰς (*into*) stands before κεφαλὴν (*head*). If the genius of the English tongue permitted it to be translated, the entire clause would stand thus: This *has become for* the corner-stone. In the Greek, the preposition expresses *design* and *result*—that is, a *designed result*—a meaning which, according to Buttmann, εἰς sometimes has. That ἐγενήθη (*has become*), though a passive, may be rendered as above (with an intransitive sense), see Buttmann, pp. 51, 52; and that, though an aorist, it may express by the implication of the context, "the continuance of the action, and its working down to the present time," see Buttmann, pp. 197, 198.

10. They were οὐ λαός (*a not-people*); λαός (*people*), οὐ (*not*). The latter word standing before the former is an instance of what is called *negatived substantives*. The peculiarity is distinctly recognized by Winer: "οὐ combined with nouns into one idea, obliterates their meaning altogether (Rom. 10: 19; 1 Pet. 2: 10), all quotations from the Old Testament." It is more neatly expressed by Buttmann: "Examples of negatived *substantives—i. e.*, of substantives transformed by the negative into their opposites, and blending with it, as it were, into a single word, occur only in Old Testament quotations. The negative then is always οὐ, because compounds of the sort are formed in Hebrew with לֹא. Rom. 9: 25; 1 Pet. 2: 10; ... Rom. 10: 19."

13, 18. ὑποτάγητε — *submit yourselves* (ver. 13) is the aorist passive, with the sense of the middle voice; "a pure reflexive," as Buttmann says of the same word in James 4: 7. *Humble yourselves* (1 Pet. 5: 6; James 4: 10); *joined themselves* (Acts 5: 36); but here the manuscripts differ. On the general subject (the use in the New Testament of the aorist passive in a reflexive sense), see Winer, ₰ 39, p. 261, Huther on this (ver. 13), and Buttmann, pp. 51, 52. Anticipating in part the consideration of ver. 18 and 3: 1, it may be added that the participle ὑποτασσόμενοι—*be subject* (ver. 18), *be in subjection* (3: 1) stands in both cases in connection with ὑποτάγητε—*submit yourselves* (ver. 13), thus: *Submit yourselves to every ordinance of man . . . servants being subject to masters, . . . wives being subject to their husbands.* Though participles, they are not improperly translated into English as if they were verbs.

21. Christ suffered *for* you. Did Christ suffer for men in the sense of suffering for their good? or did he suffer for them in the sense of suffering in their place—that is, was Christ the sinner's substitute? The difference is very great, and involves the entire question of the way of salvation. The Revisers of 1611 use the same *for* to translate two different Greek prepositions, ἀντί and ὑπέρ. But there are passages in which the former means, *in place of* (Luke 11: 11; 1 Cor. 11: 15; Matt. 20: 28); are there any in which the latter has the same meaning? That it is generally used in the sense of *for, for the good of*, is evident; but that it is never used in the sense of *instead, in place of*—that is, that it never conveys the idea of substitution, is more probably, than ought to be affirmed. See Philemon, ver. 13: "Whom I would have retained with me, that *in thy stead* (ὑπερσοῦ) he might have ministered unto me"; "as his representative—substitute" (Hackett), and the same interpreter cites 2 Cor. 5: 21: "For he made him to be sin *for us*" (ὑπὲρ ἡμῶν). Winer, after giving to ὑπέρ in several passages the meaning *for, for the benefit of*, adds: "In most cases, one who acts in behalf of another takes his place (1 Tim. 2: 6; 2 Cor. 5: 15); hence, ὑπέρ is sometimes nearly equivalent to ἀντί, instead, *loco*" (*in place of*). He refers to the very decisive Philemon 13. One is surprised to hear Winer say after this, in a note, "Still, in doctrinal passages relating to Christ's death (Gal. 3: 13; Rom. 5: 6, 8; 14: 15; 1 Pet. 3: 18, etc.), it is not justifiable to render ὑπὲρ ἡμῶν and the like rigorously by *instead of*. 'Αντί is the more definite of the two prepositions. 'Υπέρ signifies merely *for* men, for their deliverance; and leaves undetermined the precise sense in which Christ died for them." Robinson admits the sense *instead of* in Philemon, and thinks it may be the meaning in 2 Cor. 5: 20; Eph. 6: 20. Compare 1 Pet. 3: 18. The question, however, in what sense Christ died for sinners does not turn wholly upon the meaning of a preposition. See upon ver. 24.

24. The Greek for *bare* is ἀνήνεγκεν, from ἀναφέρω—ἀνά (*up*) and φέρω (bear); to bear up from a lower to a higher place. Where the Common Version says *on*, the Greek uses ἐπί (*upon*). The verb and the preposition taken together mean *bore up upon*, and as sacrifices were carried up to the altar and offered (compare James 2: 21), it has been insisted that Peter here views the cross as an altar, and represents Christ as bearing our sins up to the cross to sacrifice them there. See Col. 2: 14. But the cross of Christ is never represented in the New Testament as an altar; and neither in the Old Testament, nor in the New, are our sins viewed as the sacrifice which is brought to the altar. (Huther.) *Bearing our sins he ascended the cross* is another way of expressing the meaning. ἀναφέρω does not always mean to bear *up*, in the sense of taking the object to a higher place. See Heb. 9: 28; Isa. 53: 12; in the latter of which verses the word is used in the Septuagint for נָשָׂא and סָבַל. "But there is no necessity for regarding the case as anything more than the very common one of ἐπί, with an accusative; when the verb of motion, appropriate to such a construction is suppressed, and it is to be only mentally supplied: *bare our sins in his body* [when lifted up] upon the tree." (Lillie.) The Revised Version has in the margin, "Or, *carried up . . . to the tree*," a suggestion made by the American Committee. Farrar ("Early Days of Christianity") makes substantially the same, but less elegant, rendering: "Carried up our sins in his own body on to the tree." The marginal reading of the Revised Version may be accepted, without attributing the idea of altar and sacrifice to the verb.

CHAPTER III.

LIKEWISE, ye wives, *be* in subjection to your own husbands; that, if any obey not the word, they also

1 In like manner, ye wives, *be* in subjection to your

Ch. 3: SECOND SERIES OF EXHORTATIONS (continued).

1. THIRD EXHORTATION (*particular*), addressed to wives whose husbands are unbelievers. **Likewise.** Beginning a new exhortation, it directs to the preceding one (2:18), but it must not be understood as hinting that the "subjection" of wives to their husbands is of the same nature as that of servants to their masters. **Be in subjection.** As in 2: 18, the exact translation is, *being subject*, and, like the participle in that place, must be connected with the verb in 2: 13. **Your own.** No such contrast between their own husbands and other men is intended as to imply warning against being led into illicit connections, though some strongly insist that there is. On the other hand, the original word, which is not a mere possessive pronoun, seems intended to express something more than the mere fact that they *are* their husbands. See Critical Notes.

The duty enjoined can neither be reasoned away nor ridiculed away. The same requirement is made by the Holy Spirit through Paul. (Eph. 5: 22-24; Col. 3: 18; 1 Tim. 2: 11, 12; Titus 2: 5.) That Paul was never married is nothing to the purpose; it is certain that the Spirit of God could give a just command to wives through an unmarried apostle; but as if to rebuke mockers of Paul, a married apostle is authorized to say the same thing. "It is certainly a noticeable coincidence that these exhortations should be found exclusively in the Epistles addressed to Asiatics, nor is it improbable that they were more particularly needed for them than for Europeans." But in Rome, Athens, and Corinth, the relation of husband and wife had long been so very unlike what it ought to have been, that to us there seems to have been no less necessity for exhorting Christian wives there to be in subjection to their husbands, than Christian wives in Asia Minor; and no less necessity for exhorting husbands to love their wives. The silence referred to by the writer above cited is of little consequence; it was not to be expected that such a singling out of classes would be made in every epistle. The prominence recently given to the subject of man's relation to woman should make us more desirous to ascertain, fearlessly, the teachings of the Bible. These can be indicated only in the briefest manner.

BEFORE THE FALL.

1. The subordination of the woman to the man was ordained by the Creator. The man was created first; the woman next. The man was created from the earth; the woman "from the body of man. By this the priority and superiority of the man, and the dependence of the woman upon the man, are clearly established as an ordinance of divine creation." (Keil.) See Gen. 2: 7, 21, 22. "To create another human being wholly distinct in substance from himself, would introduce into the world a being independent of himself, antagonistic to him, and having no hold on his sympathy as part of himself." (Dr. T. J. Conant.) 2. This original authority of the husband and subordination of the wife, so far at least as it is based upon the ground that the man was created first, is recognized by Paul. (1 Tim. 2: 13.) 3. Nature teaches that unless the marriage tie may be dissolved upon every difference of opinion which may arise between the husband and the wife, some means must be used for adjusting the difference. One way of effecting this would be *force*—the method most prevalent among those not enlightened by Christianity. The weaker—be it the man or the woman—would be under the necessity of yielding. But the use of force is forbidden by nature. Another way remains—*i. e.*, subordination either of the man to the woman, or of the woman to the man. Had the woman been created first, and had the man been formed out of one of the woman's ribs, it is clear that the woman should have been regarded as having the authority, and then the man would have been under obligation to receive the woman's decision in case of difference of opinion. 4. That this subordination of the woman to the man, even while both were without moral fault, was to be maintained in love by the woman, and that the superiority of the man was to be maintained

in tenderness, and not in lordly supercilionsness, is clear from two facts: *a.* That the woman was made from the man. *b.* That she was to be a helpmeet for him—"a helper suited to him" (Conant); "'a help of his like' (Keil)—'that is, a helping being, in which, as soon as he sees it, he may recognize himself.'" (Delitzsch.) In her subordination Eve was not restive, and in his superiority Adam was not exacting.

After the Fall.

1. The woman loses sight of the relation in which she stood to Adam, and, in independence of his authority, does what will issue in destroying the purer form of the love which had existed between them. She should have done nothing which would seem like aiming to be her husband's co-ordinate, much less what would seem like aiming *to get the upper hand of him.* "Adam might have done the same thing." Possibly, but it is the business of the interpreter to deal with the actual rather than with the possible. This disregard of her relation to Adam as her constituted superior, is not, indeed, the main thing in her sin, but it is that with which we are just now concerned. 2. "Thy desire shall be to thy husband, and he shall rule over thee." (Gen. 3: 16.) This foretells the subordination of the wife as it was to become in consequence of the fall. Subordination, in this new form, intensified by human passion on both sides, is here represented as a punishment of the woman for her sin. How fearfully has the prophecy been fulfilled! In Pagan and Mohammedan countries the wife has failed to recognize in any religiousness of spirit her subordination to the husband. The husband has equally failed to recognize the tender nature of the authority with which he was originally invested.

> I will be master of what is mine own;
> She is my goods, my chattels; she is my house,
> My household stuff, my field, my barn,
> My horse, my ox, my ass, my any thing;
> And here she stands, touch her whoever dare.

This is true, not only of the half-civilized and the savage, but also of Athenians and Romans. The wife has been rebellious, and no wonder; the husband has been a tyrant, and no wonder.

After the Coming of Christ.

1. Christianity aims to restore the husband and the wife to the right relation. It requires the husband to love his wife (Eph. 5: 25, 28; Col. 3: 19) as a companion, a helper, an adviser; and it aims to make the wife worthy of such love. It aims to bring to an end (1 Cor. 9: 5; Gal. 3: 26-28) that separation of interests which has so marked domestic life since the fall, and to make the interests of the husband and the wife as completely one[1] as that between Christ and the Church. "Not a rivalry with the functions of man, but an elevation of her own functions as high as his" (Gladstone), is the further aim of Christianity. But Christianity does not purpose to accomplish this by reversing the original relation. It therefore says most distinctly that the husband is the head of the wife (Eph. 5: 23), even as Christ is the Head of the Church, and enjoins upon the wife submission to the husband. Without making the wife the co-ordinate of the husband, it gives her substantial equality with him. When the husband recognizes all this as the aim of Christianity, and when the wife also recognizes it, happiness will mark the domestic state. "Authority, kindly exercised, and subordination, quietly acknowledged, promote the development of the affections, to which there is nothing more dangerous than rivalry." (Hugh Davey Evans, LL. D.)

2. In spite of the elevating influence of Christianity upon woman, views have been urged upon the public which, if generally adopted, would sling domestic life into chaos. The viler doctrines promulgated can never, perhaps, be generally received; but the tendency of some modern views is to turn married life back into that state of separate and rival interests which has been the curse of both the husband and the wife wherever revealed religion has been unknown or disregarded. Secretiveness, and even deception in either toward the other, may thus come to characterize the relation which, more than any other of an earthly kind, Christianity requires

---

[1] See the speech of Queen Katharine to the king, in Henry VIII., act 2, scene 4, in illustration of conscious loyalty to a husband.

CH. III.] I. PETER. 43

may without the word be won by the conversation of the wives;
2 While they behold your chaste conversation *coupled* with fear.
3 Whose adorning, let it not be that outward *adorning* of plaiting the hair, and of wearing of gold, or of putting on of apparel;

own husbands; that, even if any obey not the word, they may without the word be gained by the [1] behaviour of their wives; beholding your chaste [1] behaviour *coupled* with fear. Whose *adorning* let it not be the outward adorning of plaiting the hair, and of wearing jewels of gold, or of putting on apparel;

1 Or, *manner of life*.

---

to be distinguished for openness and confidence. Peter's direction, then, viewed in the light shed upon it from other parts of the word of God, is at once most important and just. Reduced to the last point, there remains this: When, after mutual presentation of views upon a given course, agreement is impossible, the woman should yield to the opinion of her husband, those cases excepted in which she would sin by so doing; and in yielding, should feel herself not dishonored, but honored; because doing precisely that which Christianity requires. In yielding to her husband, she yields to him who is the wise Author of the relation. Submission to the final decision of the husband may be pointed and poisoned by the accusation that the decision is unjust; in which case, the very quintessence of obstinacy can be seen through the thin disguise of submission. It may be added that in much that has recently been said concerning woman's subordination to man, the entire tendency is to disregard the teachings of the Scriptures as of no account. But the Bible is as good authority upon this question as upon the duty of man to do all in his power to effect the intellectual and religious elevation of woman.

That if any. 'That' indicates the reason why they should submit. **Also** is misplaced; it should stand before *if*, and be changed into *even*, thus: *that even if any (some) obey not*. It may perhaps be inferred that the husbands of most of them were believers. But even if some obeyed not, it was possible that they might be won, etc. **Obey not.** It seems to imply positive rejection of the word. (2: 8 and compare 1: 22.) **Without the word.** Peter uses no article—'*Without word.*' He refers, not to the word as publicly preached, but probably to talking by the wives themselves; not that all speaking to their husbands is forbidden, but he suggests as the chief means of winning them their **conversation**—i. e., *walk, conduct—*

The silence often of pure innocence
Persuades, when speaking fails.

Sharp criticism of the husband on account of his defects, even if they are moral defects, and a habit of complaining at her lot, will not only not win him to the gospel—it will make his rejection of it the stiffer. Paul says: "Faith cometh by *hearing*, and hearing by *the word* of God"; and so if the husband shall be won by means of the holy walk of the wife, it will be none the less true that the word will lie at the basis of the other instrumentality.

2. While they behold. See on 2: 12. **Your chaste,** etc.—*your deportment chaste in fear*—'chaste' used in the general sense of *pure*, as in James 3: 17. **Fear**—awe either toward God or toward the husband; more probably the latter. As the husband is exhorted (ver. 7) to honor his wife, the fear is far from slavish. It is holy apprehension of doing anything which shall appear to conflict with the duty enjoined in ver. 1, and so creating an obstacle to his conversion.

3. In this and ver. 4, submission to their husbands is still enjoined, but this is done by exhorting them to the exercise of qualities which will certainly lead to it—meekness and quietness of spirit; and to these qualities they are exhorted negatively, in contrast with that vanity which would lead them to make the adornment of their persons, their *bodies* indeed, the chief object of concern. Literally, *whose adorning let it be, not the outward of plaiting the hair*, etc. In the Common Version 'adorning' is repeated, and is printed in italics. The repetition is necessary, in order to express what the Greek says without repetition, and that very necessity makes the italics needless: *Whose adorning let it be, not the outward adorning, . . . but let it be,* etc. **Plaiting**—*braiding*, not for convenience, which might be allowable, but for ornament. **Gold**—*golden ornaments, jewels of gold*. (Revised Version.) **Apparel**—*garments* (plural in the original), worn for show; no reference to convenience. 'Plaiting,' 'wearing,' 'putting on.' Notice the activity of women in this sort of self-adorning. Vanity makes

44 I. PETER. [Ch. III.

4 But *let it be* the hidden man of the heart, in that which is not corruptible, *even the ornament* of a meek and quiet spirit, which is in the sight of God of great price.
5 For after this manner in the old time the holy women also, who trusted in God, adorned themselves, being in subjection unto their own husbands:
6 Even as Sarah obeyed Abraham, calling him lord:

4 but *let it be* the hidden man of the heart, in the incorruptible *apparel* of a meek and quiet spirit,
5 which is in the sight of God, of great price. For after this manner aforetime the holy women also, who hoped in God, adorned themselves, being in
6 subjection to their own ¹ husbands: as Sarah obeyed Abraham, calling him lord; whose children ye now

1 Or, *husbands (as Sarah . . . ye are become), doing well, and not being afraid.*

---

nimble fingers. Notice also the very emphatic position of 'not'; yet the negative thought which it introduces is not the leading one; that is introduced by 'but.' (Ver. 4.) The meaning of this prohibition will escape us, unless we bear in mind the extravagant love of ornament which characterized the Oriental mind, and the great irreligiousness which led to it. The Egyptian monuments tell surprising tales of female vanity, and the inspired prophet speaks of "the bravery of their tinkling ornaments about their feet, and their cauls, and their round tires like the moon, the chains, and the bracelets, and the mufflers, the bonnets, and the ornaments of the legs, and the head bands, and the tablets, and the ear rings, the rings, and the nose jewels, the changeable suits of apparel, and the mantles, and the wimples, and the crisping pins, the glasses, and the fine linen, and the hoods, and the vails." (Isa. 3: 18-23.) It is what Calvin calls the *morbum vanitatis quo mulieres laborant* (in Luther), *the disease of vanity under which women labor*, that Peter blames. Woman's love of ornament is a root of all evil, not less than man's love of money. Women may sin by wearing too little clothing as well as by wearing too much ornament. As the remedy for love of money in man is holiness (1: 15, 16; 2: 9), so also is holiness the remedy for love of outward adornment in woman. Giving too little attention to the decoration of their bodies will not, probably, very soon become a besetting sin of women.

4. The apostle tells them what their adorning ought to be. **The hidden man of the heart.** This is the general form of expressing the contrast with outward adorning. The ornaments in which their irreligious neighbors delight appeal to the eye; this, the man of the heart, is 'hidden,' pertains to what is within. Compare Rom. 7: 22 (the inward man); Eph. 3: 16 (the inner man); 2 Cor. 4: 16 (the inward man). **In that which is not corruptible,** etc., may be rendered: *in the incorruptibleness of a meek and quiet spirit.*

It is this of which the hidden man consists. Instead of fondness for outward ornament, they should adorn themselves with meekness (Matt. 5: 5) and quietness; and, unlike gold and superfluous apparel, such qualities are not corruptible—are imperishable. With such virtues they cannot fail to be submissive to their husbands. This spirit, whatever may be said of the world's judgment, is **in the sight of God of great price.** God is infinitely able to estimate the respective values. Man judges by a false standard. 'Great price,' *costly;* applied by Paul (1 Tim. 2: 9) to "array" (raiment), and by Mark (14: 3) to "spikenard." Compare ver. 3, 4, with 1 Tim. 2: 9, 10.

5. **For** strengthens the main exhortation (ver. 1) and the subordinate one of vs. 3, 4. **After this manner**—in the way just described. He draws an illustration from the times of the Old Testament. **Trusted in God**—*hoped.* The comma of the English (both the Common and the Revised Version) ought not to have been inserted between 'also' and 'who'; the connection is closer than the comma indicates. It was not holy women only who adorned themselves, but holy women 'who hoped in God.' According to the commonly received Greek, hoped *upon* God; but according to valuable manuscripts, hoped *in* God. They were adorned within. **Being in subjection.** See on the same in ver. 1. Submitting themselves to their own husbands was one of the manifestations of their meekness and quietness. **Their own.** See on the same in ver. 1, and in Critical Notes.

6. An eminent example is seen in Sarah, the wife of their distinguished progenitor. **Even**—a needless insertion. **Obeyed.** The original term is a mild one, *listened.* She *listened* to him, and it is implied that she listened to him in submissiveness of spirit. **Calling him lord** (Gen. 18: 12); doubtless the customary way of addressing him. Sarah was not faultless. In the affair of Hagar and Ishmael she showed more independence than was delicate, and more feeling than was necessary.

I. PETER.

whose daughters ye are, as long as ye do well, and are not afraid with any amazement.
7 Likewise, ye husbands, dwell with *them* according to knowledge, giving honour unto the wife, as unto the

are, if ye do well, and are not [1] put in fear by any terror.
7 Ye husbands, in like manner, dwell with *your wives* according to knowledge, giving honour [2] unto

[1] Or, *afraid with*........ [2] Gr. *unto the female vessel, as weaker.*

A meek and quiet spirit even then would have been more womanly, and better would it have been had she respectfully and gently declined to unite with her liege lord in one or two instances of deception. Yet she was usually so decorous and obedient that the apostle deemed her worthy of imitation by all pious women. "There be many women *now-a-days* that break away from their husbands." Compare 1 Sam. 25: 10. **Whose daughters.** The Greek means *children*, whether sons or daughters. Whose children ye are (*became* at the time of their conversion, but implying that they are so now), in the sense of spiritual descent. **As long as**—inserted by the Revisionists of 1611 to aid in bringing out what they supposed to be the meaning; but reference to time is erroneous. Nor ought *if* (Revised Version) to be supplied, as if they became Sarah's spiritual children on condition that they do good; nor *because*, as if they became children of Sarah because they do good. The meaning may be expressed thus: Whose children ye became, *as shown by your well-doing*—that is, in "their entire course of life, with especial reference to their marriage relations." (Huther.) **Are not afraid**, etc., is, literally, *fearing no frightening, no dread;* or, as some, not quite exactly, would say, *fearing no fear*. "Feared exceedingly" (Mark 4: 41), is, literally, *feared a great fear.* In 1 John 5: 16 is a similar peculiarity, "sin a sin"; in Col. 2: 19, "increaseth with the increase." It is an intense form of expression, and was not very seldom used in the Hebrew language before it came into use in the Greek. The peculiarity, though not quite so marked, is found here also. The apostle exhorts them not to fear that which, in itself, is adapted to make them fear; or, not to fear those who may attempt to make them fear. The men of the world, or, as the context requires, their ungodly husbands, may oppose; but they are not to fear. Some take from 'as' to 'ye are' as a parenthesis; thus: being in subjection to their own husbands (as Sarah obeyed Abraham, calling him lord, whose children ye are become), doing well, and not being afraid. This assumes that the participle for 'doing well' is to be connected with 'women' in ver. 5. If this is the right construction (which is by no means certain), it follows that after speaking of the 'holy women' of former times, the writer pauses a moment to illustrate by the case of Sarah as one of the class, and then, resuming, completes his description of the holy women, characterizing them as 'doing well,' etc. The Revised Version has this form in the margin as an alternative reading, and Westcott and Hort's Greek Testament has the same.

7. FOURTH EXHORTATION (*particular*); addressed to husbands. **Likewise**—directs to the exhortation given to wives at ver. 1, and hints that husbands are under obligations to their wives, as well as wives to their husbands. The form of the obligation is in part different. Husbands, neither here nor elsewhere, are required to be in subjection to their wives. The spirit of the obligation is the same—that is, the same in so far as both the husband and the wife are to be controlled by love. **Dwell with them**—refers to general daily intercourse. **According to knowledge.** In your marriage relations show intelligence and judgment. **Giving honour,** etc. In this part of the verse the meaning is not well given. Translate: *Dwelling according to knowledge with the female vessel as the weaker, rendering honor* [to them] *as also fellow heirs.* 'Vessel.' The husband is a vessel as well as the wife; but the wife is the weaker vessel. The word is applied to men (1 Thess. 4: 4); to human beings without distinction of sex. (Rom. 9: 21.) 'Weaker.' Not the man is a weak vessel, and the woman a weaker one. No such comparison is intended, and such a comparison would spoil the appeal; for it is just because the man is here assumed to be a strong vessel that he is exhorted to discharge his obligations to the woman. 'The weaker' cannot mean weaker in mind, for that women as a class would prove themselves, under equally favorable conditions, constitutionally inferior to men as a class, has not yet been shown to be even probable. Every cen-

weaker vessel, and as being heirs together of the grace of life; that your prayers be not hindered.
8 Finally, *be ye* all of one mind, having compassion

the woman, as unto the weaker vessel, as being also joint-heirs of the grace of life; to the end that your prayers be not hindered.
8 Finally, *be ye* all likeminded, [1] compassionate, lov-

[1] Gr. *sympathetic.*

tury has been brilliant with women of mental capacity which quite overtopped that of a large majority of men. The wife is the weaker vessel because she has been made subordinate. In harmony with this subordination she is inferior to man in strength of body. "But Peter speaks of the woman as the weaker vessel without intending thereby disparagement or offence to the sex, or to any particularly strong-minded or strong-bodied member of it. It is no insult to the vine to say that it is weaker than the tree to which it clings; or to the rose to say that it is weaker than the bush which bears it." (Lillie.) **Giving honour unto the wife**—expresses the chief thought. The wife's submission, then, is not dishonorable. **And as being fellow heirs**, etc. Not fellow heirs with one another, but with their husbands. The wife is to receive the incorruptible possession (1: 4), as well as the husband, which is a good reason for rendering honor—*i. e.*, by esteeming her. See Rom. 8: 17; Eph. 3: 6; Heb. 11: 9. **Grace of life**—grace consisting of life. **Your prayers**—perhaps family prayers offered by the husband or by both. Of Philip Henry it is said that "he and his wife constantly prayed together morning and evening; and never, if they were together at home or abroad, was it intermitted." (Dr. Mombert in Fronmüller.) Inference: Their married life must have been harmonious. They must have constantly borne in mind the relation which each was required to maintain toward the other, without, however, being distinctly conscious of a purpose to do so. Private prayers may be included. **Hindered**—cut into, cut in pieces, from which came the meaning—*impede, hinder.* (Huther.) Some say, prevented from rising to the throne of God; but Peter is aiming to prevent their prayers from being omitted. What may cause them to be omitted? Not dwelling according to knowledge with the wife as the weaker vessel, and not honoring her as a fellow heir, etc. The disharmony which will result will cut prayer to pieces; the services will be wholly omitted. The same thing might happen if the wife should be unmindful of her own obligation; but Peter plies the wife with one kind of argument, and the husband with another kind.

8. Exhortations to distinct classes having been closed, the apostle concludes this second series with exhortations to all, growing out of their relations to persecutors. It is remarkable that in this section the most simple practical hints are found in juxtaposition with one of the most difficult passages in the Bible. Working quietly and openly among the easy things of the Christian life, the apostle suddenly plunges (18-20) out of sight into a subject of the most difficult nature. **Finally**—indicative not of the termination of the Epistle, but of a purpose to avoid further particulars, and to utter thoughts of a general nature. **All**—every individual of every class named. What follows is expressed by means of five adjectives, no other word being used. It is a beautiful cluster of virtues—*united, sympathetic, brotherly, compassionate, humble;* or, using the more active form—*like-minded, sympathizing, brother-loving, tender-hearted, lowly-minded.* **Like-minded** refers more to feeling than to opinion, yet union of heart tends to create greater union of opinion. Opinions, however unlike, ought not to bristle with prejudice. Christendom has long needed more oneness of doctrine, but much more has it needed oneness of heart. Even true churches have always needed this divine exhortation (Rom. 12: 16; 15: 5; 2 Cor. 13: 11; Phil. 2: 2; 1 Cor. 1: 10; Eph. 4: 3); how much more has Christendom needed it! Making infants church members in the early ages of Christianity at length filled churches with unregenerate persons, and the practice continuing to the present day, doctrines and rites have been forced upon men by assemblies, councils, emperors, popes, and legislatures, concerning which the Scriptures say nothing whatever. The divisions of Christendom are the progeny, not of Christianity, but of the world. **Having compassion**—*sympathizing, sympathy*—brought into our language from the Greek, is *feeling with.* The readers are dissimilar, socially and intellectually, yet each is required to make the joys, and espe-

one of another; love as brethren, *be pitiful, be courteous*:
9 Not rendering evil for evil, or railing for railing: but contrariwise blessing; knowing that ye are thereunto called, that ye should inherit a blessing.
10 For he that will love life, and see good days, let him refrain his tongue from evil, and his lips that they speak no guile:
11 Let him eschew evil, and do good; let him seek peace, and ensue it.

9 ing as brethren, tenderhearted, humbleminded: not rendering evil for evil, or reviling for reviling; but contrariwise blessing; for hereunto were ye called,
10 that ye should inherit a blessing. For,
He that would love life,
And see good days,
Let him refrain his tongue from evil,
And his lips that they speak no guile:
11 And let him turn away from evil, and do good;
Let him seek peace, and pursue it.

cially the sorrows of others, his own. (Rom. 12: 15; 1 Cor. 12: 26; Heb. 13: 3.)

So two, together weeping, make one woe.

Sympathy is a rational emotion; may be much developed; and, though often moving with great rapidity, may become, under the influence of the moral judgment enlightened by the Scriptures, a permanent power, bearing the soul forward with planet-like order through the entire course of life. Mock suffering (the theatre) and suffering described (fiction) are but feeble stimulants to sympathy. Tears may be wasted when sympathy is hoarded. **Love as brethren**—*brotherly*, in the Greek, *philadelphoi*. A philadelphian is a lover of his brethren. (1: 22; 4: 8; Rom. 12: 10.) The English, *love as brethren*, may leave an erroneous impression. **Pitiful**—*tender-hearted*, so translated in Eph. 4: 32. **Courteous.** This stands for a word which has much less manuscript authority than another, which is properly rendered as above, *lowly-minded*. The trait is to be manifested toward one another (3: 5; Phil. 2: 3), and especially toward God. (5: 6; Acts 20: 19.) The opposite is self-conceit, which is self-esteem with its eyes shut against God. The wolf may dwell with the lamb, but self-conceit with humility never.

9. The previous verse refers to their relations to each other, this to their relations to the unregenerate world; yet the virtues enjoined in ver. 8 have an anticipatory reference to what was about to be said concerning their relations to the world. **Evil for evil**—evil deeds; **railing**—words. Peter knows that his Lord did neither (Matt. 26: 62, 63; 27: 12); and he remembers what a wrong use he himself once made of the sword. (Matt. 26: 51.) **But contrariwise**—*on the contrary*. Do directly the opposite, and talk directly the opposite. Implore **blessing** upon them. bodily and spiritual, temporal and eternal. Wonderful precepts! and with the strength of Christ as easily obeyed as any others, if

one has the lowliness of mind enjoined at the close of ver. 8. Pride is the spur of retaliation. **Knowing.** The Greek has little reason for being accepted as genuine. Read thus: *Because to this end ye were called, that ye should inherit blessing;* that ye should come into possession of the blessings of the gospel provided for this life and the next. They were called (2: 21) by the Holy Spirit. If they are possessors of such blessings, surely they ought to implore blessings on those who maltreat and malign them.

10. The Old Testament (Ps. 34: 12-16) again lends its aid to the apostle of the New, for the purpose of strengthening the exhortations of ver. 9. The usual form of quotation is wanting, yet with slight variations the words are those of David, as reproduced in the Septuagint. For is Peter's, and connects the quotation with the preceding verse. **He that will love life.** 'Will' is not the usual auxiliary sign of the future. Read: *He that desires to love life;* or, *that would*. It takes for granted that life may be one of true happiness. The thought is peculiar. It is Peter's rather than David's; for David says: "He that desireth life." Peter gives prominence to *loving* life. The pessimist, if consistent, hates life. **To see good days** is to experience them—that is, to have them and enjoy them. Notice the use of the word in Luke 2: 26; Heb. 11: 5; John 3: 3. 'Good days,' in this life—the possession of none but believers. Even the sorrow of those who love God cannot make good days bad days. (Rom. 8: 28; 2 Cor. 4: 16; 6: 10.) **Let him refrain,** etc.—as if it were impossible to desire to love life, if the tongue were allowed to have its way. See James 3. **Guile,** *deceit.* See on 2: 1, 22.

11. Eschew, etc.—*turn away from evil.* It is a general, comprehensive precept, referring to evil of whatever kind. **And do good,** also a comprehensive precept, but it enjoins a positive virtue. "Went about doing

12 For the eyes of the Lord *are* over the righteous, and his ears *are open* unto their prayers: but the face of the Lord *is* against them that do evil.
13 And who *is* he that will harm you, if ye be followers of that which is good?
14 But and if ye suffer for righteousness' sake, happy *are ye:* and be not afraid of their terror, neither be troubled;
15 But sanctify the Lord God in your hearts: and be

12 For the eyes of the Lord are upon the righteous And his ears unto their supplication: But the face of the Lord is upon them that do evil.
13 And who is he that will harm you, if ye be zealous of that which is good? But and if ye should
14 suffer for righteousness' sake, blessed *are ye:* and
15 fear not their fear, neither be troubled; but sanctify in your hearts Christ as Lord: being ready always to

good," was said of Christ by this very apostle. (Acts 10: 38.) The farmer who merely abstains from sowing bad seed will reap nothing. **Seek peace**—a more particular direction. See Matt. 5: 9. To live peaceably in heaven with all will be easy; to live so here with all is scarcely possible (Rom. 12: 18); yet we are not only to seek peace, but we are to **ensue** (*pursue*) it. We are to make a vigorous and determined effort to make others peaceable and peaceful, and this is most easily done by being peaceable and peaceful ourselves. Much freedom must be granted to one another to do the usual work of life in the way preferred—in the family for example, and in the place of business, if peace is to thrive. There is no better trade to which to put a child than peace-making. In affairs moral and religious, we must be "first pure, then peaceable" (James 3: 17), yet persecution for religious opinions, even in the mild form of uncharitableness, is utterly contrary to the spirit of Christ.

12. For. This, too, is Peter's word, for David's. It points to the ground upon which the exhortations of ver. 11 rest—namely, the Lord's relation to the righteous and the wicked. **Are over**—*are upon;* that is, turned upon. **Unto their prayers**—*toward* them. 'Against,' 'upon'—the same word in the Greek as stands before the word for *righteous.* The contrast, then, between the Lord's course toward the righteous and toward the wicked is not expressed in the preposition, nor in *face.* The contrast is expressed by **but**—and the contrast how great! **Lord.** As nothing in the context requires it to be applied to Christ, it may have the reference which it has in the Psalm from which the words are taken.

13. Intensity is given to the thought by the interrogative form. Peter once had sharp experience of the power of questions. (John 21: 1 -17.) The apostle would here confirm the exhortation to do good. **Will harm**—too feeble. The rendering is stronger in Acts 7: 6, 19 (*entreat evil, evil entreated*); in 12: 1 (*vex*); in 18: 10 (*to hurt thee*). **Followers**—

imitators. But valuable manuscripts have a word which means *zealous*—*if ye are zealous of that which is good.* There are two possible meanings of the first part of the question: Who is he that will be *able* to do you evil? and, Who is he that will be *disposed* to do you evil? If the latter is the meaning, the question must have been asked in view of the supposition that usually the world will not be disposed to persecute those who lead a truly Christian life; but it can scarcely be said that in apostolic times this was usually the case. If the former is the sense, it implies that no one can do them any real and essential evil. God will parry the blow. Which is the correct view is uncertain. See Isa. 50: 9; Rom. 8: 31, 33, 34.

14. But and if—a "barbarous" translation (Lillie), an "innocent archaism" (Schaff). The English Revisers, as the latter reminds us, naturally adhere to these archaisms. Read: *But if also ye should suffer.* **For righteousness' sake**—on account of their Christian life. See *righteous* in ver. 12, *a good conscience and good conversation* in ver. 16, and *well doing* in ver. 17. **Happy**—*blessed,* which is less suggestive of hap, luck, chance. 'Happy' has taken on a Christian meaning, but even now it has less aroma than *blessed.* The sentiment which Peter here expresses fell upon his ear from the lips of Christ when upon the Mount (Matt. 5: 11.) Persecution will make these Christians more blessed here, and this fragrant result of suffering will extend into the next life, never to be diminished, but ever to be augmented. Be **not afraid of their terror**—*fear not their fear;* be not afraid of the terror with which they would harass you. See on ver. 6. These words and the first clause in ver. 15 may be a "free translation" of Isa. 8: 12, 13.

15. But sanctify—*reverence as holy.* Compare "Hallowed be thy name." (Matt. 6: 9.) **The Lord God**—*Lord the Christ;* or perhaps better, *the Christ as Lord,* according to the approved reading. The exhortation stands ready always to *give* an answer to every man that asketh you a reason of the hope that is in you, with meekness and fear:

16 Having a good conscience; that, whereas they speak evil of you, as of evil doers, they may be ashamed that falsely accuse your good conversation in Christ.

17 For *it is* better, if the will of God be so, that ye suffer for well doing, than for evil doing.

in contrast with the one immediately preceding: Fear not *them*, but fear *as holy the Christ as Lord.* Isa. 8: 13 is literally: "Sanctify Jehovah of hosts." For *Jehovah* Peter uses *Lord*. Thus the apostle enjoins the duty of sanctifying Christ as Jehovah, which *may* be a proof of Christ's Deity. Had Peter, at an earlier period, had more reverence for the Lord, he would not have feared men, and denied him. Compare Matt. 10: 28. He has been qualified by bitter experience to exhort others. Fearing God makes one superior to the fear of men. Some fear the world even when the world bears no sword. **In your hearts**—otherwise there is no reverence. **And be ready**—*being ready.* The Greek for 'and' is not genuine. They must not only reverence Christ *in the heart*, but must also be ready to make an *oral* expression. **To give an answer**—literally, *be ready for an apology*—that is, for a "defence" (Phil. 1: 7); "what clearing of yourselves" (2 Cor. 7: 11); "answer" (2 Tim. 4: 16.) The use of the word implies that those who are supposed to ask for the reason of their hope, ask with little sympathy, not to say with some opposition. (Ver. 14, 16.) The answer given is therefore of the nature of a defence. **Always**—never unprepared, never unwilling, never timid. **Every man**—without respect to his position or his character. **A reason of**—a reason *concerning*. **The hope**—the hope in Christ, with all the blessed results. See on 1: 3, 13, 21. Be ready to make us full a statement as the circumstances may require. As they are to be always ready to do it, it follows that the reference is not specially to the first profession of faith. Lips which opened then, but never afterward, would seem to have opened mechanically, not under the sweet influence of a renewed heart. Too many are like the silent letters of our language—nothing would be lost if they were all dropped out. **With meekness**, etc. In several manuscripts the Greek is preceded by a word meaning *but* or *yet*, which makes the contrast more striking. They must be ready with a defence, *but* the

give answer to every man that asketh you a reason concerning the hope that is in you, yet with meekness and fear: having a good conscience; that, wherein ye are spoken against, they may be put to shame
17 who revile your good manner of life in Christ. For it is better, if the will of God should so will, that
18 ye suffer for well-doing than for evil-doing. Be-

defence must be made in the right spirit. They must avoid the appearance of arrogance, and must fear lest their defence be such as to do more harm than good.

16. Having a good conscience. This connects with 'ready.' (ver. 15.) A good conscience is a conscience unstained with conscious guilt, or with unforgiven sin, or with intention to do wrong. It implies that the conscience has been made white through faith in Christ. Without a good conscience, their readiness for defence would be false. **That whereas,** *wherein*, or, in the matter in which. It is similar to the form of expression in 2: 12, upon which see note. **Your good conversation in Christ**—*good manner of life in communion with Christ.* **Be ashamed**—desirable even if nothing more should come from it. Oh, that the consciences of all were so pure that the accusations were false and the accusers ashamed!

17. For. In ver. 16 the apostle virtually exhorts them to have a good conscience, and now he gives a reason in support of the exhortation. **If the will of God be so,** literally, *if the will of God should will it.* The noun refers to the will of God as a faculty, and the verb to exerting the faculty. 'The will of God' refers to the suffering. The form of the verb implies the *possibility* that such may be God's will. Should it be his will that you suffer at all, it is better to suffer for the reason that you do well than for the reason that you do ill. See 2: 20 and comments. **Better**—more for the honor of Christ, better for yourselves, for such suffering will bring the usual blessed result—sanctification. Or, let *better* be explained by 2: 19-21.

18-20. THE DESCENT OF CHRIST TO HELL. Such is the title which a large majority of interpreters, whether Roman Catholic or Protestant, would prefix to this section, with what reason may appear after examination. No passage in the New Testament, none perhaps in the Bible, has been considered during at least fourteen hundred years more difficult. The main statement, with the subordinate

D

18 For Christ also hath once suffered for sins, the just for the unjust, that he might bring us to God, being put to death in the flesh, but quickened by the Spirit;
19 By which also he went and preached unto the spirits in prison;

cause Christ also [1] suffered for sins once, the righteous for the unrighteous, that he might bring us to God; being put to death in the flesh, but quickened in the spirit; in which also he went and

[1] Many ancient authorities read *died.*

clauses, has received almost innumerable explanations. Many of the people, while disinclined to accept the view that Christ, in the interval between his death and resurrection, descended to the abode of lost spirits and preached to them, yet have been so bewildered by what Peter is made by our translators and many of the expositors to say, that they have settled down in despair of ever arriving at a satisfactory view. The meaning is made no plainer by the Revised Version. Some of the reasons for the interpretation about to be given will be found in the Critical Note.

For, *because.* It indicates that the apostle is to give a reason for something, and that something is implied in ver. 17—namely, the duty of bearing up under suffering in welldoing. This duty is urged by two considerations: 1. Christ suffered; 2. He preached to wrong-doers. The wrong-doing is set in a stronger light by presentation of the circumstances under which it continued to be committed. To preach to such men required long-suffering. **Also** is to be connected with *suffered for sins.* Notice the striking contrast between their suffering for well-doing and Christ's suffering for sins. The appeal, which is from the greater to the less, is one of incomparable strength. **For sins,** *on account of sins.* **Once.** It implies only once. See Heb. 9: 26, 28; Rom. 6: 9, 10. It may be referred to the entire period of his earthly suffering, but the context shows that the apostle was thinking chiefly of his final sufferings. **The just for the unjust,** *the righteous for the unrighteous.* **Hath suffered,** should be *suffered,* for Peter refers to what occurred and was completed at some previous time. Some manuscripts give another reading, which means *died,* and this is put in the margin of the Revised Version. Many critics prefer it. 'For' the unjust. See Critical Note on the same preposition in 2: 21. The idea of substitution is clearly indicated in the context, even if it is not expressed in the preposition itself. **That he might bring us to God.** Men are separated from God—that is, they are

in want of that life which consists of communion with God. So far, then, as respects themselves, the object of Christ's suffering is to restore them to God's life—that is, to bring them into constant communion with their Creator. The verb implies very near approach to God. The scientific saying, *Omne vivum ex vivo (all life comes from life)* fails of verification in man viewed as a being of spiritual capacities; for in man there is no life to generate life. See Eph. 2: 5 ("when we were *dead . . . quickened* us"). "The spiritual life is the gift of the living Spirit." (Drummond, "Natural Law in the Spiritual World," *Biogenesis.*) **Being put to death in the flesh, but quickened by the Spirit;** *in spirit* is the more correct rendering. The meaning is not, that flesh as mere flesh died, and that the spirit as mere spirit was made alive, but that the death of Christ was the death of Christ in flesh, and that the quickening of Christ was the quickening of Christ in spirit. The Common Version, *by the Spirit* (as if there were allusion to the Holy Spirit), is here wrong. In the Greek the contrast is more strongly expressed. See Rom. 1: 3, 4; 1 Tim. 3: 16. As pre-existent, Jesus Christ was glorious in his "spiritual essence," but through all his earthly life that glory was partly veiled in flesh, and in flesh he was put to death. But at his resurrection, (compare ver. 21) he was quickened *in spirit*—that is, he came into repossession of the glory of his spiritual nature. That this quickening in spirit occurred at the resurrection, not between the death and the resurrection, is clear from Rom. 1: 4. How, then, could Christ be said to have gone *in* that spirit (ver. 19) to the abode of the lost between his death and his resurrection? But whether he went at all is to be seen chiefly in ver. 19, 20.

19. By which—*in which* spiritual nature. **Also**—not, as Lange and some others, *even.* It looks back to the *also* of ver. 18, thus: Because Christ *also* suffered, etc. (the one fact); he *also* preached (the other fact). These two facts are reasons why the readers should bear up under suffering in well-doing.

20 Which sometime were disobedient, when once the longsuffering of God waited in the days of Noah, while

20 preached unto the spirits in prison, who aforetime were disobedient, when the longsuffering of

He went, etc. Translate the remainder of the verse and the first clause of ver. 20, not as in the Revised Version, but, *he went and preached to the spirits in prison when formerly they were disobedient.* Those who heard the preaching, heard it when they were living in disobedience. They rejected the preaching, were lost (ver. 20, last clause; 2 Pet. 2: 5), and now, while Peter is writing, are in prison, disembodied, and are therefore spoken of as spirits. **In prison.** See Rev. 20: 7; Matt. 5: 25. The word is of frequent occurrence in the New Testament, and means *a place of confinement.* Here it means the place in which the wicked are punished after death. It is very necessary to the correct understanding of this passage, to notice that the word does not express the idea which the ancient classics attached to *hades,* and the ancient Hebrews, sometimes, to *sheol*—namely, the place of disembodied spirits, good and bad. The conception of such a place is entirely foreign to the New Testament. In the New Testament, hades is the place in which the wicked are punished (Luke 16: 23); in the Common Version, *hell*, transferred in the Revised Version, *hades.* The good are not there. They are in heaven, called, in three instances, *paradise.* (Luke 23: 43; 2 Cor. 12: 14; Rev. 2: 7.) Jesus died before the robbers. (John 19: 32, 33.) Those who affirm that Christ went to hades—*descended to hell* (the phrase found in some of the most widely-accepted creeds), and there preached to the wicked, invariably imply that he went immediately. But if he went immediately, he must have torn himself from his *impenitent* hearers just as their attention was becoming aroused, in order to fulfill his promise by meeting a *penitent* in paradise. The contradiction between the words of Jesus (Luke 23: 43), "Verily I say unto thee, to-day shalt thou be with me in paradise," and the representation made by Peter, *as commonly explained,* is complete. Christ could not have been with the saved robber in Paradise, and, at the same time, with the lost antediluvians in "hell." A very remarkable attempt has recently been made[1] by Dr. Davidson, of London, to save Peter as witness to a second probation for the antediluvians, by denying the authenticity of the words in Luke. The denial is based upon the one fact that the words were wanting in the copy used by Marcion, a heretic; and though admitting that Epiphanius says that Marcion "cut them off," Dr. Davidson will not admit that Epiphanius is in this to be believed. The scholar may do well to consult the Critical Apparatus in the Eighth Edition of Tischendorf's Greek Testament. Marcion took liberty with the text of Luke, which is not to be justified. ("Westcott on the Canon.") If the interpretation of Peter now to be given is correct, there is no contradiction between the apostle and the evangelist. But the question turns chiefly on the meaning of the next verse. **Preached.** The original word is not the word which means to preach the gospel; it is more general, meaning to *proclaim*, to *announce*, from which some have inferred that it was the preaching, not of glad tidings, but of condemnation. But the more general word is so often used to express the preaching of the gospel (Matt. 4: 17; 10: 7; 11: 1; Mark 1: 38), that this may be its import here. **Went.** Great weight has been attached to this word in support of the view that Christ *went in person* to the prison of the lost. But the word does not necessarily imply personal locomotion. See Gen. 11: 5–7, and especially Eph. 2: 17. Such language would have been entirely admissible (for it would have been in harmony with the genius of the Greek tongue), had Peter desired to say that Christ brought himself into connection with the persons in question, either by his Spirit, or by means of some pious inhabitant of the earth.

20. Which sometime were disobedient —*when formerly they were disobedient.* See the translation above and Critical Notes. The preaching occurred at the time of the disobedience, not thousands of years afterward. That it occurred long after the disobedient were swept away has been taught by the majority of expositors, including some recent distinguished interpreters of Germany. The common view is held in most remarkable disregard of the construction of the Greek.

---

[1] See *The Christian Register*, March 19, 1885.

the ark was a preparing, wherein few, that is, eight souls were saved by water.

God waited in the days of Noah, while the ark was a preparing, [1] wherein few, that is, eight souls, 21 were saved through water: which also [2] after a true

[1] Or, into which few, that is, eight souls, were brought safely through water........[2] Or, in the antitype.

In the next two clauses, Peter makes a more distinct statement of time and persons. **Once.** For this the Greek has scarcely any manuscript authority. **When the long suffering of God,** etc. The spirits who were in prison when Peter was writing these words were persons who lived their earthly life in the days of Noah. God's forbearance toward sinners is often mentioned in the Scriptures— e. g., Rom. 2: 4; 9: 22; and here much vividness is added to the description by **waited,** especially in the original, where the word for *waited* is intense, *to wait out, to wait long for.* God waited one hundred and twenty years (Gen. 6: 3), not, as some say, seven days. (Gen. 7: 4.) "This sentence, as we may gather from the context, was made known to Noah in his four hundred and eightieth year, to be published by him as a 'preacher of righteousness' (2 Pet. 2: 5) to the degenerate race." (Keil.) He was six hundred years old when the flood came. What long suffering does God still manifest in waiting for the repentance of sinners! **While the ark was a preparing**—*an ark being in the process of building.* Here the time of the long suffering is very exactly given. Every blow of the ax and the hammer was a call to repentance. 'Ark.' Gen. 6: 14-16. See Matt. 24: 38; Luke 17: 27; Heb. 11: 7. **Wherein**—*in which,* though strictly the original preposition is such as to imply that they first *went into* it. **That is, eight**—a tragical explanation! **Souls.** In most cases this word is not a mere equivalent for a personal pronoun—*e. g.,* "And I will very gladly spend and be spent for your souls" (Common Version, *for you,* 2 Cor. 12: 15), but the word gives prominence to their spiritual nature as that which was the chief subject of regeneration. The use of the word *soul* instead of *you* contributes to vivacity. (Winer.) The verse before us, however, is one of the few in which the Greek for *souls* may have no special significance, in which it is equivalent, that is, to persons. 'Eight.' (Gen. 7: 7.) **Saved by**—*through, by means of.* In the margin of the Revised Version is the alternative rendering—*into which few, that is, eight souls, were brought safely through water.* But in the next verse the apostle represents water, in baptism, as saving us, and therefore, if the contrast is to be deemed pertinent, it was water through which, *by means of which,* Noah and his family were saved. But how could they be said to be saved by means of *water?* Was not the *ark* the means? Notice again the preposition (εἰς)—*into* which few (*going*) were saved by means of water. The apostle associates the idea of *going into* the ark with the idea of *being saved by water.* It is impossible to separate the one idea from the other, though, if we make the mistake of interpreting according to the mere letter, we shall say that only the water without its relation to the act of *going into* the ark was the means of their being saved. But *from what* were they saved? Clearly, that from which all the others were *not* saved—that is, from perishing, from death. They were indeed delivered from the prevailing corruption, but this is not the fact here intended. The *infants* that perished by drowning were as truly saved from the prevailing corruption as the "eight." Punishment (in the case of all but the infants) did indeed follow the drowning, but the first and palpable fact is that they perished by loss of life. Noah and his family were saved. They continued to live. Farrar hits in this case nearer than he sometimes does, for he says: "Perhaps this means 'by water as an instrument'—*i. e.,* because the water floated the ark."

Thus we learn that those to whom Christ preached were the unbelieving people of Noah's time. But *how* did he preach? That is a question of little importance, and one on which the interpretation of the passage as a whole ought not in any degree to be made to turn. Peter himself does not answer it, yet Christ may have preached through Noah's preaching, for *the Spirit of Christ* was in the prophets, and testified, etc. (1: 11.) Or he may have preached by an influence exerted more directly upon their minds. See John 1: 4, 5 for proof that before the incarnation the Word was in the world, and wrought upon the souls of men. [See note on John 1: 4, 5 for a slightly different view.—A. H.] Those words show that whatever light the antediluvians had, came from Christ before he became flesh. Yet the preaching was more than the general influence of the word upon men before his incarnation.

21. The water by which Noah was saved suggests to Peter the water of baptism. The meaning of the accepted Greek is, *which* (water), *as an antitype* (as something resembling it, as a like figure), *is now saving you also—namely, baptism*. Antitype may not imply that the flood was a type of baptism in the usual sense of the word *type*. It may express only the idea of resemblance to the flood. As water saved Noah, so baptism is now saving you. *You* is the rendering of the genuine Greek. But what is meant by baptism saving them? There are a few passages in the New Testament which seem to teach, like this, that baptism precedes in the order of time forgiveness, regeneration, salvation. On the other hand, there are many passages which certainly do teach that baptism must not precede, but follow. To the latter class belong, for example, Matt. 3: 6-8; 28: 19, 20; Mark 16: 16; Acts 2: 41 (presenting an argument of cumulative force, because the number of cases in which baptism followed the spiritual change was three thousand); 8: 12; 8: 30-39; 9: 17, 18; 10: 43-48; 16: 14, 15, 29-34. Besides these and other proof-texts, the general spirit of the New Testament implies that baptism is preceded by regeneration. The chief passages which seem to teach the precedence of baptism, or, as some would say, regeneration or forgiveness of sin *in* baptism, are, besides the one before us, the following: "Except a man be born of water, and of the Spirit"—more exactly, of water and the Spirit (John 3: 5); "Arise and be baptized, and wash away thy sins, calling on the name of the Lord" (Acts 22: 16); "Repent and be baptized, every one of you . . . for the remission of sins." (Acts 2: 38.) Ought these special exceptions to the general rule to govern the interpretation of the very numerous passages above cited, or ought the many passages to govern the interpretation of these few? If the latter, then the few passages cannot mean that water-baptism is a condition of baptism by the Spirit, and the doctrine that men must be baptized in order to be born again is unscriptural. Equally unscriptural, therefore, is the view that regeneration cannot be expected to occur "on the sea or in the chamber, on the highway or in the field, in the mill, the shop, or the store"—"at any point of time in man's life." After coming to a result by this general law of *interpreting the few passages by the many*, one may examine each of the few passages in detail, and it will be seen that not one of them teaches the doctrine of baptismal regeneration, so strongly pronounced by Professor Adams to be the "keystone of the arch" of all the Christian doctrines, including even "the atonement of our blessed Redeemer."[2]

Administered as it always ought to be, in its primitive form, baptism is a vivid reproduction in figure, in symbol, of the great FACT, *already accomplished*, that the soul, having been regenerated by the Spirit of God, has been buried to sin and been raised to holiness; and a vivid representation in figure, in symbol, of the twofold EVENT, yet future, the burial and resurrection of the body, the latter guaranteed by the resurrection of Christ. The figurative representation of the *bodily* change is so vivid, that the change seems by faith to be occurring *now*—that is, in the very act of being baptized; and the figurative reproduction of the *spiritual* change is so vivid that this change also seems by faith to be brought forward to the same point. One might as truly say, therefore, with Christ, *Ye must be born of water and the Spirit*; or, with Ananias, *Be baptized, and wash away thy sins*; or, with Peter, *The like figure whereunto even baptism doth also now save us*—as to say, Believe, and be baptized. The latter direction is plain—not figurative, not symbolic, and therefore it expresses exactly *the time-relation of faith and baptism;* the former directions are not plain, but are symbolic, figurative, and therefore the exact time-relation *is not given*. Thus the interpretation of the few, and, it may be added,

---

[1] Prof. Wm. Adams, of the Episcopal Church ("Regeneration in Baptism").
[2] For an explanation of the passages supposed to teach baptismal regeneration, the reader is referred to the Appendix to the Commentary on the Gospel of John.—A. H.

21 The like figure whereunto *even* baptism doth also now save us, (not the putting away of the filth of the flesh, but the answer of a good conscience toward God,) by the resurrection of Jesus Christ:

likeness doth now save you, *even* baptism, not the putting away of the filth of the flesh, but the ¹ interrogation of a good conscience toward God, through 22 the resurrection of Jesus Christ; who is on the right

¹ Or, *inquiry*; or, *appeal*.

obscure, passages by the many, concerning which there is no obscurity whatever, is justified. Baptism, then, is the symbolic representation of what literally took place before. "*It pictures in the present* what has been experienced in the past. . . . The past is presented again emblematically in baptism, as if it were present." (President A. Hovey.) Coming "to the baptismal font," the soul "comes to ratify in the appointed way its own previous act of surrender." (Lillie.) Thus, not more necessary is it here than in the other passages with which it has been classed to see the doctrine of baptismal regeneration. **Save us** (*you*), as well as Noah and his family. **Now** contrasts the present time with that of Noah. **Doth save**—not, *saved*, or *will save*. The present may here be used to express the general fact that baptism saves; or, it may denote continuance of action, *is saving you*. In the latter case, it denotes the spiritual influence of baptism continued through life. Such continued influence will be greater or less, according to one's clearness of spiritual perception. It is to be feared that with many persons it is painfully small.
Baptism. The act denoted by this word is an immersion of the entire body. As regeneration had respect to the *entire* man, as the entire man in regeneration is buried to sin and is raised to holiness, and as the bodies of the regenerate are to be buried and to be raised from the grave, the rite is beautifully and wonderfully expressive. (Rom. 6: 3, 4; Col. 2: 12.) "And how, as for a moment the prostrate form of the disciple disappears beneath the wave, is the whole solemn story of our death in Christ silently rehearsed!" (Dr. A. J. Gordon, "In Christ.") "There can be no doubt," says Dean Goulburn of the Episcopal Church, "that baptism, when administered in the primitive and most correct form, is a divinely constituted emblem of bodily resurrection."
Not the putting away, etc.—a definition, first negative then positive, of what baptism is. Heb. 9: 10, 13 makes it not improbable, that Peter had Jewish ceremonials in his eye. In any case, baptism as such has no effect in improving the outward man, though millions have been taught to think otherwise. **But the answer**, etc. The difficulties of the passage pertain chiefly to the word translated *answer*. It is certain that this translation is incorrect, but as the word occurs nowhere else in the New Testament, scholars are not agreed as to its meaning. The Revisers show their own uncertainty by translating "interrogation," and putting in the margin, "Or, *inquiry*, or *appeal*." Question, request, inquiry, seeking after, asking, are the chief meanings assigned. It is also queried whether the 'good conscience' is already the possession of him who requests or whether it is the object of the request. Some translate: *The inquiry of a good conscience after God*; some, *the question directed to God for a good conscience*; some, *the asking of a good conscience*, meaning, *the asking in which we address God with a good conscience*, our sins being forgiven and renounced; some, *the stipulation* (promise) *toward God of a good conscience*. It is clear that with such variety of translation, positiveness relative to the meaning would be unseemly. On the whole, *inquiry* or *requirement* is perhaps the best rendering: *Baptism is the requirement of a good conscience toward God.* Baptism is something which a conscience, made sensitive and pure relative to the will of God requires, or, something concerning which it makes inquiry. **A good conscience** is a conscience sprinkled with the blood of Christ and also purified by the Spirit. (Heb. 9: 14; 10: 2, 22.) It is such a conscience which makes request. It became such before baptism, which implies that the subject had already been regenerated. **By the resurrection of Jesus Christ.** *Through* is here better than *by*. Connect with *saves* and notice its relation to *quickened in spirit*. (Ver. 18.) It gives the means by which baptism is made symbolically so efficacious. See 1: 3. There seems to be a silent reference to Christ's death. All turns on the question whether Christ rose from the dead. (1 Cor. 15: 14-17.)

Before leaving this part of the chapter, a

Ch. III.] I. PETER. 55

22 Who is gone into heaven, and is on the right hand of God; angels and authorities and powers being made subject unto him.

hand of God, having gone into heaven; angels and authorities and powers being made subject unto him.

---

brief quotation from Dean Stanley's "Christian Institution" (Chap. I., "Baptism"), may not be amiss: "Baptism was not only a bath, but a plunge—an entire submersion in the deep water, a leap as into the rolling sea or the rushing river, where, for the moment, the waves close over the bather's head, and he emerges again as from a momentary grave. . . . This was the part of the ceremony on which the apostles laid so much stress. It seemed to them like a burial of the old former self and the rising again of the new life. . . . The essence of the material form is gone. There is now no disappearance as in a watery grave. . . . It is but the few drops sprinkled." Saddening as is the departure from apostolic practice, by which a "human invention" (Dean Stanley) has been introduced into the Christian world in place of that which God requires, the Dean expresses himself with entirely too great positiveness, since the apostolic act of baptism is retained throughout the large Greek Church, and is practiced by a great company of believers in the United States, by many in England, and many in other countries, and is pretty rapidly working its way into nearly all the evangelical churches of Christendom.

22. The ascension of Christ, hitherto implied (1: 21), is now affirmed. Thus, in this unique passage (19-22) has the apostle swept from the spiritual activity of the unincarnated Word, in the earlier period of human history, through the deep vale of earthly suffering, to the triumphal appearance on the mediatorial throne. The Sufferer is Sufferer no more. The groundwork of appeal to suffering Christians is complete. **Who is gone into heaven,** etc.—*who is on the right hand of God, having gone into heaven,* is more exact, as in the Revised Version. (Rom. 8: 34; Mark 16: 19; Heb. 1: 3; Col. 3: 1.) To sit on God's right hand is a peculiar honor granted to Jesus Christ. See Ps. 110: 1, quoted by our apostle in his discourse on the Day of Pentecost. (Acts 2: 34, 35.) "Supreme dominion is most clearly meant"; "his being seated on the mediatorial throne as the result and reward of his sufferings"; "the sacred writers never speak respecting the Logos (Word, John 1: 1) considered simply in his *divine* nature, as being seated at the right hand of God; but only of the Logos *incarnate*, or the Mediator, as being seated there." (Stuart on "Hebrews," p. 559, 1833.) See Hackett, "Acts" (belonging to the present Series), 2: 34, who makes an ampler quotation from Stuart. **Angels and authorities and powers**—not any class of human beings, whether on earth or in heaven, but heavenly beings. Of their difference and employments we know little. But see Heb. 1: 14. The three classes may be mentioned in the order of their rank; their rank may be the same. We may know more of them hereafter. More study of God and less inquisitiveness concerning angels would have made some people wiser. Paul uses the same or similar words. See Eph. 1: 21; Col. 1: 16. However exalted the beings are, they are **made subject** —*are subjected* to Christ. Thus Christ as Mediator is over all. (Heb. 1; Col. 1: 18.)

CRITICAL NOTES.—CHAPTER III.

1. ἰδίοις is here, and in most other places, properly translated *your own*—that is, it expresses more emphasis than the Greek personal pronoun. Denied by Meyer; Fronmuller goes to the other extreme. Lillie takes the medium view, as Ellicott also on the parallel passage (Eph. 5: 22), the latter saying, "*Your own husbands*—those especially yours, whom feeling, therefore, as well as duty, must prompt you to obey. Compare 1 Pet. 3: 1. The pronominal adjective ἰδίοις ('*your own*') is clearly more than a possessive pronoun (De Wette), or, what is virtually the same, than a formal designation of the husband. . . . It seems rather both here, and in 1 Pet. 3: 1, to retain its proper force, and imply, by a latent antithesis, the *legitimacy* (compare John 4: 18), *exclusiveness* (1 Cor. 7: 2), and *specialty* (1 Cor. 14: 35) of the connection. . . . It may still be remarked that the use of ἰδίοις in later writers is such as to make us cautious how far in *all* cases in the New Testament (see Matt. 22: 5; John 1: 42), we press the usual meaning." It is not the classic way of expressing the possessive and reflexive sense, but it *is* the way of the New Testament writers.

20. The New Testament of the Bible Union, the Common Version, and the Revised Version, translate the words relative to preaching to the spirits in prison in essentially the same way. They all use a relative pronoun and a verb: *Which* (who) *were disobedient*. In the same way are the words translated by perhaps the majority. If this rendering is correct, there is no escape from the conclusion that Christ preached to the sinners of Noah's day two thousand years after they died. If the interpretation, which is now to be controverted and rejected is deemed to be necessary (and that is the plea) as a defense of the character of God, it would seem to be the duty of those who take that view to reconcile the hypothesis with the remarkable fact that God permitted those sinners to suffer *two thousand years* before using any means whatever to bring them to repentance. That two thousand years was a short period compared with eternity is not at all to the purpose. If giving them "another chance" was necessary as a vindication of divine goodness, it is impossible to see the justice of postponing the offer so long.

An examination of the construction, made by President S. C. Bartlett, appeared in the "New Englander," October, 1872. The subject is discussed in the "Bibliotheca Sacra," by Prof. Cowles, and in the "Presbyterian Quarterly," by Dr. Nathaniel West. Dr. Bartlett's article was examined, and its main position rejected, by Dr. W. W. Patton, in the "New Englander," July, 1882. To this President Bartlett rejoins in the "Bibliotheca Sacra" for April, 1883. It is important to see the points at issue. *Unto the spirits which were disobedient* (τοῖς πνεύμασιν ἀπειθήσασιν). Here is a noun with the article, followed by an aorist participle without the article. It is admitted that if the participle had the article, it could properly be translated with a relative pronoun and verb. Then antecedency of time would not be expressed, and Christ might have preached long after the disobedience. As the participle has no article, it cannot properly be translated *who were* disobedient. That the aorist participle without the article should be translated in some other way than by using the relative pronoun and the verb, is clear from the teachings of grammarians and from usage.

I. The grammarians are agreed in recognizing the aorist participle when connected with a verb as expressing what occurred before the action of the main verb, as Winer, Buttmann, Kühner, Goodwin, and many others. The grammarians more or less distinctly recognize also the difference between the aorist participle with the article and the aorist participle without the article. With much unanimity they teach, that with the article the participle is *attributive*—attributes some quality; and without the article is *predicative* —predicates or affirms something; and in the latter case, whatever else may be included, expresses *antecedency of time*.

II. Usage is very clear in support of these distinctions, and this must be the last ground of appeal. President Bartlett cites chiefly from Matthew. We may notice the usage in the Acts. "*When* they had fasted," *having* fasted (13:3) (aorist). "*When* Paul and his companions loosed they came"; or, as in the Revised Version: "Paul and his company set sail *and* came"; "*Having* put to sea they came." (13:13.) (Hackett.) In both cases the aorist was required, because the act preceded the act of the verb. Either of the three ways of rendering in the last instance expresses antecedency. "David, *having* served, *after* he had served, fell asleep." (13:36.) "The apostles, *having* heard, *having* sent, they ran in." (14:14.) The *hearing* and the *sending* took place before the running (aorist therefore). "Whom ye slew and hanged." (5:30.) Overlooking the aorist of the participle, the Common Version makes the Jews first to have slain Jesus, and then to have hanged him on a tree! Whom ye slew, *having* hanged him, or more freely, *by* hanging him. Many more cases could be cited from the Acts. This usage pervades the New Testament. President Bartlett has "counted more than a hundred in the first sixteen chapters of Matthew, all denoting preliminary action." Winer (§20, 1) cites 1 Pet. 5: 10: "Peculiarly instructive," he says, "respecting the use and the omission of the articles with participles": "But the God of all grace, *who hath called us, after* that ye *have suffered* awhile." Here are both forms, a participle with the article (*attributive*), and therefore properly translated by means of a pronoun and a verb (*who hath called*); and a participle without the

CHAPTER IV.

FORASMUCH then as Christ hath suffered for us in the flesh, arm yourselves likewise with the same

1 Forasmuch then as Christ suffered in the flesh,

article, and therefore correctly translated not with the pronoun but with some sign of time, as *when* or *after*. Were the three English Versions, already mentioned, as regardless of Greek usage here as they are in the verses before us, they would say, not *after* that ye have suffered, but *who* have suffered. Then we should have, *who called us who suffered*. But the apostle prays that the readers may be perfected, stablished, and strengthened, *after* they have escaped; hence the aorist participle without the article. The usage of the Greek language, then, as appears from these and very many other instances which might be cited, shows that the translation, unto the spirits *which were disobedient*, cannot be sustained. The Greek should be rendered in such a way as to show that the act expressed by the participle occurred before and at the time of the preaching, thus: He preached unto the spirits *when formerly they were disobedient*; or, "on their being once upon a time disobedient." The participle tells us *when* Christ did the preaching—*when the sinning was done*, not thousands of years afterward. See additional confirmation of this view in a note in Smith's "Dictionary of the Bible," p. 2786, American edition, by Prof. Thayer.

"Probably," says President Bartlett, "the Vulgate (or, rather, Itala) is largely responsible for the acceptance of the common rendering; and it was facilitated by the doctrine of the descent into hades, which, at a later period, found its way into the 'Apostles' Creed,' and thus into the 'Articles of the Church of England,' the Lutheran 'Formula of Confession,' and even into Calvin's 'Institutes.' The theological bias of Christendom has favored the erroneous rendering." It is deeply to be regretted that the doctrine of Christ's "Descent to Hell" should still be taught as a doctrine of Scripture. See Huther, Fronmüller, with an Excursus by Dr. Monbert in the English translation, Farrar in "Early Days of Christianity," and many others. Farrar, with no examination, in the work cited, of the Greek construction, pronounces the doctrine of Christ's "Descent into Hades" ("Descent into *Hell*," three pages further on) as "inestimably precious," and complains of "the torturing of the passage and of the human perversity expended upon it." It is in support of the dogma of a second probation—that is, a probation after death—that fresh interest in the passage has recently been awakened in certain quarters in our own country; but, if the Greek bears the interpretation here most heartily accepted, that doctrine finds no countenance in this part of our Epistle. If there are any sinners to whom God grants a second probation, they are not such sinners as the contemporaries of Noah. These were giants in wickedness. They had light enough to make their guilt of awful dye. They were among the last persons to whom Peter would represent God as granting another probation; for mark carefully what he says in his Second Epistle. (2:5): "God *spared not* the old world, but saved (preserved) Noah, the eighth person, a *preacher of righteousness*, bringing in the flood upon the world of the ungodly." See also what Christ himself says in Matt. 24: 38, 39.

> In religion,
> What damned error, but some sober brow
> Will bless it, and approve it with a text
> Hiding the grossness with ornament.

Ch. 4: 1-6. SECOND SERIES OF EXHORTATIONS (*continued*).

The exhortations arising from the relation of the Christians to persecutors are continued. Ver. 1 has general connection with the entire section (3: 18-22), but is closely related to ver. 18.

1. **Forasmuch then as Christ hath suffered**—*Christ, then, having suffered*, is more literal. We have already been reminded by similar allusions, that Peter once repelled the thought that his Lord was to suffer, saying, "This shall not be unto thee." (Matt. 16: 22.) Four times since the opening of the Epistle has he given special prominence to the fact. (1: 11; 2: 21; 3: 18; 4: 1.) He had been instructed (Matt. 16: 21; Luke 9: 31), but his self-confidence was strong; and, besides, he held the opinion, then prevalent, that the Messiah, whenever he

mind: for he that hath suffered in the flesh hath ceased from sin;
2 That he no longer should live the rest of *his* time in the flesh to the lusts of men, but to the will of God.
3 For the time past of *our* life may suffice us to have wrought the will of the Gentiles, when we walked in lasciviousness, lusts, excess of wine, revellings, banquetings, and abominable idolatries:

arm ye yourselves also with the same ¹ mind; for he that hath suffered in the flesh hath ceased ² from 2 sin; that ᵃ ye no longer should live the rest of your time in the flesh to the lusts of men, but to the will 3 of God. For the time past may suffice to have wrought the desire of the Gentiles, and to have walked in lasciviousness, lusts, winebibbings, revel- 4 lings, carousings, and abominable idolatries: where-

1 Or, *thought*........ 2 Some ancient authorities read *unto sins*........ 3 Or, *he no longer . . . his time*.

might come, was not to die. His present convictions respecting the necessity of Christ's sufferings are as strong as Paul's. **In the flesh**—*as to the flesh*, in that state. Christ's death is included in the suffering. **Arm yourselves likewise**—*do ye also arm yourselves*. As ships and chariots were equipped for battle, so they *also* as well as Christ are to be morally furnished. **The same mind**—*same thought* or *disposition*. Christ had the disposition to suffer, and they must be equipped with the same. The disposition will be as *armor* in which to meet their persecutors. He who has no mind to suffer, who assumes that suffering is unnecessary, that so far as it springs from man it is even unjust, is like an unarmed man on the field of battle. Not seeking suffering as merit, but calmly awaiting it, is imitation of Christ! **For he that . . . from sin** has the nature of a parenthesis. It is to be referred, not to Christ, but to the Christian. He who with conscious reference to Christ's disposition to suffer, has himself suffered in the flesh, has been made to cease from sin (*sins*, Wescott and Hort), has been transferred from sin to holiness. Through suffering. sin has ceased to rule over him. [Does not the expression "suffered in the flesh" (ὁ παθὼν σαρκί) refer to death? The suffering of Christ just referred to was a suffering of death. The clause may be regarded as parenthetic.—A. H.] **For us** (ὑπὲρ ἡμῶν) is to be rejected. *Hath ceased* (πέπαυται) may be taken in the passive sense: he *has rest* from sin, *is preserved* from sin.

2. That. Connect with 'arm yourselves.' The third person singular (*he*) is no reason why the clause may not be connected with one containing a word in the second person plural, for in the Greek there is no pronoun whatever. It may therefore be rendered as in Revised Version: That *ye* may no longer . . . *your* time. It assigns the *end* of the arming. **The rest**—an impressive hint that a part of their earthly life has gone beyond

their control. **In the flesh.** It marks them as still being in this life. It is not used, as Paul often uses it, in the sense of *depraved nature*. **To the lusts**—*according to*, and lusts of the grosser kind. (Ver. 3, 4.) **To the will**—*according to*. How opposite these rules of life! so opposite that the former is not a rule; sin is defiance of all rule. Compare Eph. 2: 12; Gal. 5: 17; Rom. 6: 20. The obligation to live 'according to the will of God,' presupposes that will to be righteous. The contrast between men and God is as great as between lust and infinite purity. **No longer** holds a very emphatic position.

3. May suffice—a striking way of hinting that their former mode of life ought not to have existed at all, but it is also a rhetorical softening of the description. **Us.** This seems to class the writer himself with the others; but (1) it need not be supposed that *all* the readers, much less Peter, had been addicted to these different kinds of vice, and (2) the Greek for *us* is rejected as of little authority. **Will** (*desire*) **of the Gentiles**— a proof, say some, especially as they had been guilty of idolatry, from which the Jews had certainly become free, that the readers were Gentiles. It may be sufficient evidence that some of the readers were Gentiles, as other expressions are proof that some of them were Jews. 'The will of the Gentiles' and 'the will of God'—thoroughly antagonistic, and this fact is the foundation of missions. **Walked** —customary. **Lasciviousness.** The Greek of all the nouns is plural, which, perhaps, indicates the variety of the forms of evil. **Excess of wine.** The correct rendering is simply *wine-drinkings*, or, as in the Revised Version, *wine-bibbings*. **Revellings, banquetings**—*carousings*, riotings after supper, "the guests often sallying into the streets with torches, music, frolic, and songs in honor especially of Bacchus." **Abominable idolatries**—unlawful idol-worship, including the terrible immorality connected with it. It

4 Wherein they think it strange that ye run not with them to the same excess of riot, speaking evil of you;
5 Who shall give account to him that is ready to judge the quick and the dead.

in they think it strange that ye run not with them into the same ¹excess of riot, speaking evil of you:
5 who shall give account to him that is ready to judge
6 the quick and the dead. For unto this end ²was the

1 Or, *flood*,.......2 Or, *were the good tidings preached.*

was unlawful, for it was contrary to the will of God. Compare this description with that of Paul. (Rom. 1: 19-32.) Peter and Paul failed to make the discovery made by the sharp eyes of some modern religionists, that there is about as much truth at the bottom of idolatry as in Christianity. See Critical Notes.

4. Wherein. The original, being in the singular, it is difficult to refer this to the various vices with which it stands in such close relation. Some refer it to 'suffice' (ver. 3), and would express the meaning thus: *They think it strange that it suffices you to have wrought the will of the Gentiles.* Some refer it to what follows: **That ye run not with them,** etc. It may be referred to what precedes, taken as a whole, yet the prominent thought is that the unconverted Gentiles think strange, are surprised (the surprise manifesting itself in slander) at the change from such habits of wickedness to their present mode of life. The text gives a graphic description of the torrent-like excitability of men who are borne by their passions into evil. **To the same**—*into* the same. **Excess** (*flood*) **of riot**—outpouring of debauchery. It is a metaphor of great strength. The form of expression was doubtless drawn from what was observed in the rushing of flood-waters into excavations of the land. Their wicked neighbors and townsmen were amazed that they did not still rush with them into the outpourings or overflowings of debauchery. They slandered them for it. These are not the sins in which most Christians of modern times indulged before their conversion, and therefore they are not the sins into which they are in greatest danger of running with the ungodly. Running with the world is possible without running with it into the grosser evils. The more velvety forms of social sin are now, in Christian countries, the more dangerous. The life of God in the soul of man includes morality; but morality, and that of a high order, is possible without life.

5. Give account. An account (see on 3: 15) was sometimes demanded of Christians by men of the world, even by opposers; but these shall give account to Christ. A solemn sight will it be when all who rejected Christ and slandered his people are standing before the Judge, and are required to make a report of their manner of life and of their reasons for pursuing it. Matt. 12: 36. Compare Heb. 13: 17. **To him.** Christ is to be the Judge. (Acts 10: 42; 2 Tim. 4: 1.) Sometimes he is said to be the Being through whom God will judge. (Acts 17: 31.) **The quick and the dead**—those who are alive and those who are dead. Of course, it includes those who may be alive at Christ's second coming and all who may have died. Thus are meant all human beings whatsoever. **Ready.** Some explain this word by "the end of all things is at hand" (ver. 7), as if the readiness consisted in being about to do it, which is a good explanation on condition that the latter words are evidence that Peter was expecting the coming of Christ to be very near. But even without such reference the words are solemnly significant. Jesus Christ is ready by *personal qualification* to ascend the tribunal at any moment when the purposes of God relative to the salvation of men shall have been accomplished.

Heaven is above all yet; there sits a judge
That no king can corrupt.

6. It is sufficiently surprising that the Roman Catholic Church should here, as in 3: 19, 20, find purgatory, but it is more surprising that as there so here even some Protestant scholars should as easily find "Christ's Descent to Hell." Recently men of rationalistic and men of "broad church" views have been fired anew in support of the latter interpretation. If this passage teaches the doctrine of a second probation, the *Descent to Universalism* would seem to be less difficult. Their interpretation proceeds upon two unproved assumptions: 1. That God has no right to punish men who have never heard the gospel. But see Rom. 1: 19, 20. 2. That even those who may have heard and rejected, ought to have "another chance." Two more prelimi-

6 For, for this cause was the gospel preached also to them that are dead, that they might be judged according to men in the flesh, but live according to God in the spirit.

gospel preached even to the dead, that they might be judged according to men in the flesh, but live according to God in the spirit.

nary remarks may be made: 1. That even if it were impossible, as perhaps it is, to arrive at entirely satisfactory results, it is certainly impossible to obtain from the text, by any process of interpretation which will not put it into contradiction to the teachings of Christ, and to other teachings of the apostles, the doctrine that Christ descended to hades to give the lost "another chance" to be saved. 2. The advocates of the "Descent" are utterly and hopelessly at variance among themselves relative to the object for which the "Descent" was made; whether to preach to the antediluvians who perished in the flood impenitent, or to those who perished repenting at the last moment; whether to all sinners of the ancient world, or to Old Testaments saints; and whether the object was to preach the gospel, or to preach condemnation.

For. It gives the verse a particular connection with 'to judge the quick and the dead,' and a general connection with the entire section beginning at ver. 1. There the exhortation is, to arm themselves with the same mind that Christ had—namely, the mind to suffer—a thought which lies with great weight upon the heart of the writer; for he knows that they have already suffered, and evidently believes that yet greater sufferings await them. In *this* verse he continues to encourage them. **For this cause**—*for to this end*. The end is introduced by '*that.*' **Also**—to those who are dead as well as to those who are still living. Some translate by *even ;* preached *even to them* who are now dead. **Them that are dead**—more briefly and exactly, *to the dead.* The chief question here is, Who are meant by the dead? The dead spiritually? or the dead physically? The latter is clearly the meaning in the closing word of the previous verse, and this may lead us to presume that is the meaning here. But not all the dead are meant, for to many of the dead the gospel had never been preached. The reference is to *dead believers.* **That,** etc. All that follows, to the close of the verse, expresses the end for which the gospel was preached to those *now dead ;* namely, **that they might be judged,** etc. But how could the gospel have been preached to them for such an end? The pertinency of the statement in the last clause is easily seen, but not the pertinency of what is said here. The difficulty may be removed by supposing that the sign used to express the end (*that*), passes over the former of the two clauses and connects itself only with the latter. Upon that view the meaning may be given thus: that though they might be judged according to men in the flesh, yet, etc. In support of this view may be adduced Rom. 6: 17: "But God be thanked that ye were (that *having once been*) the servants of sin, ye have obeyed," etc.

But in what sense might these now deceased Christians have been judged according to men in the flesh? Two different answers have been given: 1. Their death may be called a *judgment* or *condemnation*, since death comes upon all men, Christians not excepted, as condemnation for sin. 2. They may have been *judicially condemned to death*—martyrs. Though they may have been judged in the one way or in the other, yet the gospel was preached to them that they might *live according to God in the spirit*. **According to men** —*after the manner of men*. Thus the readers may be encouraged to bear up under their sufferings by the consideration that those who have already died, whether unjustly condemned by the judicial power, or adjudged to the death of the body in the ordinary course of nature—that they **live in . . the spirit.** The life was eternal; it was the life of the spirit; it was a divine life, for it was **according to God;** and the gospel was preached to them that that very end might be accomplished. The writer is far from confident that this interpretation of the most difficult passage in the Epistle is correct. He is not satisfied with any interpretation which he has seen; but, as it would conflict with a great multitude of passages, he is utterly unable to accept the explanation that the apostle teaches a second probation.

Ch. 4: 7-5: 9. THIRD SERIES OF EXHORTATIONS.

This series pertains to their general church

7 But the end of all things is at hand: be ye therefore sober, and watch unto prayer.

7 But the end of all things is at hand: be ye therefore

life. It is pervaded with deep solemnity, being tinged with thoughts in reference to the end of all things (ver. 7), the second coming of Christ (5: 4), and the judgment. (ver. 17, 18.)

7. First Exhortation. But does not contrast what follows with what precedes; it is rather an index to another line of thought. The verse contains a proposition and an exhortation; the exhortation being clothed in the form of an inference. To the proposition is given the prominent place, though, in fact, the exhortation is the main thing. **The end of all things.** See on 'the last time' (1: 5); on the appearing of Jesus Christ (1: 7); and also on 'the revelation of Jesus Christ' (1: 13). The words before us cannot possibly be referred to the time of each man's death. To what can they refer but to the supposed coming of Christ? **Is at hand**—more exactly, *has come near*. But in what sense do Peter and Paul and other apostles teach that the end of all things has come near? One view, which, perhaps, is the correct one, has been lucidly expressed by Hackett on Acts 3: 20. The importance of the subject will justify the quoting of almost the entire passage : "Nearly all critics understand this passage as referring to the return of Christ at the end of the world. The similarity of the language to that of other passages which announce that event demands this interpretation. The apostle enforces his exhortation to repent, by an appeal to the final coming of Christ, not because he would represent it as near in point of time, but because that event was always *near to the feelings and consciousness* of the first believers. It was the great consummation on which the strongest desires of their souls were fixed, to which their thoughts and hopes were habitually turned. They lived with reference to this event. They labored to be prepared for it. They were constantly, in the expressive language of Peter, *looking for and* (in their impatience as it were) *hastening the arrival of the day of God*. (2 Pet. 3: 12.) It is then that Christ will reveal himself in glory, will come "taking vengeance on them that know not the gospel," and "admired in all them that believe" (2 Thess. 1: 8, 10), will raise the dead (John 5: 28, 29), invest the redeemed with an incorruptible body (Phil. 3: 21), and introduce them for the first time, and forever, into the state of perfect holiness and happiness prepared for them in his kingdom. The apostles, as well as the first Christians in general, comprehended the grandeur of that occasion. It filled their circle of view, stood forth to their contemplations as the point of culminating interest in their own and the world's history; threw into comparative insignificance the present time, death, all intermediate events; and made them feel that the manifestation of Christ, with its consequences of indescribable moment to all true believers, was the grand object which they were to keep in view as the end of their toils, the commencement and perfection of their glorious immortality. In such a state of intimate sympathy with an event so habitually present to their thoughts, they derived, and must have derived, their chief incentives to action from the prospect of that future glory. As we should expect, they hold it up to the people of God to encourage them in affliction, to awaken them to fidelity, zeal, perseverance, and, on the other hand, appeal to it to warn the wicked and impress upon them the necessity of preparation for the revelation of the final day. For examples of this habit the reader may see Acts 17: 30, 31; 1 Tim. 6: 13, seq.; 2 Tim. 4: 8; Titus 2: 11, seq.; 2 Pet. 3: 11, seq., etc. Some have ascribed the frequency of such passages in the New Testament to a definite expectation on the part of the apostles, that the personal advent of Christ was nigh at hand; but such a view is not only unnecessary, in order to account for such references to the day of the Lord, but at variance with 2 Thess. 2: 2. The Apostle Paul declares there, that the expectation in question was unfounded, and that he himself did not entertain it or teach it to others. But while he corrects the opinion of those at Thessalonica, who imagined that the return of Christ was then near, neither he nor any other inspired writer has informed us how remote that event may be, or when it will take place."

[It is doubted by many whether Dr. Hackett's view of 2 Thess. 2: 2 is correct, though it is still defended by able scholars. Thus, the Revised Version by the Bible Union translates ἐνέστηκεν, *is at hand;* the Revised English Bible, *were close at hand;* Prof. Noyes,

8 And above all things have fervent charity among yourselves: for charity shall cover the multitude of sins.

fore of sound mind, and be sober unto ¹ prayer: 8 above all things being fervent in your love among yourselves; for love covereth a multitude of sins:

¹ Gr. *prayers.*

were close at hand. But Alford translates the word, *is come;* Ellicott, *is now come.* With the former agree Robinson in his Lexicon (s. v. ἐνίστημι) and Grimm, "Lexicon Græco-Latinum in Libros N. T." In favor of the view assumed by Dr. Hackett to be correct is the consideration that, according to 1 Thess. 4: 16, the advent of the Lord was to be in visible glory, and the Thessalonians could scarcely have supposed that he had thus come in already. Or, if they had adopted so erroneous a view, it would have been most effectually refuted by assuring them that Christ's Presence was to be a visible one at his coming.—A. H.]

Be ye therefore sober. In view of the end be sober, of *sound mind.* It is opposed to erratic, insane views of things. Control yourselves in the use of the appetites and passions. **Watch.** See on the word *sober* (1: 13), where the original is the same as here. **Unto prayer**—*unto prayers.* 'Prayer' is to be connected with 'be sober' as well as with 'watch'; be sober unto prayers as well as watch unto prayers. 'Unto' indicates the *end* of the soberness and watchfulness; namely, 'prayers'; that is, they are to be in such a state of mind that the spirit of prayer shall be kept alive and be strengthened. The plural is no evidence of allusion to public written prayers. Compare Eph. 6: 18; Matt. 26: 41. Praying may precede watching, as watching may precede praying. The two cannot well be separated. Had Oliver Cromwell's army done all the praying which it is reported to have done, without any watching, its victories had been ignominious defeats. Yet watching without praying is almost sure to lead into some tempestuous Euroclydon. (Acts 27: 14.) Had Peter watched, not all the demons of perdition would have been able to make him deny Christ; had he prayed more, he would have watched more, and so would have remained steadfast. His exhortation was indeed prompted by an impressive view of Christ's second coming, yet his own sad fall must have made him conscious of a stronger impulse to give it.

8. SECOND EXHORTATION. It is more closely related to that of ver. 7 than it appears to be. Be sober and watch; **have, rather, having fervent charity.** *In connection with* sobriety and watchfulness have *charity (love).* **And** is to be rejected from the text. **Above all things.** But the love which is here set so high is mutual love, love to God not being mentioned. Love to one another is put not above love to God, but above all the duties which they owe to each other. Without mutual love, the churches of which they were members would be disintegrated or petrified. In either case, all other duties toward one another would go undone. The love must not be merely negative, only saving them from biting and devouring one another (Gal 5: 14, 15), but it must be 'fervent' (*intense*). See on 'fervently,' 1: 22. Compare 1 Cor. 13: 4-7; 14: 1. Such love should be *cultivated.* The true construction is: *Above all things having your love toward one another intense.* They are not exhorted to love, but to love with intensity. **For charity shall cover** (*covereth*) **the** (rather, *a*) **multitude of sins;** a reason given, enforcing the duty. Proverbs 10: 12, is: "Hatred stirreth up strifes; but love covereth all sins." The latter half is to be understood in the light of the former half, for they are in contrast. Hatred produces and inflames strife; love neither inflames nor produces sin; more than this, which is only negative, it keeps down sin, prevents it from rising; or, if it is rising, quenches it as a garment may smother an outbursting flame. Such being the meaning of the passage in Proverbs, this must be substantially the meaning here. 'A multitude.' One virtue may be more than a match for many sins, not in itself, but as nourished by the life of God, as, in the strictest sense, originating in that life. It is sin in another which is meant. Some Roman Catholic expositors deny this, and the denial is believed by some to be the natural offspring of extravagant views relative to personal merit. Sinners need mercy, since they have no merit. Perhaps the latter half expresses forgiveness of sin committed; or, it may express the effect of love in preventing the committal. Peter

Ch. IV] I. PETER. 63

9 Use hospitality one to another without grudging.
10 As every man hath received the gift, even so minister the same one to another, as good stewards of the manifold grace of God.
11 If any man speak, *let him speak* as the oracles of God; if any man minister, *let him do it* as of the ability

9 using hospitality one to another without murmuring:
10 according as each hath received a gift, ministering it among yourselves, as good stewards of the
11 the manifold grace of God; if any man speaketh, *speaking* as it were oracles of God; if any man ministereth, *ministering* as of the strength which God

---

learned this precious truth from his Lord. See Matt. 18: 21, 22. He had asked how often he ought to forgive an offending brother, and probably thought he put the number high when he asked, "till seven times"? "Seventy times seven," was the Lord's reply. So Peter, well qualified to say it, tells his readers that love covereth a *multitude* of sins.

9. One of the *manifestations* of the love enjoined in ver. 8. **One to another.** It should be kept in mind that the Epistle is directed to many, and these scattered in different provinces. (1:1.) It follows that opportunities for showing hospitality would not be few. Hospitality is sometimes shown by savages, but is purest and most constant where Christianity exerts its strongest influence, whether in the city or in the country. Compare Rom. 12: 13; Heb. 13: 2; 3 John 5; 1 Tim. 3: 2; 5: 10. See a singular illustration of inhospitableness in Diotrephes. (3 John 9, 10.) Jesus extolled the virtue in Peter's hearing (Matt. 25: 35, 36), but condemned selfish forms of it. (Luke 14: 12-14.) Wisdom is necessary lest hospitality be withheld from the worthy and conferred upon the worthless. **Without grudging.** To grudge was formerly to *murmur openly*, but it now means what it was beginning to mean even when the Common Version was made (Trench, *Authorized Version*), to *repine inwardly*. The Revised Version renders, *murmuring*. The Greek seems to be used in one case (John 7: 12, compare 13) to express "whispering, low and suppressed discourse." (Robinson.) If given at all, hospitality should be given with cheerfulness. It is possible to give it with hypocritical cheerfulness, in comparison with which it would be better to imitate certain Samaritan villagers. (Luke 9: 53.) Of the two, he who gives hospitality and murmurs when the guest has gone that he came, and he who refuses to give it to one who needs it, the former would seem the more richly to deserve *the fire*. (Luke 9: 54.) But it is difficult to know his state of mind before commanding the fire to descend; so false are his words and face.

10. Another manifestation of love. **The gift**—a *gift*. In the times of the early Church,

miraculous endowments were conferred at baptism, and these were *charismata* (gifts). See Rom. 12: 6-8; 1 Cor. 12: 4, 28. But the apostle may also refer to natural endowments and the usual endowments of grace. Whatever gift any Christian has should be used, not merely or chiefly for his own advantage, but for the good of others. The entire church should have the benefit of it. He should '*minister*' it, should employ it in the service of others; should not deem it beneath him to do so. **Even so** is an unnecessary insertion. **As good stewards**—as is fitting men who do not possess the gifts in their own right. They are but stewards; they hold the gifts in accountability to him who is the Lord of stewards—God. The Christian who has an impressive view of this cardinal fact, and *acts accordingly* in all his church relations, is probably as near perfection as he will ever be in this life. The **grace** is **manifold**—various, many-colored, because of the variety of the gifts which grace confers.

11. Two kinds of gifts are specified, *speaking* and *ministering*. **If any man speak.** Speaking in the church, to which alone is the reference, was either in the form of prophesying, or teaching, or exhorting. (Rom. 12: 6-8.) **As the oracles of God.** What he speaks he must speak, not as if it were woven out of himself, but as communications from God, drawn either from the Old Covenant or from the New. [Does not λόγια θεοῦ (*oracles of God*) taken in connection with χάρισμα (*gift*, ver. 10) point to *inspired* communications, uttered by one who has the gift of prophecy, rather than to communications taken from inspired sources?—A. H.] **Let him speak as.** The words supplied 'let him speak,' are connected by some with 'minister' in ver. 10, which will be made clear by supplying *ministering*, thus—*as ministering the oracles*. Whatever the gift, he must minister it for the good of others. But it is better to supply, as in the Common Version and the Revision, 'let him *speak*,' or, *speaking*. If any man has the gift of *speaking*, that he must minister. **If any man minister ... as of the ability, etc.**—that

ity which God giveth; that God in all things may be glorified through Jesus Christ: to whom be praise and dominion for ever and ever. Amen.

12 Beloved, think it not strange concerning the fiery trial which is to try you, as though some strange thing happened unto you:

13 But rejoice, inasmuch as ye are partakers of Christ's sufferings; that, when his glory shall be revealed, ye may be glad also with exceeding joy.

---

supplieth: that in all things God will be glorified through Jesus Christ, whose is the glory and the dominion [1] for ever and ever. Amen.

12 Beloved, think it not strange concerning the fiery trial among you, which cometh upon you to prove you, as though a strange thing happened unto you: 13 but insomuch as ye are partakers of Christ's sufferings, rejoice; that at the revelation of his glory 14 also ye may rejoice with exceeding joy. If ye are

[1] Gr. *unto the ages of the ages.*

---

is, *as ministering of, out of, the strength*, etc. It is evident that 'minister' is here used in a narrower sense than in ver. 10. This specific ministering consisted probably for the most part of relieving the poor, the sick, and the aged. Whatever service is done must be done in conscious acknowledgment of the fact that it is done, and all the good which may result from it, in strength given from above—an exhortation always needed, so prone is religious activity to forget its divine origin. **That the end declared**; namely—that God, not themselves, may have the honor of the ability and success. **Through Jesus Christ**—since Christ is the Mediator through whom God ministers strength. **To whom**—to God, is on the whole the more probable, since *God* stands as the subject in the preceding clause. (Huther.) **Forever and ever**—one among the many instances in which the words express *unending duration*. **Amen**—as an adjective, *true, faithful;* as an adverb, *truly, verily.* It was sometimes used as a response. (1 Cor. 14:16.) At the close of doxologies, it means as here, *so be it.* Thus, even before the approaching end of the Epistle (5:11), the apostle hastens to give utterance to his overflowing spirit of praise in a sublime doxology. **Be praise** (glory) **and dominion**—whose *is the glory and the dominion.* It is not the expression of a wish; it is a declaration. See on 1:3. The article is never used either in classic or New Testament Greek by chance: it always means something. Here it hints that praise and dominion rightfully belong to God; the glory and the dominion *which are his due.*

12. Third Exhortation, growing out of their relation to persecutors. With the related thoughts it extends to the end of the chapter. **Beloved.** See on 2:11. **Think it not strange**, etc.—be not surprised at. **The fiery trial**—literally, *burning,* applied figuratively to trial, calamity, here 'fiery trial,'—a "felicitious rendering." Our translators have taken no notice of two words which stand before the Greek for 'fiery trial.' Translating them, we have the fiery trial *among you.* The trial affected, or threatened to affect, them *all;* it was among them viewed as a community. The trial may have been in part the beginning of the persecution by Nero, or it may have been the slanders of those among whom they dwelt. (2:20; 3:9, 16; 4:4.) **Which is to try you.** Putting their Christian character to *the test* for the sake of improving it was the end of the fiery trial. That the human activity employed to test them was itself sinful is no evidence that the end was not designed by the Holy One. He who passes through life without sharp trials is more to be pitied than congratulated. **Happened**—*were befalling you.* Be not surprised, for your trials are the fruit of God's purpose. Good men in all ages have been called to suffer, and blessed will be the results.

13. Rejoice. Rejoice in the fiery trial, which is better than to be surprised at it. They are not merely to "hold still" and let the test work out the intended result, but they are to rejoice. **Inasmuch**—*in proportion as,* or, *in so far as.* It may be arranged thus: *So far as ye are partakers of Christ's sufferings, rejoice.* Their enemies would persecute Christ if he were among them, for it is really he who is the object of their hatred; and, therefore, in being persecuted themselves, they are partakers of Christ's sufferings. See Col. 1:24. But the chief reference must be to the sufferings which Christ himself bore. **Shall be revealed**—should be, *in the revelation.* **Also**—should be brought in earlier than it is either in the Common Version or the Revision, thus: *that also in the revelation,* etc. It puts in contrast the joy which they are to have in the future with the joy which they ought to have now. 'The revelation'; to be made at his second coming, and the glory which will eternally follow. Compare Matt. 25:31; Col. 3:4. **Glad,** etc. Though the same strong word in the original is applied (1:6-8) to their state of mind in

14 If ye be reproached for the name of Christ, happy *are ye*; for the Spirit of glory and of God resteth upon you; on their part he is evil spoken of, but on your part he is glorified.
15 But let none of you suffer as a murderer, or *as a* thief, or *as* an evil doer, or as a busy-body in other men's matters.

reproached ¹ for the name of Christ, blessed *are ye*; because the *Spirit* of glory and the Spirit of God 15 resteth upon you. For let none of you suffer as a murderer, or a thief, or an evil-doer, or as a meddler 16 in other men's matters: but if *a man suffer* as a

¹ Gr. *in*.

---

this life, yet here it seems to be put in contrast with the weaker term, rendered 'rejoice.' They should rejoice now, and doing so, they will rejoice exultingly then. Peter learned long before to do what he here exhorts others to do. He is not a mere theorist. A golden experience makes golden utterances. The possibility of rejoicing in trials has had many signal illustrations in the history of the Lord's people, not only in martyrdom, but in sickness and poverty. The writer once had acquaintance with a Christian woman who was remarkable for spirituality and for sweetness of disposition under long protracted and painful sickness. In one of his calls, he ventured to ask how she thought she could receive the announcement that she was to lie in such suffering *seven years more?* With quiet firmness, and with what no one who knew her could doubt was the result of profound self-knowledge, she replied: "It would make no difference to me—just as my Saviour chooses." Seven years more of suffering were allotted her—confined to the bed fourteen years—but her spirit continued to the last in the same sweet harmony with the will of God.

14. A confirmation of ver. 12, 13, by a distinct reference to the *reproach* (railing), as caused by their relation to Christ. **Be reproached**—*are reproached*. **For the name of Christ.** The meaning is made clear by Mark 9: 4 (a cup of water to drink *in my name, because ye belong to Christ*). In our passage the original preposition is the same as in Mark, and instead of *for the name* might stand *in* the name. Peter might have added, as Jesus added, the explanatory words, "because ye belong to Christ." **Happy**—*blessed.* See on the same word, 3: 14. **For** (*because*)—points to the proof that they are blessed. **The Spirit of glory**—the Holy Spirit; and he is called the Spirit of glory as Christ is called the Lord of glory (1 Cor. 2: 8), and God the Father of glory. (Eph. 1: 17.) The glory of the Spirit is seen in his nature and work. Notice the contrast implied in *reproach* and *glory.* To you belongs reproach; to the Spirit, glory. On the other hand, the glory of the Spirit becomes yours, **resteth upon you.** The enemies of Christians are in truth the only ones that have reason to regard themselves as objects of shame. The Christians could have avoided reproach by continuing with the men of the world, but they would not have gained the abiding glory of the Spirit. **And of God.** If we translate *even* instead of 'and,' we make *Spirit of God* explanatory of *Spirit of glory.* "The Spirit of glory and (consequently) the Spirit of God—the Spirit of glory, which is no other than the Spirit of God himself." Meyer, § 20, p. 132. The Revised Version translates with *and.* The reference is both to the Holy Spirit and to God the Father. The remainder of the verse has little manuscript authority, and is rejected by leading critics.

15. **But**—*for.* Peter introduces the warning with this particle, in order to impress upon his readers the fact that the blessedness can be theirs only on condition that sufferings come upon them as Christians. Should they be guilty of murder, or of theft, or, speaking more generally, of any kind of immorality, and suffer in consequence, that will change the case; no blessedness can be theirs, for the Spirit of glory and of God will not rest upon them. **As.** The supply of this word before **thief** and **evil doer** is unnecessary. It stands before **busybody**—and this for the purpose of giving that word special prominence. 'As,' as being a **murderer.** But what the apostle means by the Greek, represented by 'busybody,' is not quite clear. Only here is the word found in the New Testament, and in Greek classics it is unknown. According to its etymology it means an overseer of other men's matters; the last part of the compound being the very word which is sometimes, though erroneously, rendered *bishop;* and so, figuratively, it may be one who, 'as it were, plays the bishop in another's diocese.' (Cited by Lillie.) *Busybody* or *intermeddler*

16 Yet if *any man suffer* as a Christian, let him not be ashamed; but let him glorify God on this behalf.
17 For the time *is come* that judgment must begin at the house of God; and if *it* first *begin* at us, what shall the end *be* of them that obey not the gospel of God?
18 And if the righteous scarcely be saved, where shall the ungodly and the sinner appear?
19 Wherefore, let them that suffer according to the

is probably not far from correct. Paul showed similar anxiety relative to the Christians in Thessalonica. (1 Thess. 4: 11; 2 Thess. 3: 11.) Robinson suggests as probable that Peter intended to warn them against being indiscreet zealots relative to heathen manners and customs. There might have been some danger at that point. Busybodies are even now not wholly unknown. Advancing civilization seems to do little in restraining the fertility of the brood.

16. Peter likes to reiterate the thought that the suffering must be suffering which is borne on account of Christ. **As a Christian.** The disciples were called Christians first in Antioch. See Acts 11: 26; also Acts 26: 28; James 2: 7. 'The origin of the term is left in some uncertainty. It has been thought that the name was invented by the Romans or by the Greeks. It would not have been applied first by the Jews, for they would not have admitted the implication of the term, that Jesus was the Messiah. It is improbable that the Christians themselves assumed it; such an origin would be inconsistent with its infrequent use in the New Testament. The term may not have been at first opprobrious, but distinctive merely.' (Hackett.) **Glorify God.** See ver. 11, and 2: 20; compare 2: 12. **On this behalf.** Another and preferred reading gives, *in this name*—that is, the name of Christian.

17. For. What follows is given as the reason for not being ashamed on account of their sufferings and for glorifying God. **For the time,** etc.—*for it is the time of the beginning of judgment.* Even the Christians must be regarded as under judgment; for their trials, though a ground of joy, yet being needed to free them from sin, are in some respects a judgment. See Matt. 24: 9-13. The fiery trial (ver. 12) *begins* the judgment of believers. Compare Jer. 25: 29; Ezek. 9: 6. "Begin at my sanctuary." But the judgment of Christians will not issue in their destruction. Christians will be saved. (Ver. 18.) **At the house**—*from* the house. The preposition indicates more than the English *at*. It begins

Christian, let him not be ashamed; but let him
17 glorify God in this name. For the time *is come* for judgment to begin at the house of God: and if *it begin* first at us, what *shall* be the end of them that
18 obey not the gospel of God? And if the righteous is scarcely saved, where shall the ungodly and sin-
19 ner appear? Wherefore let them also that suffer

at and goes onward toward others. (Luther.) **House of God**—the church. 1 Tim. 3: 15; compare 2: 5. Think of Ananias and Sapphira. **If first at us.** The apostle conceives the judgment as beginning from Christians first, because the first act in the drama is the persecution which they suffer. He now brings out the chief thought, which, for the sake of emphatic contrast, is preceded by reference to the judgment of Christians. **The end**—the final issue. **Obey not**—disbelieve, implying opposition. **Gospel of God**—good news proclaimed from God by the Messiah and the apostles. (1 Thess. 2: 9.) It is also called the gospel of Christ. (Rom. 15: 19.) It is called so by Mark (1: 1), who wrote in some sense under the supervision of Peter himself. The apostle purposely uses such comprehensive language that he may include, not only the immoral, but the moral, if rejecting the gospel.

18. A more solemn development of the reason for not being 'ashamed.' It is a quotation of the Greek translation of Prov. 11: 31, which varies from the Hebrew. **The righteous.** It is in the singular number, meaning *the righteous 'man'*; he who has become righteous, not necessarily sinless, through faith in Christ. Even such a man is **scarcely, with difficulty, saved.** The pitfalls of life are many, and his sight has not become perfect. He is saved (Phil. 1: 6), but notice the difficulty as implied in Phil. 2: 12, and see 2 Pet. 1: 10. Compare 2 Pet. 1: 11. An *abundant* entrance is possible, after all. How striking that no answer to the solemn questions is attempted! WHAT THE END? WHERE APPEAR? Some are attempting to answer them by saying that the end will be eternal bliss; they will appear among the holy ones of heaven: if not immediately, yet after an indefinite period of suffering. Peter answers not, which is the most solemn way possible of saying that the 'end' will be eternal death, and the *place where* will be the one prepared for the devil and his angels. (Matt. 25: 41.)

19. Wherefore—in view of all that has been said concerning suffering, especially the

will of God commit the keeping of their souls *to him* in well doing, as unto a faithful Creator.

according to the will of God commit their souls in well-doing unto a faithful Creator.

CHAPTER V.

THE elders which are among you I exhort, who am also an elder, and a witness of the sufferings of

1 The elders therefore among you I exhort, who am a fellow-elder, and a witness of the sufferings of

---

blessed results of suffering. "Also" is found in the Bible Union and the Revised Versions, and should have appeared in the Common Version; let them *also* that suffer. **According to the will of God.** Their sufferings must be those of true Christians (ver. 15, 16), for then they can be sure that they suffer according to God's will, and then, *also*, they will be able to commit *their souls* to a faithful Creator. [May not the reference be to martyrdom chiefly or exclusively? See Luke 23: 46; Acts 7: 59.—A. H.] **Commit the keeping** of—*entrust their souls.* Expunge 'the keeping of.' **Souls.** See on the same word 1: 9, and especially as used 3: 20. As should not be retained. Read—*entrust their souls to a faithful Creator in well doing.* Thus Peter would impress upon them the fact of the divine faithfulness; God will do all that he has promised to do. Persecution may destroy the body, but it cannot touch the soul. In **well doing.** They must continue to do well, and then there will be no inconsistency between the life and entrusting their souls to God.

This chapter, while precious in practical precepts, and while occasionally re-echoing in subdued notes the praise and exultant joy of the sections preceding, is characterized, as are no other parts of the Epistle, by great solemnity.

CRITICAL NOTE.—CHAPTER IV.

3. The manuscripts differ considerably in the Greek of this verse. Besides the instance already noted, the rejection of (ἡμῖν) *us*, it should be mentioned that (τοῦ βίου) *the life* is wanting in many of the best manuscripts. It is rejected by Lachmann, Tregelles, Tischendorf, and Westcott and Hort. θέλημα (*will*) is rejected for βούλημα, which, however, is also properly rendered *will.* κατεργάσασθαι (*to have wrought*) has but feeble support, but there is good authority for κατειργάσθαι.

Ch. 5. THIRD SERIES OF EXHORTATIONS (*continued*).

The remainder of the final series divides itself into two parts: the first (1-5) addressed to elders and to younger persons; the second (5-9) to the readers generally.

1. The elders. Another and accepted reading gives, *elders therefore. Presbyter* is the Greek in English spelling, and partly upon the original word as used here and elsewhere is based the conviction of some, that the Presbyterian form of church government is the Scriptural form. But in the primitive churches the minister was sometimes called *elder*, and sometimes *bishop.* The explanation is not difficult. The original word for *elder* (Πρεσβύτερος) was of Jewish origin (Ex. 3: 16); the original word for *bishop* (ἐπίσκοπος) was of Greek origin. It was natural, therefore, in writing to Jews to use *elder,* and in writing to others to use *bishop.* Every minister was a bishop, and every minister was an elder. See Acts 20: 17, and compare ver. 28; Titus 1: 5, and compare ver. 7. *Bishop* and *elder,* then, were applied to the same church officer, and no other church officer was known except *deacon.* The office of apostle was temporary. It was of such a nature that it could not be transmitted: it was impossible for an apostle to have a successor. Were a list of qualifications of the bishop and of the elder to be arranged in two columns, one could write either *bishop* or *elder* over either, and neither would be inappropriate. It is not improbable that the elders as a class consisted of men somewhat advanced in age, for the churches were yet to make the discovery that it was not well to put themselves under men of experience. On the contrary, it was necessary to guard the churches against thinking too lightly of young men. 1 Tim. 4: 12: "Let no man despise thy youth." **Among you.** The readers are supposed to belong to different churches (1: 1), and one or more of these elders may have been connected with each church, or possibly some of the smallest churches had no elders at all of their own, but were visited by elders of some large church. **I exhort**—a tender word. **Who am also an elder**—*who am a fellow-elder.* Though an apostle (1: 1; Matt. 10· 2), Peter puts himself in genuine humility upon an equality with elders. Never, by act

Christ, and also a partaker of the glory that shall be revealed:
2 Feed the flock of God which is among you, taking the oversight *thereof*, not by constraint, but willingly; not for filthy lucre, but of a ready mind;

Christ, who am also a partaker of the glory that 2 shall be revealed: Tend the flock of God which is among you, ¹exercising the oversight, not of constraint, but willingly, ²according to *the will of* God; 3 nor yet for filthy lucre, but of a ready mind; neither

1 Some ancient authorities omit *exercising the oversight*........2 Some ancient authorities omit *according to the will of God.*

or word, does he show that he considers himself superior in rank to other preachers, whether elders or apostles. **Witness of the sufferings of Christ**—both eye-witness and preacher. (Acts 5: 32.) He had seen his Master's entire course of suffering. It is difficult to believe that having bitterly repented of his denial, he did not see the crucifixion itself, though in the anguish of his spirit he may have stood afar off. This is the sixth time that he has made distinct mention of his Master's sufferings. What he saw he preached. **And also**—*who am also*, as in the Revised Version. It is an emphatic connection of the two ideas of suffering and glory, and connection of the two is a favorite thing with the apostles. (4: 13; 2: 20; 1: 7; Rom. 8: 18.) **The glory that shall be revealed.** Col. 3: 4; 1 John 3: 2. The glory of Christ which will shine out at his second coming and onward through eternity—shine upon his people, and shine out from them, is meant. Of that glory of Christ the apostle has the most beautiful assurance that he is even now a sharer. Equally strong may be, and ought to be, the conviction of all the elect.

2, 3. Feed. The original is more comprehensive. It includes feeding, watching over, guiding, protecting. *Tend* includes all. How affectionate is this apostolic echo of the Lord's command to Peter himself: *Feed (tend) my sheep.* (John 21: 16.) The elders must instruct, comfort, reprove, guide, the several churches, and the individual members of which they are composed. **Flock.** See on 2: 25. Once straying like sheep, they need even now the faithful care of divinely appointed shepherds. **Of God.** How penetrating the appeal! Can they neglect the flock which belongs to God? **Among you**—in the different provinces (1: 1) where you live. The elders were among the Christians (ver. 1), **and the Christians were among the elders. Taking the oversight.** The original word is akin to *episcopos* translated in 2: 25 *bishop*, but it would be as great an error to translate it *perform the duties of a bishop* as was committed in using *bishop* in

2: 25. It means substantially what the Common Version says. It is taking the spiritual care of those over whom they are placed, and this is intended by the apostle as an explanation of *tending*. After all, it is doubtful whether the words should appear. The Revisers accept the Greek as the correct reading, and translate *exercising the oversight*, yet say in the margin that some omit the words. The Greek is rejected by Westcott and Hort. The spirit in which the oversight is to be taken is presented with rhetorical fullness in a threefold antithetical form: (*a*) Not by constraint, but willingly; (*b*) Not for filthy lucre, but of a ready mind; (*c*) Neither as being lords over God's heritage, but as being ensamples to the flock. **Constraint**—*necessity*. They are to perform their duty not under an impulse from without, but under an impulse from within; their service must be rendered *willingly, heartily.* He who would gladly escape from the ministry if he could escape without loss of reputation or bread, is but a minister in mask. Paul indeed says (1 Cor. 9: 16), that necessity is laid upon him, but *necessity* is not used in the same sense as here. He was willingly impelled (ver. 17) by consciousness of obligation. It was an inward, not an outward, necessity. **Filthy lucre**—*sordidly* (an adverb in the original); that is, for the purpose of making money. The money made, would, under the circumstances, be filthy lucre. The elders had the right, as the apostles had, to a support from the churches (1 Cor. 9: 7-14), but they were not to make even a support the motive for entering or continuing in the ministry. Constitutional love of gain, habitual "anxiety to save," is a disqualification for the Christian ministry. Compare 1 Tim. 3: 3; 6: 5-10; 2 Tim. 4: 10, and remember Judas Iscariot. It is equally true that a spendthrift cannot be a "good minister" of Christ. Penuriousness and extravagance, though like two oxen, pulling hard apart, yet draw under the same yoke. **Of a ready mind**—*readily* (here, also, in the Greek, an adverb, corresponding to the ad-

3 Neither as being lords over *God's* heritage, but being ensamples to the flock.
4 And when the chief Shepherd shall appear, ye shall receive a crown of glory that fadeth not away.

as lording it over the charge allotted to you, but
4 making yourselves ensamples to the flock. And when the chief Shepherd shall be manifested, ye

verb above named, *sordidly*) or, better, *willingly*. It implies *cheerful* alacrity. He who works in the ministry sordidly, will soon find the filthy lucre a clog. **Neither as being lords over God's**—*neither as lording against or over*. "God's" is an insertion by the translators. The participle for *lording* is combined with a preposition, the meaning of which is *down, down upon*. The combined words express *intensity* of action. Lording *down upon* is lording *against;* or as one may say in good English, lording *over*. The preposition causes the verb to express greater arrogance and severity. **Heritage**—*the heritages*. The article points them out as well known; they are the churches over which the elders preside. The Greek originally meant *lot, portion*, what is conferred as inheritance or possession. (Acts 26: 18; Col. 1: 12.) It is the Greek word from which *clergy* (κλῆρος) was derived, and therefore some, hastening to give the word a meaning which it never had in apostolic times, have considered the apostle as requiring the elders not to lord it over the clergy. To apply the word to national churches is an equally great mistake, for a national Christian Church is a body of which Peter "died without the sight." **Being ensamples**—*becoming examples*. Their influence must be that of *a* pure and gentle life. **Flock.** As this answers to *heritages*, it may be seen that the latter must refer, as above, to churches. As Dean Howson says (*Horæ Petrinæ*), "Nothing could be more simple, more lowly, more affectionate. No contrast in literature is more striking than the difference between the style of St. Peter's own epistles, and that in which his so-called successors have often written. Here is no trace of any consciousness of a divine grant of supreme jurisdiction. If the plenitude of teaching and of ruling were vested in St. Peter and his successors, we should surely find the assertion of it here. But we do not find it here."

This exhortation to elders seems like a warning prophecy of the changes which were to come. The sessions of a Presbyterian Church, consisting of the pastor and ruling elders, is

a judicatory for the exercise of government and discipline.[1] It has power to receive members and power to exclude.[2] These elders hold office through life. The power of the people has been lost, however, chiefly through the rise of Episcopacy. Within one hundred years after the apostles, the original oneness of bishop and elder began to disappear; *bishop* came to be applied to a small class of ministers, while other ministers continued to be called *elders;* the bishops grew in ambition, dared to call themselves the successors of the apostles, arrogated the exclusive right to ordain, and claimed that the Holy Ghost would not be given through any other fingers than their own. Diocesan power became metropolitan power, metropolitan power became patriarchal power, and patriarchal power became papal power. Bishops deposed bishops. Councils came into vogue, and, becoming the tools of the higher clergy, had the arrogance to demand of the churches the acceptance of creeds hammered out upon their own anvils. It is not surprising that in view of the quarrels and lust of bishops an ancient idolater said: "Make me a bishop, and I will surely become a Christian."
Ecclesiastical monarchy still prevails. In the papal form of development it has brought upon itself the strongest condemnation by that quintessence of all arrogance—infallibility. Millions of human souls are ground into the dust by being denied that right "of private judgment in matters of religion in opposition to authority," which, as the Roman Catholic Archbishop Spalding says,[3] "is the fatal source of all this mischief"—"American infidelity and indifference."

4. This verse states the certainty of the blessed result which will accrue to the elders, if they shall obey the exhortation just given. The reward will be conferred at the appearing of the chief Shepherd, Christ himself, called in 2: 25 *the Shepherd;* in Heb. 13: 20 *the great Shepherd,* and by himself (John 10: 14) *the good Shepherd.* **Chief.** The elders, then, are shepherds in the service of Christ. But Christ is the Shepherd of all the flock—that is, all the

---

[1] "The Form of Government." Book 1, Chap. 5. [2] *Id.,* Book 1, Chap. 9: 7. [3] "Miscellanea," p. 383.

5 Likewise, ye younger, submit yourselves unto the elder. Yea, all *of you* be subject one to another, and be clothed with humility: for God resisteth the proud, and giveth grace to the humble.

shall receive the crown of glory that fadeth not 5 away. ¹Likewise. ye younger, be subject unto the elder. Yea, all of you gird yourselves with humility, to serve one another: for God resisteth the

1 Or, *Likewise . . . elder; yea, all of you one to another. Gird yourselves with humility.*

---

elect. **Shall appear**—*shall be manifested.* It refers to the second coming, viewed by Peter in his consciousness as near, though, perhaps, not viewed as near in time. See on 4: 7, and see Col. 3: 4; 1 John 2: 28. **A crown**—*the crown;* no other like it. *Ye shall receive the amaranthine crown of glory,* is the literal rendering. In 1: 4 occurs *fadeth not,* the original of which is akin to the Greek used here. Whether the apostle has in his eye the beautiful conception of a never-fading flower (amaranth) "is very doubtful" (Lillie), but Huther otherwise. 'Crown.' Probably Peter has in mind a wreath of flowers; nor is it improbable that he thinks of those in the Grecian games on whose heads such a wreath was placed in token of victory. Still, as we are reminded, such flower-wreaths were used among the Jews. **Glory**—the bliss of heaven, the chief element of which will be the life of God poured into the soul through Christ. This figurative method of representing the rewards of the future is one which the New Testament writers freely use. See 1 Cor. 9: 25, *an incorruptible crown;* 2 Tim. 4: 8, *a crown of righteousness;* James 1: 12, *the crown of life.* What activity and what powers of endurance under trial should ministers of the gospel manifest!

5. **Likewise.** Compare the use of this word in 3: 1, 7. It implies that, as the writer had an exhortation for the elders, he now has one 'likewise,' *also,* for the younger. **Younger**—in age, not in office, in support of which latter view has been adduced the case of the young men who buried Ananias and Sapphira. (Acts 5: 6, 10.) But who are the *elders?* The elders of ver. 1?—that is, elders in office? But why should Peter select only the younger in age as needing an exhortation to submit to elders in office? It is replied that the younger would be more inclined to have their own way. Probably; but it would be strange if the other members, the middle-aged, were wholly superior to the necessity of similar exhortation. It is quite in accordance with the practice of the New Testament writers to use the same word twice in different senses,

even though the words may stand near each other. 'Elder' may therefore be understood as *elder in age.* That would include all the other members, whether in or out of office. It is, then, an exhortation to those who are younger in age to submit to those who are older in age. Peter's knowledge of human nature should be noticed. The exhortation is needed now. Deference toward the older members of a church by the younger is a virtue which has never been known to grow too rank. A few passages may aid in the cultivation of so beautiful a trait of Christian character. See 1 Kings 12: 6-8; Prov. 16: 31; 20: 29; Job 32: 7; Lev. 19: 32.

Yea, all. The apostle here speaks more generally. What he requires of the younger in their relation to the elder, he requires of *all* in relation to *all*—a marvel of practical theology. The rich must submit themselves to the poor, not less than the poor to the rich; the learned to the ignorant, as well as the ignorant to the learned; and even the elder to the younger, equally with the younger to the elder. See Luke 22: 24-26. "Contradictory and absurd" the world cries; but he who is "clothed with humility" sees the reasonableness and harmony of it all. **Clothed.** The original, found nowhere else in the New Testament, is a peculiar word; not the word which the Greeks commonly used to express the simple idea of being clothed. Some think the word was derived from the name of a slave's frock, and infer its peculiar appropriateness to express *humility.* This is too artificial. Others give it a meaning almost the opposite—*ornament yourselves.* The word is more probably derived from one which expresses that by means of which a garment is fastened, and so, according to some, it enjoins the duty of being *girded* with humility. The question is one pertaining only to the *shade of* meaning which the word may have as a figurative one. The general meaning is clear enough, and is expressed by Bengel thus—"*Put on and wrap yourselves in,* so that the covering of humility cannot possibly be stripped from you." **With humility.** The

6 Humble yourselves therefore under the mighty hand of God, that he may exalt you in due time:
7 Casting all your care upon him; for he careth for you.
8 Be sober, be vigilant; because your adversary the devil, as a roaring lion, walketh about, seeking whom he may devour:

6 proud, but giveth grace to the humble. Humble yourselves therefore under the mighty hand of God, 7 that he may exalt you in due time; casting all your 8 anxiety upon him, because he careth for you. Be sober, be watchful: your adversary the devil, as a roaring lion, walketh about, seeking whom he may

---

duty is also enjoined in Eph. 4: 2; Phil. 2: 3; Rom. 12: 16. Often had Peter learned the lesson from his Master. (Matt. 16 1-4; Mark 10: 15; John 13: 14-17.) As so often before, the exhortation is supported by a citation from the Old Testament—that is, from the Septuagint translation of Prov. 3: 34. Compare Luke 1: 51, 52. The passage is cited also by James. (Jas. 4: 6.)

6. **Therefore**—because to the humble grace is given. **Under the mighty hand of God.** This is the more forcible, because enjoined upon all without respect to position. It refers to the endurance of sufferings, which is evident from ver. 7. They must bear with humility the sufferings which God, as with a mighty hand, lays upon them. See Deut. 3: 24. Exaltation to spiritual honor is most desirable, and that they must consider as the end. **In due time**—whenever God shall see fit to do so. It may occur partly in this life, but it will certainly occur in the next life. The worlds were made *by* the mighty hand of God, and are held *in* his mighty hand, but in suffering the Christian is *under* his mighty hand.

7. **All your care**—*anxious* care. The original word is akin to that found in Matt. 6: 25, "Take *no thought*"; thought, when the Common Version was made, having strictly the meaning of *anxiety*, or *solicitous care*. (Trench.) They were to throw off upon God all their burden of anxiety. **For he careth for you.** The Greek does not have such related words as appear in the English, *care*, *careth*, but for rhetorical emphasis it brings into proximity the two pronouns rendered respectively *him* and *he*, thus—Casting all your care upon *him*, for to *him* belongs care for you. Compare the beautiful exhortation in Ps. 55: 22, "Cast thy burden upon the Lord and he shall sustain thee," with which, evidently, Peter was familiar. No sweeter thought has yet been uttered in the ear of these suffering Christians.

8. The requirement to throw off upon God their burden of solicitude implies no grant of carnal security. **Be sober**—twice before.

(1: 13; 4: 7.) See on the former. **Be vigilant**—*watch*. Notice the rapid energy of the style. He hastens from the former to the latter without stopping to use a connecting particle; and if the critics must be followed, or rather as the best manuscripts ought to be followed, *because* must be expunged, and this makes the swiftness and energy of the thought still greater. With characteristic power, and flashing as if in heated remembrance of his own narrow escape (Luke 22: 31, 32), he says—*Be sober! watch! the devil seeks you!* **Your adversary.** An antagonist in law was called an 'adversary' (*antidikos*), and the term was applied in a general sense to any one who put himself in hostility to another. The Scriptures everywhere recognize, Christ himself recognized, the existence of a being, who, though once in possession of a will in harmony with God's, is now hostile to the Creator, especially in his work of saving men through Christ; and this is the being to whom the apostle refers. **The devil.** It points out the antagonist by a well-known name. *Satan* is of Hebrew origin. (Job 1: 6.) *Diabolus* (devil) of Greek origin. The attempt to disprove the personality of such a being has been a failure. Satan would have been better pleased had the people been led to believe the attempt successful. **As a roaring lion**, etc. See Gen. 49: 9, where Judah is called a lion's whelp. Christ is called a Lion (Rev. 5: 5), but, as Augustine says, cited by Huther, "*Christus leo propter fortitudinem, diabolus propter feritatem; ille leo ad vincendum, iste leo ad nocendum.* (Christ is a lion on account of his courage, the devil on account of his ferocity; the former is a lion to conquer, the latter to injure.) ' Roaring,' which is frequently referred to in the Old Testament as a terrible characteristic of the lion, adds power to the description. Smiling, however, is as easy for the devil as roaring—an adept at both, and whichever doing, is bent on evil. **Walketh about**—*is walking;* his custom. He was walking *very near* where Peter himself was at the time of his fearful sin. He is continually in

9 Whom resist stedfast in the faith, knowing that the same afflictions are accomplished in your brethren that are in the world.
10 But the God of all grace, who hath called us unto his eternal glory by Christ Jesus, after that ye have suffered a while, make you perfect, stablish, strengthen, settle *you*.

9 devour: whom withstand stedfast in ¹your faith, knowing that the same sufferings are ²accomplished 10 in your ³brethren who are in the world. And the God of all grace, who called you unto his eternal glory in Christ, after that ye have suffered a little while, shall himself ⁴perfect, stablish, strengthen

1 Or, *the*......2 Gr. *being accomplished*......3 Gr. *brotherhood*......4 Or, *restore*.

motion. He is above the necessity of taking rest, which is not contradictory to Matt. 12: 43 ("When the unclean spirit is gone out of a man, he walketh through dry places, seeking rest"); for these words do not indicate ceasing from the pursuit of victims, but they show the opposite—the restlessness of a demon when cast out of a man. **Seeking whom**—or, possibly, *some one*. **He may devour**—or *swallow down*. The figure expresses ruin, and implies ruin of body and soul. Satan desired to have Peter himself. (Luke 22: 31.)

9. As in ver. 8 the apostle guards them against the indolence which might result from casting their care upon God, so now he guards them against the danger of trusting in the activity enjoined. They must **resist,** but they must resist **stedfast,** *firm*, **in the faith.** No resistance of the devil will be successful which is made in their own strength—still another clear echo of Peter's experience. Christ once prayed that *his* faith might not fail. Here, too, the case of Ananias and Sapphira is solemnly instructive. It was this very apostle, who, after bitter experience of the sinfulness of yielding to Satan, and after the deepest sorrow for doing so, faithfully reproved those corrupt members of the Church in Jerusalem. "Ananias, why hath Satan filled thine heart to lie to the Holy Ghost?" Fearful illustrations of the consequences of not resisting the evil one! (James 4: 7.) When seeking whom he may devour he walks, when resisted he flees: the spirit is the same. Peter sees him walking about; James sees him fleeing. **Knowing.** Their knowledge of the fact will lead them to cultivate the habit of *considering* it. **The same afflictions** which they are suffering **are accomplished** (continuance of action) upon their **brethren,** their *brotherhood*, literally. See 2: 17. Considering the fact of the sufferings of their brotherhood in the world will be one means of strengthening their faith, and of qualifying them to resist. What suffering believers have been able to do and to bear, may be seen in Paul and his companions (2 Cor. 4: 8-10; 6: 9, 10), and even in many of the Old Covenant time. For the latter, see Heb. 11. Peter and James (4: 7), as well as Peter and Paul, are in harmony. The brotherhood of Christians, viewed as a general fact, is a precious one: brotherhood in suffering will be followed by brotherhood in eternal glory. *The third series of exhortations is ended.*

10, 11. A promise and a doxology. The Common Version gives the expression of a wish rather than a promise, but the tense of the Greek now generally adopted is the future: *will* make you perfect, *will* establish, etc. **All grace.** *All* the grace which is shown toward men is God's grace; or it may refer to *variety* in the gifts which result from grace. **Grace.** See on the same word in 1: 2. **Hath called**—should be, *called*. They were called at a given time in the past—that is, when they were regenerated, as in 2: 9. Compare 2: 21. **Unto his eternal glory.** Notice that it is *his* (God's) glory to which they were called; therefore the meaning is, that they were *to share* God's glory. The same rich thought is expressed by Paul in 1 Thess. 2: 12; 2 Thess. 2: 14. They share it here, but the fullness of the gift is reserved for the future. **By Jesus Christ**—*in* Jesus *Christ*. It expresses not instrumentality, but communion with Christ's life—a favorite idea. Westcott and Hort with some others consider 'Jesus' as not supported by sufficient manuscript authority. **After that ye have suffered a while** (*a little time*). *The perfecting*, etc., is indeed carried on *while* they are suffering, which thought has been elsewhere expressed, but the apostle conceives the grand result as occurring *after* the sufferings. But another explanation is more usually given; that which connects the suffering with being called unto his glory, thus: *who called us unto his eternal glory, after we have suffered.* Suffering precedes glory. **Make you perfect.** The Common Version takes no notice of an emphatic pronoun; *himself* will make you

[CH. V.] I. PETER. 73

11 To him be glory and dominion for ever and ever. Amen.
12 By Silvanus, a faithful brother unto you, as I suppose, I have written briefly, exhorting, and testifying that this is the true grace of God wherein ye stand.
13 The *church that is* at Babylon, elected together with *you*, saluteth you; and *so doth* Marcus my son.

11 ¹you. To him *be* the dominion ²for ever and ever. Amen.
12 By Silvanus, ³our faithful brother, as I account *him*, I have written unto you briefly, exhorting, and testifying that this is the true grace of God: 13 stand ye fast therein. ⁴She that is in Babylon, elect together with *you*, saluteth you; and *so doth*

---

1 Many ancient authorities add *settle*.. ..2 Gr. *unto the ages of the ages*..... .3 Gr. *the*......4 That is, The church, or the sister.

---

perfect. It excludes all others. 'Perfect,' *will fully furnish*—that is, such as one should be, deficient in no part. (Robinson.) See Heb. 13: 21. **Stablish**—will make firm. (2 Thess. 2: 17; 3: 3.) It is the same word in the Greek as is found in Luke 22: 32: "Strengthen thy brethren." How his Lord's command must have imprinted itself upon the apostle's heart! So the exhortation given to Peter is by Peter transformed into one of the richest of promises. **Settle you**—*will ground* you upon an immovable foundation. The original word is used in Matt. 7: 25, "founded" upon a rock, and in Eph. 3: 17, "grounded," in love. Here, also, Peter flashes onward in quick, sudden strokes, without connecting particles. The Greek for 'settle' is omitted by Westcott and Hort. As to the doxology, see on 4: 11.

12. Silvanus—the same, probably, as is mentioned in Acts by the name of *Silas*. The Epistles always use the form found here. It was not unusual for Jews to have two names. Saul was also called Paul. *Silas* was probably the Jewish and *Silvanus* the foreign name; yet it need not be supposed that he was never called Silas except in Palestine or by Jews. Silvanus stood high among early Christian laborers. He is classed with Paul, Barnabas, and Judas Barsabas, as a *leading* man among the brethren. (Acts 15: 22.) He was appointed to one of the most important services of apostolic times. (Acts 15: 1-31.) He was a public teacher. (Acts 15: 32.) He was Paul's companion on his second missionary tour. He was imprisoned with Paul at Philippi, where, with the apostle, he poured forth thanksgiving to God in songs constructed probably from poetic portions of the Old Testament. (Acts 16: 19-40.) How long he continued to labor with Paul, or what special object brought him into this brief connection with Peter, is unknown. Peter writes the Epistle by him—that is, he sends by him the Epistle which he himself wrote. **Have written**—*wrote*. The Epistle is nearly completed,

and the apostle conceives it as finished. See Crit. Notes. **A faithful brother**—*the* faithful brother; a pleasant testimonial. Upon the "sharp" disagreement of Paul and Barnabas concerning Mark, Silas was preferred by Paul as a co-worker instead of Mark, who was chosen by Barnabas. (Acts 15: 37-40.) As Mark was closely allied with Peter (for example, in the preparation of the gospel which bears his name), it would not have been strange had Peter's special relation with Mark led him to show a touch of unsanctified human nature toward Silas; but *Silas is the faithful brother*. Some connect 'unto you' with *write*, and some (the Common Version) with *faithful*. It is not easy to decide which the apostle intended. But See Crit. Note. **As I suppose.** Too weak, or if this translation is retained it must not be considered as showing doubt. The apostle says he *thinks*, he *considers*, he *accounts* (Revised Version) the brother as faithful; and this is a judgment formed upon what he knows of his Christian character. **Briefly.** He could have written more, for his heart is full of desire for their comfort and growth under sufferings. **Exhorting and testifying.** See Introduction, II. **This is the true grace**—not the grace of which he has been writing, but that which they received at their renewal. 'Grace' —divine favor, implying always that those to whom it is shown do not merit it. 'True'— having reality, a veritable existence. It is not intended as a contrast with error of doctrine. (Huther.) It has been supposed that the apostle here refers to Paul, and intends to say that Paul's preaching, which they are supposed to have heard, was true; but there is nothing to justify that view. **Wherein ye stand.** Some manuscripts give another form of the verb, which several critics accept: *in which stand*.

13. The church that is ... you. The English reader will notice that these words are in italics. For these the Greek has no corresponding words. The Sinaitic manu-

14 Greet ye one another with a kiss of charity. Peace *be* with you all that are in Christ Jesus. Amen.

script, which is at least one of the oldest, has the Greek word for 'church' after Babylon, but the manuscripts in general have no noun whatever. Literal rendering: *The co-elect in Babylon saluteth you.* The two principal views are: 1. That Peter's wife is meant (1 Cor. 9: 5); 2. A Christian church. The former view seems unentitled to acceptance, since it is difficult to see how it could be necessary to add *in Babylon.* It would seem to be enough to say, *the co-elect saluteth you.* But it would have been very natural to add the name of the place, if a church were meant. Notice the correspondence between *co-elect* here and *elect* in 1:2. The consideration by itself, however, is by no means decisive. **Babylon.** Most Roman Catholic expositors insist that *Rome* is meant. But if Rome is meant, 'Babylon' is used figuratively; yet in this very simple, unimaginative close of the Epistle, such a figurative (symbolic) form of expression would have been contrary to the way in which the human mind usually works. Not Babylon in Egypt can be meant, for that was scarcely more than a military post. Babylon in Chaldea was still sufficiently large to be a place of some importance, and it is known to have been a place of residence for Jews. It is true that according to Josephus, many of the Jews had been driven away, but there is no reason to suppose that there were none remaining. That is probably the Babylon to which Peter refers. It is singular that Roman Catholics should incline to apply to Rome the name of *such* a city as Babylon, but it is intended to help a theory which greatly needs all possible support. **Marcus**—son of a Mary who lived in Jerusalem (Acts 12:12), and into whose house Peter went after his release from prison; *John* Mark (Acts 12:12; 15:37); *John* (Acts 13:5, 13).; *Mark.* (Acts 15:39.) *John* was his Jewish, and *Mark* his Roman name. Mark was a cousin to Barnabas (Col. 4: 10), which may have influenced the latter's choice. (Acts 15: 37.) His reluctance to accompany Paul on one of the apostle's missionary journeys was a fault (Acts 13:13), but Paul's magnanimous reference to him (2 Tim. 4:11) is worthy of special note.

14 Mark my son. Salute one another with a kiss of love.
Peace be unto you all that are in Christ.

He was with Paul in Rome when the latter was a prisoner. (Col. 4:10; Philemon 24.) He was doubtless the writer of the gospel which bears his name. **My son**—spiritually; probably converted by Peter's means.

14. **Greet**—*salute.* **A kiss of charity**—*of love.* A *holy* kiss. (Rom. 16: 16; 1 Cor. 16: 20; 2 Cor. 13: 12; 1 Thess. 5: 26.) This sign was not to be given them as from Peter, but Peter exhorts that they give it to **one another,** and, as Meyer suggests on 1 Cor. 16: 20, they probably gave it immediately after reading the Epistle. This was not merely a form of salutation; it was a method of expressing their *Christian love,* and "was, specifically, a recognition or ratification of one another's Christian character. The kiss, as a token of love or friendship or respect, was as common in Oriental countries as shaking hands is in Europe and the United States. Esau kissed his father (Gen. 27: 27); Laban his sister's son (Gen. 29: 13); the woman who was a sinner kissed the Saviour, applying the token to the feet as expressive of her humility; Simon violated custom in *not* kissing Jesus (Luke 7: 45, 'Thou gavest me no kiss')." The Epistle concludes with the expression of desire that **peace** may be with them. **All that are in Christ Jesus**—all that are in communion with him, all who have become sharers in his spiritual life. '**Jesus**' and **Amen** have little sanction from manuscripts.

CRITICAL NOTE.—CHAPTER V.

The objection to connecting ὑμῖν (*you*) with ἔγραψα (*wrote*) is that the former is brought in so early, standing between Διὰ Σιλουανοῦ (*by Silvanus*) and τοῦ πιστοῦ ἀδελφοῦ (*the faithful brother*). Translated in the order of the Greek: *By Silvanus to you the faithful brother, as I suppose, briefly I wrote.* But the objection seems greatly weakened, if not wholly removed, by comparing the arrangement with a similar one in Gal. 6: 11: "Ἴδετε πηλίκοις ὑμῖν γράμμασιν ἔγραψα (*ye see how large to you a letter I wrote*). Here it is evident that ὑμῖν (*you*) must be connected with ἔγραψα (*wrote*). Such, therefore, may be the connection in the verse before us.

INTRODUCTION TO THE SECOND EPISTLE OF PETER.

I. WAS PETER THE WRITER?

It would be an error to affirm that the Epistle to the Hebrews, if not written by Paul, was forged, for it does not profess to have been written by him. But the Epistle which goes under the name of "The Second Epistle of Peter" must have been forged if not written by Peter. The question before us is therefore one of great importance. As is the case with all the other epistles, the sources of evidence are either external or internal.

I. EXTERNAL. This is not very strong. The Epistle has been accepted since A. D. 363 as belonging to the Canon of Scripture. The decision to receive it was made by the Council of Laodicea. But this is not evidence that Peter wrote it. Quotations from the Epistle in the earliest Christian writings would afford strong evidence in its favor, but it is affirmed that no quotations can be found. "The Epistle is not quoted," says Farrar, "and is not *certainly* referred to by a single writer in the first or second century. Neither Polycarp, nor Ignatius, nor Barnabas, nor Clement of Rome, nor Justin Martyr, nor Theophilus of Antioch, nor Irenæus, nor Tertullian, nor Cyprian can be proved to allude to it. . . . During the first two centuries the only traces of it, if traces they can be called, are to be found in the Pastor of Hermas, and in a recently discovered passage of Melito of Sardis: but even these are of so distant and general a nature that it is impossible to determine whether we should regard them as reminiscences of the language of the Epistle, or accidental approximations to it." ("Early Days of Christianity.") On the other hand, in works of most of the above-named writers, several of whom, because following first after the apostles are called Apostolic Fathers, Dietlein thinks he has discovered many allusions. Not a few, however, besides Farrar, think that Dietlein is entirely mistaken.

A serious difficulty ("entirely new and very formidable," "Early Christianity") arises from resemblance to the writings of Josephus. In "The Expositor" for 1882, an English periodical, the authorship of our Epistle is discussed in three articles by Rev. Edwin A. Abbott, D. D. In the first article is considered the question, "Had the author read Josephus?" in the second, "Had the author read St. Jude?" in the third, "Was the author St. Peter?" The nature of the question at issue in the first article is expressed by Dr. Abbott as follows: "If it could be shown that the author had borrowed from some work of which the date is known to be late—*e. g.*, the "Antiquities" of Josephus, published in A. D. 93, the date of the Epistle would then be determined to be after 93 A. D., and the author of the Epistle would be known to be not St. Peter." Dr. Abbott attempts to prove that the author of the Epistle had read the "Antiquities" of Josephus. If his attempt has been successful, it is certain that the Epistle was not written by Peter, for Peter died many years before Josephus wrote his "Antiquities." That the author of our Epistle imitated Josephus, not Josephus the author of the Epistle, appears clear to Dr. Abbott for the following reasons: "It exhibits, 1. A very large number of similar words and phrases in the two authors; 2. All the phrases and words on which stress has been laid above are words and phrases rare or non-existent in the New Testament and LXX, and therefore completely out of the author's natural sphere; 3. The groups of similarities between the Epistle and the 'Antiquities' are found in just those portions of the latter which our author would be likely to have studied; 4. Besides parallelism of thought in the two passages selected above to exhibit the parallelism of language, we find two others in which our author agrees with Josephus in diverging from, or at all events adding to, the Bible narrative." These considerations, which are given at the close of Dr. Abbott's article, are illustrated by previous citations from the two writers. An examination of Dr. Abbott's "Discovery" would be out of place in the present work, but the writer may take the liberty of saying that it is by no means certain that the author of our Epistle borrowed from Josephus. The arguments against that view are so weighty that the people of God need not feel called upon to consider the Epistle as the work of some other than the Apostle Peter. He feels constrained to add that Dr. Abbott's third article,[1] "Was the author St. Peter?" is so extravagant in its representation of the *style* of the Epistle as to amount to a caricature. It were possible so to translate almost any paragraph of the Bible as to justify the application of "vulgar pomposity" and "verbose pedantry" to the original. "He leadeth me beside the gentle liquidities" (Ps. 23: 2), is scarcely an adequate illustration of the unfairness and absurdity of many of Dr. Abbott's renderings of the Epistle of Peter. We give one instance, and to those who desire to pursue the subject farther, we suggest the reading of Farrar's article in "The Expositor" of the same year, in which he makes an examination of Dr. Abbott's third article. The Common Version (2: 22) is—*The dog is turned to his own vomit again; and, the sow that was washed to her wallowing in the mire.* Dr. Abbott translates (?), "The dog having returned to his own evacuation, and the sow having bathed to her wallowance." A more *judicial* treatment of the entire question is desirable. The spirit of the mere advocate is not favorable to ascertaining truth.

Such are some of the difficulties drawn from external sources. As in the case of one or two other books of the New Testament, this Epistle was longer in coming into general acceptance. To this fact there is a favorable side, for it shows that Christians of early times were not disposed to receive in haste every book which might profess to be inspired. It may be added that the Epistle is received by a large number of modern scholars even in Germany, though in part, perhaps chiefly, on internal grounds. Even Farrar, though deeming the difficulty arising from the similarities between the Epistle and Josephus as "very formidable," does not reject it.

But something of a more favorable kind concerning even external evidence remains to be said. 1. In the works which have come from one of the greatest of the Fathers, Augustine, bishop from A. D. 395, is "a list of the books of the New Testament exactly agreeing with our present Canon." (Westcott, "On the Canon of the New Testament.") 2. Jerome, A. D. 390, has a Catalogue in which occurs the Second Epistle of Peter, and the doubts which some had relative to the authenticity of the Epistle were not shared by that well-informed Father. 3. Receding from this date toward the apostolic age, we find a Catalogue of all our present books in the works of Gregory Nazianzen, A. D. 328-389. 4. Eusebius, A. D. 270-340, was one of the celebrated Christian men of early times. He

---

[1] [In Prof Salmon's "Introduction to the Books of the New Testament" the reader will find a satisfactory answer to the argument of Dr. Abbott against the genuineness of the Second Epistle of Peter.—A. H.]

INTRODUCTION TO THE SECOND EPISTLE OF PETER.

was a voluminous writer, a historian, and it is through him that we obtain knowledge of the opinions of many who lived before him. From his works it is clear that he was acquainted with the Second Epistle of Peter, and that, because it appeared useful to many, it was generally read. Yet it must be admitted that while he did not reject it as spurious, Eusebius was not prepared to admit it to an equal footing with the books which are now received. 5. Origen, in Eusebius. This Father was born in Alexandria, Egypt, A. D. 185, and died at Tyre, A. D. 254. In the Greek text of his writings are no quotations from Second Peter, but in the Latin translation by Rufinus are many—*e. g.*, 1 : 4. "Peter," he says, "has left behind one Epistle generally acknowledged; perhaps also a second, for it is a disputed question." In the Latin Homily on Joshua 7 is the following: "Peter, moreover, sounds loudly on the twofold trumpet of his Epistles." It is clear that Origen did not reject our Epistle as spurious; he only held its genuineness as not entirely settled. Too much dependence, however, must not be placed on the Latin translation. 6. Firmilian, A. D. 256, Bishop of Cesarea, in Cappadocia, speaks in a letter to Cyprian of Paul and Peter as condemning heretics in the epistles; but as First Peter makes no allusion to heretics, it may be inferred that he alludes to Second Peter. 7. Clement of Alexandria, A. D. 165–220, gave, according to Eusebius, "explanations of all the Canonical Scriptures without omitting the disputed books." (Westcott.) One of the disputed books was Second Peter. By some this testimony is thought to be slightly weakened by a remark of Cassiodorus, but by others not at all. 8. Tertullian, born in the last of the second century, and Cyprian, converted to Christianity A. D. 246, make no allusion to it. 9. Justin Martyr, A. D. 138, and Irenæus, who died about A. D. 202, are believed by some to make unmistakable allusions to our Epistle; but by others, as seen above, the references are not deemed certain.

II. INTERNAL. As already remarked, the Epistle is Peter's, or it is a forgery. That it is not a forgery may be safely concluded from the following considerations: 1. *Its general tone.* Though some of its views are peculiar, yet the entire Epistle is in harmony with other Epistles known, on abundant historical evidence, to be authentic. In this respect the writer has made no slip by which one might be led to suspect forgery. But it is also positively spiritual, devout, and trustful. It contains nothing puerile, nothing feeble, which is far more than can be said of most of the writings which immediately followed the apostolic age. It has been confidently affirmed that not one of the Apostolic Fathers could have produced a writing evincing such intellectual ability and such elevated spirituality. It must, therefore, have been written before their time—*i. e.*, in the apostolic age itself. 2. *The writer is confident that he shall soon die.* Yet it is *possible* that one might deliberately allow one's self to forge even in the face of approaching death; for many a man has died with a lie on his lips, but in such cases that particular sin has been in accordance with the entire life. It is morally impossible that an Epistle which is throughout unexceptionable in morality and piety, should have been written by one whose approach to death was marked by one of the boldest falsehoods ever told. 3. The writer professes to have been with Christ at the Transfiguration, which was one of the falsehoods told, if he was not with him. But the difficulty of supposing it to be a falsehood is expressed above. 4. In ver. 1 the writer distinctly avows himself to be Simon Peter, a servant and an apostle of Jesus Christ, and the objection to calling this a falsehood is also to be seen above. The supposition that the Epistle is a forgery is too nearly absurd to allow its acceptance. Then it was written by Peter. Some writers have laid much stress upon the fact that the Epistle is, in style and spirit, very unlike the First; but, though the differences in these respects are indeed striking, they are not more so than is to be seen in the writings of many an author, even when the writings were composed with no longer interval of time than is supposed to have existed between these two Epistles. This objection, without others of more weight, may well be offset by the striking resemblances.

II. PLAN AND OBJECT.

The Epistle consists of two parts, and each part of two sections. In section first (1 : 1–11) of part first, after the address, the readers are reminded of the gifts conferred upon them by divine power; are exhorted to bring forth certain specified virtues, and to be earnest in securing the salvation to which God has elected them; they are assured that on that condition they shall not fail of entering into the kingdom of Christ. In section second (12–21), the writer gives the reason which prompted him to write, and assures the readers that what he has taught relative to the Second Coming of Christ is true. In section first (2 : 1–22) of part second are described certain false teachers, libertinists, licentious men, and their overthrow and punishment are foretold. In section second (3 : 1–10), the writer describes the scoffers who deny the Second Coming of Christ, and accuses them of willful ignorance relative to the origin and the destruction of the world, and assures the readers that the coming of the Lord will certainly occur. He closes with an exhortation based upon these facts, alludes to Paul and his Epistles, and again exhorts to steadfastness.

III. IS THE EPISTLE IN PART A COPY OF JUDE'S EPISTLE?

A comparison of the two Epistles shows some remarkable resemblances. Compare 1 : 5 with Jude 3; 2 : 1 with Jude 4; 2 : 4 with Jude 6; 2 : 6–10 with Jude 7; 2 : 10 with Jude 8; 2 : 11 with Jude 9; 2 : 12 with Jude 10. The resemblance of these passages is so striking, that many have affirmed intentional copying, though with some changes; as condensation, expansion, more simplicity or less. Resemblances granted, the question is: Which Epistle was written first? As in the past, so, doubtless, in the future, there will be no oneness upon the point. The view that Peter wrote first seems on the whole to be the more probable. The resemblances and the differences constitute an interesting literary question; but they have little significance as related to the authenticity of either epistle, and none as related to our spiritual life. See on the same subject, III., Introduction to the Epistle of Jude.

IV. WHEN WRITTEN, AND WHERE?

There are no means of deciding. Possibly it was written from Rome; for, as there can be no doubt that Peter suffered martyrdom there, he probably went to Rome after he wrote the First.

THE SECOND EPISTLE OF PETER.

CHAPTER I.

SIMON Peter, a servant and an apostle of Jesus Christ, to them that have obtained like precious

1 ¹Simon Peter, a ²servant and apostle of Jesus Christ to them that have obtained ³a like precious

---

1 Many ancient authorities read *Symeon*......2 Gr. *bondservant*......3 Gr. *an equally precious*.

Ch. 1: 1, 2. INTRODUCTION. The Introduction gives the inscription, the character of the persons addressed, and the salutation. **Simon** —*Symeon*, or *Simeon*. Simon is the Greek form, and Symeon the Hebrew form. Even the Hebrew name had some variations. See Gen. 29: 33 (Simeon); 1 Chron. 4: 20 (Shimon.) Simeon is used in Acts 13: 1 by the historian, and in Acts 15: 14 by James in his speech before the assembly in Jerusalem. Simon is the form generally used. It is uncertain which is here the true reading, Simon or Symeon. The name was not uncommon among Romans and was very common among Jews. It means *hearing*. The application of the name to a child implied, at least sometimes, that God *had heard*. (Gen. 29: 33.) The man who, in the temple, took up the infant Jesus in his arms, and, blessing God, uttered the singularly rich prophecy concerning the object of the child's advent, bore the name Simeon. (Luke 2: 25.) The New Testament mentions, also, among others, Simon the "Canaanite,"¹ one of the twelve apostles, Simon of Cyrene, Simon the leper, Simon Magus, Simon the tanner, Simon the father of Judas Iscariot. **Peter.** See on 1 Pet. 1: 1. Simon, *who is called* Peter, is found in Matt. 10: 2. It has been suggested that the apostle here uses both names in conscious reference to his earlier state, and that into which he is supposed to have come afterward. The suggestion is not without a basis of possibility, but the probability of such a reference is slender. For some account of the apostle's life, and for a brief characterization, see "I. Introduction to the First Epistle." **A servant and an apostle.** In the First Epistle the official designation is briefer, "an apostle." In Jude, also, it is briefer, but there it is "servant." Paul sometimes designated himself in the longer form (Rom. 1: 1; Titus 1: 1), and sometimes in the shorter. (1 Cor. 1: 1; 2 Cor. 1: 1; Gal. 1: 1, etc.) Neither James nor Jude says "apostle"; each says "servant." Here "servant" (*bondservant*) is not used merely in the sense in which it may be applied to Christians in general; it is doubtless an official use of the term, indicating that the writer regards himself as a servant in ministerial labor, while "apostle" is the narrower term, expressing not only the form of ministerial labor peculiar to the twelve, but also the authority peculiar to them. Farrar ("Early Days of Christianity") translates "slave," which is scarcely a just representation of the Greek. See upon this question the last part of the notes on 1 Peter 2: 18. Peter's acknowledgment of himself as a servant of Christ, was an acknowledgment that Christ had the right to direct him in all his ministerial life; and it was precisely that right in which the apostle gloried. Like Peter, ministers of all times should wait for Christ's "orders," not for man's, and when the orders come should obey with promptness and alacrity. "An apostle"; one *sent away*, and while the word was applied in this general sense to the twelve, it had the special meaning implied in their peculiar official position in distinction from that of all other ministers. Peter has been called the first pope; he never calls himself pope. See further on 1 Pet. 1: 1, and also on 5: 1, on the nature of the apostleship. **Jesus Christ**—as in 1 Pet. 1: 1. Paul usually said the same, though in most cases, according to the approved reading,² he put "Christ" first, which fact has special significance. "Jesus" is the Greek form, while *Joshua* is the Hebrew form. Joshua is a shorter form of Jehoshua (*help of Jehovah, Saviour*). The Greek form is used for Joshua in Heb. 4: 8. ("For if

---

¹ The wrong spelling. The apostle here meant was not a Canaanite, for, as Dr. Schaff reminds us ("Companion to Greek Testament and English Version"), "None of the apostles belonged to the race of Canaanites." Simon the Canancan is correct. See Matt. 10: 4. Revised Version.

² Concerning different readings of Greek manuscripts, see remarks on 1 Pet. 1: 8.

faith with us through the righteousness of God and our Saviour Jesus Christ:
2 Grace and peace be multiplied unto you through the knowledge of God, and of Jesus our Lord,

faith with us in the righteousness of [1] our God and 2 *the* Saviour Jesus Christ: Grace to you and peace be multiplied in the knowledge of God and of Jesus

1 Or, *our God and Saviour.*

Jesus had given them rest.") "Jesus" was a common Jewish name, but was given to the first born son of the virgin Mary for the special reason that he was to save his people from their sins. (Matt. 1: 21.) "Christ," anointed. It is used by the New Testament writers to designate the Being who was believed by the Jews of Old Testament times as appointed *to come* (Matt. 11: 3), God's ANOINTED. It is equivalent to Messiah. "We have found the Messias, which is, being interpreted, the Christ." (John 1: 41.) **To them that have obtained,** etc. This is one of the cases, so common in the Greek, of a short method of expression. Given fully: *to them that have obtained faith equally precious with that which we have obtained.* "Them" and "us" must not be referred to Gentiles and Jews; the former refers to all who are described, whether Jews or Gentiles, and the latter to Peter himself, or to the apostles as a class. **Faith**—not Christianity as external, but that faith which Christianity inspires. Peter writes, not merely to the Christians of Asia Minor, as in his First Epistle, but to all Christians then living; and indeed, according to the intention of the Holy Spirit, to all the saints of all the ages that were to follow. Comprehensive benevolence in a forger! As to the word "General" in the title of the Authorized Version, see on the same word in the title of the First Epistle, first paragraph of the notes. **Precious.** See 1 Pet. 1: 18, 19 (precious *blood*.) Here we have **through the righteousness,** etc. Precious also is this faith as the foundation of Christian character, as investing the present life with something of the power of the future life, and as giving the possessor ability to appropriate the future life as one of unending bliss. **Like**—as precious in kind as that of Peter and the other apostles. Whether it is equally *strong* in all Christians is a question not touched. **Have obtained**—literally, *obtained by lot.* See Luke 1: 9; John 19: 24. The faith was "obtained"; it came from a source external to themselves. In no sense did they originate it; personal merit, then, is not to be thought of. **The righteousness,** etc.—not, as Fronmuller, "an attribute of God," not "the personal righteousness of believers" viewed as God's because given by him, but the entire scheme of the gospel as an exhibition of divine righteousness and mercy. Here is the germ of the doctrine so much enforced by Paul in Romans. (1: 17; 3: 21, 22, 25; 4: 13 and elsewhere.) See also Galatians, and Crit. Notes.

"Through," either *in* or *by means of.* The Greek preposition means primarily *in*, but in the New Testament often expresses *instrumentality.* The righteousness is the medium or source of faith. **Of God and our Saviour Jesus Christ**—*of our* God, etc. The question is, whether "God and Saviour" are both to be connected with "Jesus Christ"—that is, whether Jesus Christ is here called God as well as Saviour; or whether two distinct persons are meant, God the Father and Jesus Christ. In ver. 2 an evident distinction is made: *of God, and of Jesus our Lord.* See ver. 11, "our Lord and Saviour Jesus Christ," where the arrangement of the Greek is the same as here, but, which is a very important difference, *Lord* (κύριος) is used instead of *God* (θεός). See also 2: 20, "of the Lord and Saviour Jesus Christ"; 3: 18, "of our Lord and Saviour Jesus Christ." In Titus 2: 13, "of the great God and our Saviour Jesus Christ." Nowhere, unless here, does Peter apply directly to Jesus Christ the word *God,* which is a strong, perhaps decisive, consideration that he does not so apply it here. See Crit. Notes.

2. **Grace ... unto you.** See on 1 Peter 1: 2. **Though** (*in*) **the knowledge.** Peter makes free use of this word knowledge (1: 3, 5, 8; 2: 20; 3: 18), but never in the sense in which it was used by the false philosophy which soon attempted to force its way into the churches. The kindred verb was used by Christ in his memorable prayer. (John 17: 3.) Knowledge of God, in Scriptural use, is not mere speculative knowledge: it pertains to the heart quite as much as to the intellect; it implies knowledge of Jesus our Lord. A very few who, in consequence of having no written

3 According as his divine power hath given unto us all things that *pertain* unto life and godliness, through the knowledge of him that hath called us to glory and virtue:

3 our Lord; seeing that his divine power hath granted unto us all things that pertain unto life and godliness through the knowledge of him that called us
4 [1] by his own glory and virtue; whereby he hath

1 Some ancient authorities read *through glory and virtue.*

---

revelation, were ignorant of Christ, may have attained, nevertheless, to some knowledge of God, but such knowledge of God as it is possible for men to attain, is impossible if Christ is not known. Professing to know God, and at the same time rejecting Christ, is proof of great and culpable ignorance — ignorance which comes more from disease of the heart than from weakness of the head. Peter uses two words, both of which are represented in the English by *knowledge* (ἐπίγνωσις and γνῶσις). The former occurs in ver. 2, 3, 8; 2: 20; the latter in ver. 5, 6; 3: 18. The context of these verses makes it very improbable that the writer used the words in different senses, though the former may in itself include the idea of *acknowledging* in addition to the idea of *knowledge*, which is the exclusive meaning of the latter. It may sometimes be used in a stronger sense, *full* knowledge. *Knowledge* (γνῶσις) is a term which was much used in Alexandria and elsewhere. *Gnosticism* (the word is akin to that used by Peter) was one of the most dangerous errors of ancient times. It was a foolish kind of wisdom. Possibly Peter had the germ of the error in his eye. The "agnosticism" of the present is remarkable for being neither foolish nor wise, since it *knows nothing at all.*

PART I. SECTION FIRST.

Ch. 1: 3-11. The superscription and salutation being ended, the Epistle proper begins. This section divides itself thus: 1. What has been done for them; 2. What they themselves ought to do. The latter is hortatory; the former is the doctrinal foundation. The method is this: As God has done given things for them for a given end, they are earnestly to strive for given Christian traits. The second verse is closed by some with a period, and by some with a colon. The connection of ver. 3 with that verse is not so close as a comma indicates.

3. According as—*inasmuch as.* The sense is, *persuaded*, or *knowing that.* In the original, **all things** is made emphatic by being put next after the conjunction: Inasmuch as *all things have been given.* It is difficult to see what Peter could have intended in the *all things*, unless it were the promises. (Ver. 4.) These, through application to the heart by the Holy Spirit, would promote both life and godliness. **That pertain**—and therefore subserve. **Life**—spiritual life, the result of being begotten by the God and Father of our Lord Jesus Christ. (1 Pet. 1:3.) It implies blessedness, but that is not the principal thing meant. The difference between their former state of death and their present state of life is more than can be told. When men lose their prejudice against "theology," and speak as educators, as men of business, as employers or employed, they have no difficulty in feeling that men are depraved, which is what the Scriptures mean by being *dead.* Consciousness of depravity, however, is not generally as marked as consciousness of life. Reason: Depravity ever tends to diminish self knowledge, while life ever tends to increase it. Hence, one may come to have little of that unhappiness which is the natural fruit of sin; while another cannot but be conscious of the blessedness which is the fruit of life. **Godliness**—a righteous state of heart toward God, but manifesting itself in holy activity. *This* is *imparted* righteousness. As to the distinction between imparted and imputed righteousness, see note on ver. 1. **Of him**—of *God*, as in 1 Pet. 1: 15; 2: 9. The call came indeed "through" the Holy Spirit, on the ground of Christ's mediatorial work, but it *came from* God. The New Testament writers never become weary of referring the change which had been wrought upon the souls of their readers to the call of God. They give no prominence to the activity of man in conversion, except as the result of divine, effectual calling. **To glory and virtue.** Revised Version: *by his own glory and virtue.* (Westcott and Hort: διὰ δόξης καὶ ἀρετῆς, *through glory and virtue;* but they put in the margin, ἰδίᾳ δόξῃ καὶ ἀρετῇ, *by his own glory and virtue.*) Which is the true reading is uncertain. By "glory" may be meant his glorious nature, and by "virtue" his "superiority revealed in the work of salvation." "See Acts 2: 11 (the wonderful works of God)."—*Cremer*. The glory and virtue were *the means by which* they were called—means, because they were used in effecting their regeneration. It is impossible to conceive how the apostle could have more strongly represented God as the source of all which the readers have above what they had by nature. But he has yet more to say (ver. 4) as preparatory to the exhortation of ver. 5-11.

'*Virtue*' (Ἀρετή) is a word of much historical interest, the New Testament use being very unlike that which prevailed in Greek literature. Intense worldliness and Pagan viciousness are to be seen in its derivation. It is traceable to *Ares* ("Ἀρης), Mars, son of Jupiter, and Juno, god of war. Hence, it was applied to war itself. Some trace it to the word signifying *man* (ἀνήρ), and it is certain that manliness or bravery in war was the principal idea which it expressed. The Latin equivalent, *virtus*, was used by the Romans in the same way. As Trench says ("Study of Words"): "It is as if for them all virtues were included in warlike courage alone." As the same writer also reminds us, the Italians of to-day "degrade the word *virtuoso*, or *the virtuous*, to signify one accomplished in painting, music, and sculpture, such things as are the ornamental fringe of a nation's life, but can never be made, without loss of all manliness of character, its main texture and woof, not to say that excellence in these fine arts has been in too many cases divorced from all true virtue and worth." Christianity took the word 'virtue' (ἀρετή) out from the ignoble uses to which it had been consecrated, and made it the watchword of Godlike excellence. The application of the word to God is very unusual, and has led to severe stricture of the Epistle (as not Peter's) by Dr. Edwin A. Abbott. See the "Introduction, I., Was Peter the Writer?" But the same word in the plural is applied to God in the First Epistle 2: 9 ("shew forth the praises—*virtues* —of him"), and not, as Farrar ("Early Days") says it is, "in a very different sense." The sense seems to be essentially the same here as there.

4. Whereby—*by which*—that is, by which granted unto us his precious and exceeding great promises; that through these ye may become partakers of glory and power. **Are given**—*he hath given* (*granted as a gift*); **him that called us** (ver. 3)—still referring the readers to the divine source of all. **Exceeding great**—literally, *the greatest and precious*, according to the *Textus Receptus*. But the manuscripts differ. Wescott and Hort, interchanging the adjectives say, *precious and exceeding great*. So the Revised Version. Promises which are so great cannot be of little value. The promises of God to the elect are resolvable into two classes: the one pertains to the coming of a Saviour; the other, to the coming of the Holy Spirit. The latter is the complement of the former. It would not have been in accordance with the boundless sweep of the divine benevolence to give the one and withhold the other. Neither class alone would have had any practical preciousness; but conjoined, the two classes of promises are of infinite value: for they have as their object the glory of the Father and of the Son and of the Holy Spirit, in making men partakers of the divine nature. For the first promise of the first class, see Gen. 3: 15. See in many of the Psalms, in Isaiah, Jeremiah, Daniel, Joel, Micah, etc., promises of each class so great and precious as to have awakened the intensest interest of prophets and angels. (1 Pet. 1: 10-12.) **Us**—both Peter and those to whom he is writing. **That**—the end for which the promises were given; for *these* refers to *promises*, not, as some say, to *glory* and *virtue*. The contents of the promises, applied to their hearts, had already made them so far like God that they are justly called God's children. In so far as they are the children of God, they have already become partakers of the divine nature. But the change is not complete. The effect of the promises will not be fully realized till the next life. **Might be**—*may become*. Partaking of the divine nature implies no loss of their own individuality, no absorption of their personality in the personality of God. They partake of God's nature while retaining their own nature. They lose their own nature viewed as depravity, but viewed as organic and constitutional their nature cannot be absorbed into the nature of God. In regeneration God's spiritual life, not his essence, is communicated to the soul. In that sense they

of the divine nature, having escaped the corruption that is in the world through lust.
5 And besides this, giving all diligence, add to your faith virtue; and to virtue, knowledge;

takers of ¹the divine nature, having escaped from
5 the corruption that is in the world by lust. Yea, and for this very cause adding on your part all diligence, in your faith supply virtue; and in your
6 virtue knowledge; and in your knowledge ²temper-

1 Or, a....... 2 Or, self-control.

become sharers of God's nature, and only in that sense can they be said to have a new nature. See Heb. 12: 10 ("partakers of his holiness"); 1 John 3: 2 ("shall be like him"); and compare John 1: 12, 13; 1 Pet. 1: 23. *May become* implies growth, but **might** be expresses (which the apostle does not mean to express) a sudden, instantaneous, and completed participation. **Having escaped**—a strong representation, having escaped *from*. It hints their activity, but makes prominent the result of God's interposition—a wonderful deliverance, since that from which they were delivered was so terrible. **The corruption.** It describes the moral filth of the world without Christianity. (2: 12, 19.) Paul uses the same word in Rom. 8: 21 ("bondage of corruption"), contrasting it with the glorious liberty of the children of God, and in Gal: 6: 8 ("shall of the flesh reap corruption"). The fearful immorality which, with few exceptions, characterized the social life of Greece and Rome, the highest state as well as the lowest, and which has equally marked non-Christian society in all lands and all times, fully justifies the apostolic application of the term 'corruption.' The vileness of man left traces of itself in durable form on the walls of dwellings and in bronze castings, the detail of which would be indecorous to relate; and in proportion as society, after being purified by Christianity, has withdrawn from the purifying influence, it has relapsed into similar pollution. *The world's corruption, which is founded in lust,* expresses the meaning.

5-7. What God has done for them should lead them to the manifestation of appropriate Christian traits. The contrast, on the one hand, between divine power, life, and godliness, knowledge of God, divine calling, glory and virtue, precious and exceeding great promises, sharing the divine nature; and, on the other hand, the corruption, which, originating in lust, pervades the world, is a strong ground of appeal. **And besides this**—*but for this very reason also.* The connection is with 'according as' in ver. 3, thus: *Inasmuch* *as,* or, as explained above, *knowing that,* all things have been given to us by his divine power, etc.—*for this very reason* manifest the Christian virtues which I am about to enumerate. If Paul was the first Christian logician of the apostolic time, certainly Peter was the second. Paul reasoned more, but Peter, when he reasoned, reasoned as divinely as Paul. In ver. 3 and 4 we have premises which are laid in God's power, glory, and promise, and here in ver. 5-7 are practical conclusions, under the popular form of exhortation, which flow from the premises with conclusiveness, not inferior to that which marks any section of Paul's great Epistle to the Romans. **Giving all diligence**—*exhibiting* on your part earnestness. The apostle has told them in ver. 3, 4 what God has given them, and now he tells them what they ought to do. **Add.** From this word the pulpit has drawn material for its rhetoric, but the idea of arithmetical addition is not Peter's. *Furnish* or *minister,* or *supply* (Revised Version), probably expresses the sense. See ver. 11, where for "shall be ministered" (*shall be supplied,* Revised Version) is the same Greek word; 2 Cor. 9: 10, *ministereth* (*supplieth,* Revised Version); Gal. 3: 5, *ministereth* (*supplieth,* Revised Version). The preposition *in* (*ἐν*) is not, strange to say, translated at all in the Common Version, for *to* was not intended as a rendering of the Greek preposition. But *in* is the only translation which the word here admits. Thus the apostle says, *in your faith minister* (or *supply*) *virtue.* You have faith; see that it be such as to include virtue, leading to it and embracing it. By *virtue* may be meant something more specific than moral excellence, as fortitude, energy, vigor (in the Christian life, and therefore a Christian virtue). Cremer gives it the more general meaning. **And to (*in*) virtue (*supply*) knowledge.** For the meaning of 'knowledge,' as used in ver. 2, 3, see on ver. 2. While not excluding the ideas there expressed, it may here be used more distinctly of the *practical understand-*

6 And to knowledge, temperance; and to temperance, patience; and to patience, godliness; 7 And to godliness, brotherly kindness; and to brotherly kindness, charity. 8 For if these things be in you, and abound, they make *you that ye shall* neither be barren nor unfruitful in the knowledge of our Lord Jesus Christ.

ance; and in *your* ¹ temperance ² patience; and in 7 *your* ² patience godliness; and in *your* godliness ³ brotherly kindness; and in *your* ³ brotherly kindness love. For if these things are yours and abound, they make you to be not idle nor unfruitful

---

1 Or, *self control*......2 Or, *steadfastness*......3 Gr. *love of the brethren.*

---

ing which is so necessary to the successful accomplishment of the ends of their new life. They must not be satisfied with virtue. In it should be supplied knowledge. Without knowledge their virtue might be erratic. And to (*in*) knowledge (*supply*) temperance. You have knowledge; let it be such as to include temperance. By 'temperance' is meant self-control in all respects, though with special reference to the passions. See Acts 24: 25; Gal. 5: 23. And to (*in*) temperance (*supply*) patience—patience under trials, whether of cares or of persecutions—a virtue often enjoined in the First Epistle. And to (*in*) patience (*supply*) godliness—*i. e.*, right disposition toward God.

7. And to (*in*) godliness (*supply*) brotherly kindness. Let your godliness be such as to lead to and so include brotherly kindness. The Greek is the same as in 1 Pet. 1: 22 ("love of the brethren"); 3: 8 ("love as brethren"). Right disposition toward God (godliness) implies love toward Christian brethren, though it is equally true that love, Christian love, toward the disciples of Christ implies right disposition toward God. See 1 John 4: 20; 2: 9; 3: 11, 14, 17; 4: 11. And to (*in*) brotherly kindness (*supply*) charity (*love*). The latter is the more comprehensive, all mankind being its object. (1 Thess. 3: 12; Gal. 6: 10.) One of the few infelicitous renderings by the Revised Version is this final clause of the series: *in your love of the brethren love*. Twice they use the same English word *love* where the Greek uses different words: *brotherly love* or *kindness* (φιλαδελφία) and *love* (ἀγάπην). To the Greek reader of the Epistle, there could have been nothing so "intolerable" as the Revised Version gives us. The American Committee would have preferred *brotherly kindness*, and in some American editions this rendering is substituted. The sense of this clause may be expressed like that of the others: as you have love for the brethren, let it be such as to lead to *universal* love. If it is such as it ought to be, it will produce love for all mankind. It should be noticed, then, that these virtues are organically related. The relation is somewhat of a *causal* nature— that is, *faith* may cause *virtue*, and *virtue* may cause *knowledge*—not, strictly, *originating*, but causing a more abundant fruitage of what had already been originated.

8. For points to *the reason why* they should minister in their faith such virtues: they will attain to *much knowledge of Christ*. So the Spirit leads back the apostle to the very position which he took in ver. 2. There he wishes them knowledge; here he assures them that having the virtues they will have the knowledge. Such knowledge as Peter means is heart knowledge quite as much as head knowledge, and therefore the knowledge and the virtues may not always be easily distinguished. Which precedes, it is difficult to say. God's working is not limited to a given order. Know God and his Son Jesus Christ, and Christian graces will thrive; cultivate Christian graces, and knowledge of God will increase. These things—the virtues of ver. 5-7. Be in you—*are* (really) *yours*. Abound— an expressive word in the Greek—literally, *to do*, or, *be more* (than enough). Not dwarfs, but amply developed and ever developing must all these virtues be, if the result mentioned in the latter part of the verse is to be attained. If does not imply doubt. No word for 'if' is used in the original. These things *being in you and abounding* is the literal rendering. Barren—*idle* or *slothful*. They make. According to Lillie the idea is, *render*, constitute, you, establish your character as, *not idle*, not unfruitful in (*as to*) the true knowledge of our Lord Jesus Christ. A better view is that which, making *in* (εἰς) equivalent to *into*, represents the knowledge as *the aim* toward an ever greater measure of which they are continually to advance. They render you neither slothful nor unfruitful *into* the knowledge—that is, in *advancing* in the knowledge of. Yet, as hinted above, this does not imply that in no degree is practicing

II. PETER.

9 But he that lacketh these things is blind, and cannot see afar off, and hath forgotten that he was purged from his old sins.

9 unto the knowledge of our Lord Jesus Christ. For he that lacketh these things is blind, ¹seeing only what is near, having forgotten the cleansing from

¹ Or, *closing his eyes*.

---

the Christian virtues preceded by the knowledge of Christ. Notice that it is not, as in ver. 2, knowledge of *God and of Jesus our Lord*. Knowledge of Christ, then, is knowledge of God. In this verse are traces of the Lord's teaching: 'idle' in the market place (Matt. 20: 3); he becometh 'unfruitful' (Matt. 13: 22). There may have been no *conscious* reference to the Lord's use of the words, yet the words are like reflected touches of light, which the artist's pencil has left upon the canvas. See a remarkably condensed expression of the same sentiment made by the Lord to his disciples on the mountain: "Blessed are the pure in heart, for they shall see God." (Matt. 5: 8.) The *pure in heart* is expanded by the apostle, not consciously, perhaps, into the numerous virtues of ver. 5–7, and 'see God' is represented in 'the knowledge of our Lord Jesus Christ.'

9. But should be *for*. The positive (ver. 8) is offset by the negative view, and is thereby confirmed—not an uncommon rhetorical way of enforcing a truth. What is called the rhetorical way may be the natural way. The apostle perhaps knew little of rhetoric; but illumined, controlled, inspired, by the Spirit of God, he wrote according to nature. These things corresponds with *these things* in ver. 8, and therefore to the virtues specified in ver. 5–7. **That lacketh**—in striking contrast with him 'who abounds.' These virtues no man has till he has been born again, but most men have the opposite sins. **Is blind.** Applied originally to the eyes, it was applied figuratively and with great significance to the mind; and while the intellect of man is blind, it is chiefly the heart (the affections) in which blindness is seated. The blindness is alienation from spiritual things, which does indeed produce stupidity of understanding; but the latter is more the effect of the former than the cause. See Matt. 15: 14; Luke 4: 18; Rom. 2: 19; Rev. 3: 17. **Cannot see afar off**—not a waste of words, but explanatory of 'blind.' He is so far blind that he cannot see afar off (*seeing only what is near*, Revised Version); he is near-sighted. The Greek word is compounded of two, which mean *to close* or *blink the eyes*, which is a peculiarity of many near-sighted persons when, without artificial help, they desire to see a distant object. Those who lack the virtues in question are near-sighted, inasmuch as they cannot see things which are eternal and invisible. (2 Cor. 4: 18.) God is invisible (Col. 1: 15; 1 Tim. 1: 17); his attributes are invisible (Rom. 1: 20); but according to Heb. 11: 27, *the unseen can be seen*. Though lacking Christian virtues, yet one may have sharp sight relative to things which are near—of this world. **And hath forgotten.** When the heart has lost interest in the invisible, memory is brittle relative to things spiritual. It will fail to do its office respecting even the work which has been done, or is believed to have been done, on the very mind of which memory is itself one of the faculties; as, for example, the work of being cleansed from former sins. **That he was purged**—more literally, *having forgotten the cleansing*. The Greek for 'cleansing' is the same as is used in Heb. 1: 3 ("When he had *purged, cleansed*, our sins"). It was used of Jewish ceremonial washings (John 2: 6), and of the purification of lepers. (Luke 5: 14.) But in what sense is he here said to be cleansed from his sins? It should be remarked as preliminary that the case is a supposed one rather than one directly and positively affirmed, though this does not appear from the Common Version or from the Revision. The sense is this: For he to whom these *may* be wanting—he who, *by supposition*, is lacking these things. It may, therefore, refer to a regenerated soul, without necessarily teaching, in contradiction to other Scriptures, an actual and continued fall. Like many other passages, it may be of the nature of a warning against apostasy. (Heb. 2: 1-3; 4: 1; 6: 1-9; 10: 26-29.) If it refer to a regenerated person, he was cleansed from his sins in the sense of being delivered from their dominion, which deliverance was effected through the atoning death of Christ received by faith. It may not be justifiable, however, to ground so important a view upon a very delicate peculiarity of the Greek tongue. In that case it must be assumed, in harmony

10 Wherefore the rather, brethren, give diligence to make your calling and election sure: for if ye do these things ye shall never fall:
11 For so an entrance shall be ministered unto you abundantly into the everlasting kingdom of our Lord and Saviour Jesus Christ.

10 his old sins. Wherefore, brethren, give the more diligence to make your calling and election sure: for if ye do these things, ye shall never stumble;
11 for thus shall be richly supplied unto you the entrance into the eternal kingdom of our Lord and Saviour Jesus Christ.

with numerous passages which teach that no regenerated person will suffer a final, fatal fall; that being unregenerated, he belongs to that class of which there are not a few in every age, who are greatly enlightened and deeply affected by spiritual things, and at length identify themselves with the people of God by baptism, and show during a short period much interest in whatever concerns the kingdom of Christ, but, having no root in themselves, wither away. (Matt. 13:6.) Such a man *forgets* that he was, as he thought and as he appeared to others, cleansed from his old sins, such, perhaps, as are described in 1 Pet. 4: 3.

10. The arrangement of the Greek is very emphatic: *Wherefore the rather, brethren, be in earnest, sure your calling and election to make, for these things doing, not by any means shall ye fall ever.* Every word drives the nail further, and the last clinches it beyond the possibility of being drawn. **Wherefore**—in view of the assurance (ver. 8), and the warning. (Ver 9.) The **rather**—all the more in view of the assurance and the warning. **Brethren**—never used in the First Epistle, and used only here in this. He addresses in the same way those who killed the Prince of Life (Acts 3: 17); but only as descendants with himself from the founder of the nation, Abraham. The readers are his brethren as born, like himself, from above. It is even more significant than *dearly beloved* in 1 Pet. 2: 11. He and they have one Father. The **rather** (*the more*) **give diligence**—*give the more diligence*—i. e., be the more earnest. **Calling.** See on *elect.* (1 Pet. 1:2.) 'Calling' stands before **election**—not because they were first called, and then, having accepted the call, were elected; but because he is just now giving special prominence to what has been done for them in this life, not to what God did from eternity. But can *they* do anything toward making their calling and election sure? What can be surer than God's eternal purpose and God's call? But how are *they to feel sure* that they were elected and called? Ananias and Sapphira must have felt quite

confident at the time of their baptism that the question of their salvation had been settled in the counsels of God; and it had been settled, but not in the way they supposed. Dishonesty and lying spoke terribly against the supposition that they had been elected; for those who are elected are elected to holiness, not less than to heaven. The readers are to make their calling and election sure *by doing these things*—that is, by having (abounding in) the Christian virtues. So a holy life will prove to *themselves* that they were elected and called. Peter strikes hard blows at Antinomianism. **Shall never fall**—shall *not by any means ever stumble*, and so lose salvation. Peter has not forgotten his Master's doctrine. They shall never perish. (John 10: 28.)

11. This verse gives the blessed result; and this, as an expansion of the thought 'Ye shall never fall,' enforces the duty of *doing these things; (for so).* **Ministered.** The Greek for 'ministered' is the same as in ver. 3 (*add to*). **Abundantly**—*richly;* a word which, though applied to earthly things, is beautifully applied also to things spiritual. **Entrance.** Strictly, 'ministered richly' qualifies 'entrance'; yet the idea pertains to what is to come after the entrance—eternal bliss. Compare 1 Pet. 4: 18 (the righteous *scarcely* saved), and see notes, first paragraph. That one should be satisfied with the prospect of being barely able to pass through the heavenly gate, speaks poorly for his view of the "wideness of God's mercy." The gate is strait and the way is narrow which *leadeth unto life;* but the gate *at the other end* is broad to him who has been neither slothful nor unfruitful in the knowledge of Christ. **Kingdom**—a word often used by our Lord, but rare in the writings of our apostle. It expresses substantially the same as 'inheritance' (1 Pet. 1: 4); but that views heaven as related to the believer, this as related to Christ. Heaven is conceived as a kingdom over which Christ reigns, yet as embraced within certain limits; whence the expression, 'entrance into.' The conception of a kingdom into which the subjects of Christ are to enter after death is not contradictory to

II. PETER.

12 Wherefore I will not be negligent to put you always in remembrance of these things, though ye know them, and be established in the present truth.
13 Yea, I think it meet, as long as I am in this tabernacle, to stir you up by putting you in remembrance;
14 Knowing that shortly I must put off *this* my tabernacle, even as our Lord Jesus Christ hath shewed me.
15 Moreover I will endeavour that ye may be able

12 Wherefore I shall be ready always to put you in remembrance of these things, though ye know them, and are established in the truth which is with *you*.
13 And I think it right, as long as I am in this tabernacle, to stir you up by putting you in remembrance; knowing that the putting off of my tabernacle cometh swiftly, even as our Lord Jesus Christ
15 signified unto me. Yea, I will give diligence that

the idea of a kingdom in this world. (Matt. 3: 2.) The kingdom has been already set up, and Christ is even now reigning; but as it is not here in its completed form, it is represented as it is in the verse before us. See Matt. 8: 11. The conception of a kingdom consisting of persons regenerated by the Holy Spirit is expressed in Jer. 23: 5; Dan. 2: 44, and many other places. Christ's kingdom may be viewed as external, as internal, as beginning, as advancing, as completed. God the Father is represented as King, and as having a kingdom: "Our Father who art in heaven. Thy *kingdom come.*" But the kingdom is generally viewed as reigned over by Christ. Christ reigns over it as God's Vicegerent. In this mediatorial capacity, Christ must reign till he has put all enemies under his feet (1 Cor. 15: 25), and when that glorious end shall have come, he will relinquish his mediatorial character, delivering up the kingdom to God, even the Father; but the kingdom itself will continue forever. It is impossible that that should come to an end, unless those who constitute it shall all either become disloyal, or be annihilated. **Everlasting**—*eternal;* used also in Matt. 25: 46; and, what is very striking, the Greek word is there applied to future punishment as well as to future bliss.

12-21. SECTION SECOND. The reason which prompted the apostle to write, and the truth of what he has taught, relative to the second coming of Christ.

12. Wherefore—in view of all I have said, but especially in view of the grand final result. (Ver. 11.) **Will not be negligent.** Another and approved Greek reading gives the meaning, *I will, I intend,* and may be rendered freely, *I will be ready.* **These things**—the things concerning which he has been writing. Peter, so forgetful of some things in the early part of his Christian life, is deeply impressed with the importance of reminding the readers concerning all these gracious things. **Though ye know.** Memory is frail even respecting things which we know; the more worldly the more forgetful. **Present truth**—truth of the

present gospel; truth now preached by apostles, and now believed by the readers.

13. Yea—rather, *but—but* though ye know them. **Meet**—*proper* or *fit*. **This tabernacle**—*this tent,* the human body. (2 Cor. 5: 1.) Like a soldier's or a traveler's tent, the body is only for temporary use, is frail, and is easily taken down. As a tent is for human beings to dwell in, so the body is the earthly dwelling place of the immortal spirit. Hence it would be improper to apply the figure to animals. **As long as.** The apostle has no thought of "retiring." **Stir you up**—not that they were asleep, as he himself once slept in Gethsemane, but that he purposes not to allow them to sleep. Literally, 'to stir you up' **in remembrance.** As long as he shall continue to live, he will continue to put them in mind, so that his exhortations may be remembered.

14. He is the more strongly impelled to this by the fact that the opportunity to do so will soon be closed. **Knowing that shortly**—more exactly, *swiftly*, as in the Revised Version. He knows that his death is to be *sudden.* How many of the apostles left the world by means of sickness is unknown. Peter expects to die by martyrdom, as his Lord (John 21: 18, 19) **shewed** him (not *hath* shewed him), *indicated* to him. Some say he learned it by revelation made at a later time—possible, not probable. The verb is in just the tense which Peter would have used had he meant the time referred to in John. The apostle has no reluctance to call to mind the fact of his departure from this world, and the fact that he must suffer death at the hands of the wicked. He is indeed to meet him whom he once denied, but long ago he received assurance of his Master's readiness to recognize him as his penitent disciple whenever the hour of his martyrdom should come.

> For when thy deadly need is bitterest,
> Thou shalt not be denied, as I am here—
> My voice, to God and angels, shall attest,—
> Because I know this man, let him be clear.

15. Moreover—*but also.* The 'also' points to the time after he shall have gone. They

after my decease to have these things always in remembrance.

16 For we have not followed cunningly devised fables, when we made known unto you the power and coming of our Lord Jesus Christ, but were eyewitnesses of his majesty.

at every time ye may be able after my [1]decease to call these things to remembrance. For we did not follow cunningly devised fables, when we made known unto you the power and [2]coming of our Lord Jesus Christ, but we were eyewitnesses of

1 Or, *departure*........2 Or. *presence.*

must remember the things, not only before, but 'also' after, he dies. But how are they to be aided in remembering them? By this very Epistle. Some think he refers to the Gospel of Mark. That is possible, but it would meet the requirement of the case if he should be supposed to refer only to the present Epistle. **After my decease**—literally, *after my exodus*, departure, journey out of; that is, out of this world. This word (ἔξοδος) in the sense of *death* is rare, and it is an interesting fact that the death of the apostle's Master, which formed the subject of conversation on the Mount of Transfiguration, is expressed by the same word: "Who appeared in glory and spake of his *decease*" (*his exodus*). Does Peter make this uncommon use of the word because he remembers it as used then? It *may* not have been used in the conversation itself, but as Luke uses it in his narrative (9:31) it is probable that it had been used in the conversation. In ver. 11 is the opposite word (εἴσοδος, *a journey into*, "entrance"). To *go out of* such a world as this without *going into* such a world as heaven is inconceivably deplorable. **Always.** A periodical remembrance will not suffice. Alternation of remembering and forgetting is condemned. Romanism has sharp sight. It is able to see here the doctrine of the saint's intercession in heaven on behalf of saints on the earth. Peter is instructing Christians that he will intercede for them after his decease! A logical inference would be that all Christians on the earth may pray to Peter in heaven to pray to God for them. See "Path to Paradise; or Catholic Christians' Manual," pp. 141-145, Dublin, 1846, in which is a long list of persons from that of "Holy Mary" to "St. Bridget" and all the "holy virgins and widows," for whose prayers Roman Catholics are taught to pray, and in the list are the names of the apostles headed by that of Peter.

16. For. The writer now proceeds to strengthen the position which he has taken. In his teaching he gave prominence to the power and coming of Christ, and he purposes to show that that teaching was truth: 1. By what he knew had occurred on the Mount of Transfiguration; 2. By ancient prophecy. This shown, he will have justified the preceding exhortation. **Have not followed**—*did not follow.* **Fables**—*myths*, and these were **devised** (invented and wrought) **cunningly** (with great skill). A myth is a story with little or no historical basis. The myth has been defended as adapted to do the people good, but instead of healing the fever of sin it inflamed it. The Jews had their myths, as well as the Greeks and the Romans. Scarcely any people have been without a large stock of fabulous stories, and nearly all of them have been supremely silly.

> Let all the heathen writers join
> To form one perfect book;
> Great God, if once compared with thine,
> How mean their writings look!

Fables like Æsop's belong to a different class. They are simple, beautiful, and instructive. In his preface to "Antiquities of the Jews," Josephus says: "For us to other legislators" (contrasting them with Moses), "they followed fables; and by their discourses transferred the most reproachful of human vices unto the gods, and so afforded wicked men plausible excuses for their crimes." Elsewhere he speaks of Moses as having "preserved his writings from those indecent fables which others have framed." To what myths Peter referred is of no importance. **When we**—the apostles in general, and in particular John and James, those being the two who, with himself, were in the holy mount. (ver. 18.) They made known by preaching, and perhaps by their writings. It is possible that Peter includes his own First Epistle. **The power and coming of**, etc. 'Coming' (3: 4; Matt. 24: 3, 27; 1 Cor. 15: 23; 1 Thess. 2: 19) at the last day to judge the world; 'the power' displayed at that time. They are viewed as prefigured in the events of the Transfiguration, and only so is his argument pertinent. **Were eye-witnesses.** The Eleusinia were a celebrated religious festival of the

17 For he received from God the Father honour and glory, when there came such a voice to him from the excellent glory, This is my beloved Son, in whom I am well pleased.
18 And this voice which came from heaven we heard, when we were with him in the holy mount.

17 his majesty. For he [1] received from God the Father honour and glory, when there was borne such a voice to him by the Majestic Glory, This is my 18 beloved Son, in whom I am well pleased: and this voice we *ourselves* heard borne out of heaven, when

[1] Gr. *having received*.

Greeks in honor of two of their deities. Everything done was supposed to be a *mystery*, and hence the name, *Eleusinian Mysteries*. Initiation into the mysteries was considered as one of the most obligatory and sacred of all human rites. In one year, passing from the less mysteries, they were initiated into the greater, and then were called *epoptai* (ἐπόπται), the name implying that they now *look upon, see*, the mysteries. This is the word used by the apostle: we were 'eye-witnesses' of his majesty. Of course, the word is used in a Christian sense, but its use seems to imply that what he and his companions, James and John, saw on the Mount was of the nature of a *secret* or *mystery* to which *they* were admitted, in distinction from the other apostles. **His majesty**—*glory*, as seen on the Mount. The Greek word is the same as was used by Demetrius, the silversmith, who made little portable temples containing an image of Diana: "And her *magnificence* (glory) should be destroyed." (Acts 19: 27.) The glory of Christ, and the glory of the goddess Diana! Wealth of meaning in the one, and shriveled poverty in the other! "Nothing but myths," says the unbeliever. "We have not followed artfully wrought myths," says Peter. Let the Christian cling with the confidence of an apostle to the gospel as containing, not fables wrought by "the cunning craftiness" of men, but truth revealed by God himself.

17. For. He now shows, by what he had himself seen on the Mount, that his teaching relative to the coming of Christ was true. **He**—Christ. **Honor and glory.** See Rom. 2: 7, 10. 'Glory'—not the brilliant light which proceeded from the Lord's person (Matt. 17:2; Mark 9:3); this was additional to that. It came directly from *God the Father*, and it consisted of the remarkable audible expression of the Father's approval and love—an approval of him not merely as a good man, but as his beloved Son—as his Son in a sense applicable to no other being. **When,** etc.—literally, *such a voice being borne to him.*

From the excellent glory—*by* instead of 'from.' "All other expositions," says Winer, "are arbitrary." By 'excellent (*sublime*) glory' is meant, not heaven, but God himself, *the exalted Majesty.* (Winer.) **My beloved Son.** The original is very expressive, and cannot be reproduced in good English. With naked literalness it would be: *the Son of me, the beloved.* The idea may be expressed thus: *My Son, who is the beloved.* Whether the words "the Son of God" are used in the Scriptures to express the deity of Christ, or only his Messianic office, has long been a mooted question. It is certain that the Jews understood it as implying equality with God. (John 5:18.) "Thou art my Son, this day have I begotten thee" (Ps. 2:7) is clearly applicable to Jesus Christ, as is the entire Psalm; and on the surface of the passage it seems to be taught that the Sonship of Christ had a *beginning,* and if it had a beginning, the beginning may have been at the incarnation (John 1:14), or at the baptism (Matt. 3:16, 17), or at the resurrection. (Rom. 1:4.) In either case it may be only the *declaration* that he was the Son of God which is referred to. He may have been God's Son from eternity, but the declaration or recognition of the fact may have been made in time. See Crit. Note. **In whom,** etc. On *whom I let my pleasure rest* is a more exact expression of the thought; or, *my good pleasure fixed upon him.* (Winer.) See Crit. Notes. The verb expresses the feelings which God had toward him before he came into the world, while the context shows that such are God's feelings still. He who is displeased with one on whom God's pleasure is fixed, needs something more than God's goodness: he needs God's mercy.

18. This voice, not the mere sound, they guessing the meaning, but the words. **Which came.** Correctly, we *heard borne* out of heaven (American Revisers); *heard come* (English Revisers; in the margin, *brought*). **We**—Peter, James, and John. Here, unlike what is often the case, the pronoun in the original is expressed, and for emphasis, *we*

19 We have also a more sure word of prophecy; whereunto ye do well that ye take heed, as unto a light that shineth in a dark place, until the day dawn, and the daystar arise in your hearts:
20 Knowing this first, that no prophecy of the Scripture is of any private interpretation.

19 we were with him in the holy mount. And we have the word of prophecy *made* more sure; whereunto ye do well that ye take heed, as unto a lamp shining in a ¹dark place, until the day dawn, and the day-
20 star arise in your hearts: knowing this first, that

---

1 Gr. *squalid.*

---

ourselves (Rev. Ver.), not some other persons, or perhaps better, we, consciously we, heard it. **When we were with him.** It is when we are in conscious communion with Christ that we feel most deeply the force of the evidence that Christ was and is the special object of God's love. **Holy mount**—not yet certainly known. Mount Tabor has generally had the honor, but without reason. It was more probably an elevation near Mount Hermon. 'Holy': sacred in consequence of the events which occurred.

19. With the last verse he completed his first argument in support of his teaching concerning Christ's power and coming, and he now presents his second argument. The former is based upon what he had seen and heard on the Mount, the latter upon the prophetic Scriptures. **Also** (*and*) stands first in the Greek, and points to this new source of evidence. **A more sure word of prophecy.** Either of two translations is possible: 1. *We have a surer, the prophetic, word.* This makes a direct and strong comparison with something else, and the question arises, With what? With the evidence drawn from what he and two other apostles had *witnessed?* But how could he seem to disparage the strength of the first argument? Was not that decisive, and strongly decisive, of the truthfulness of his teaching? 2. *We have as surer* (more certain), *the prophetic word,* which is an equally correct rendering, and saves from all disparaging contrast with the evidence just given. Peter, then, may be understood as saying: "In consequence of what we saw and heard, and of which miraculous things you yourselves have heard, we may feel that the prophetic word is made more certain; we can have no doubt of the truth of ancient prophecy respecting the future power and coming of Christ." Many other explanations have been given, but while this is not without its difficulties, those have greater ones. **Word.** The apostle groups all the prophecies together, even all the words of the Old Testament, and views them in their unity.

To him the ancient Scriptures are as but one harmonious utterance of the Holy Spirit. (Ver. 21.) **Do well**—*are doing well.* He commends their present interest in the word. Then the rejection of the Old Testament, or any part of it, is *ill-doing.* The Christian who has little interest in the "Jewish" Scriptures is quite too ignorant of the relation between the Old Testament and the New Testament. The "Jewish" Scriptures are Christian in the sense that they as truly, though not as exclusively and clearly, as the New Testament, give forth divine music relative to the power and coming of Christ. The student of botany is not uninterested in the roots and stock of a plant. The beauty which is unfolded in the flower depends upon the stock and roots. **To take heed.** It implies, not mere attention, which in itself is merely an act of the intellect, but attention originated and continued in faith. **A light,** *a lamp.* **That shineth**—not, that *shone.* So the Old Testament still gives light. **Dark place**—the times of the Old Testament, or the earlier and less enlightened state of believers, or the world in general as it was then and as it always is, apart from the Bible. The last meaning is to be preferred. **Until**—take heed until. **The day**—omit the article. **Daystar arise.** The Greek word is phosphorus (φωσφόρος, *light-bearer*); not the sun, but the morning-star. Christ is the Morning Star (Rev. 22:16), but here the allusion is not to Christ. **Arise** (above the horizon). The time referred to is probably that of the second coming of Christ, in which, as already seen (1 Pet. 1: 13; 4: 7, 13), the apostle has so deep an interest. **In your hearts**—not implying that their hearts are now in darkness, but at the second coming the light of Christ will shine so much more brightly that one is justified in using language which seems to imply that their present state is one of darkness—a verse rich in sentiment and beautiful in coloring.

20. Knowing—connected with 'do well to take heed'—thus: to which ye are doing well to take heed, *while ye know,* or, *for ye know.*

21 For the prophecy came not in old time by the will of man: but holy men of God spake *as they were* moved by the Holy Ghost.

no prophecy of scripture is of[1] private interpretation. 21 For no prophecy ever [2] came by the will of man: but men spake from God, being moved by the Holy Spirit.

1 Or, *special*......2 Gr. *was brought*.

First—of all (1 Tim. 2: 1); first of all, in your recollection or consciousness. (Heb. 10: 34.) **This** (standing first in the Greek) gives greater prominence to what is to follow. It calls attention. **Scripture**—the Old Testament. **Any private interpretation**. Rome easily solves the difficulty which has been supposed to lie in these words. In the Douay Version is this note: "This shows plainly that the Scriptures are not to be expounded by any one's private judgment or private spirit. . . . Some may tell us that many of our divines interpret the Scriptures; they may do so, but they do it always with a submission to the judgment of the Church, and not otherwise." In "The Most Reverend Dr. James Butler's Catechism," revised by four Roman Catholic archbishops of Ireland, is the question: "How do we know with *certainty*, what God has taught?" Answer: "By the authority of his Church." Says Archbishop Spalding ("Miscellanea," p. 392): "The fatal source of all this mischief is the principle of private judgment in matters of religion, in opposition to that of authority. The distracting and disorganizing principle of individuality has set itself up against the great conservative principle of an authority, based on antiquity, and secured from error by divine promise." The interpretation of these words by the Roman Catholic Church is therefore this: that nothing in Scripture is to be explained by any individual for himself. He must take the interpretation made by the "Church," which is the Roman Catholic Church, and only that. As that body has itself often been fearfully convulsed by warring opinions, it follows that the final decision must be made by the pope. However immoral, the pope cannot err in his interpretations of God's holy word, and all other men whatsoever, relinquishing their own judgment, must rest upon his. Even Protestants, while rejecting the Romish view, are not quite agreed as to the meaning; but the best view seems to be this: "*That no prophecy of Scripture is matter of one's own explanation*—that is, the prophets do not originate their own prophecies; they receive them entirely from above, as is clear from the fact given in the next verse. Peter, therefore, must be understood as saying nothing whatever relative to *interpreting* the Scriptures.

21. **For** confirms what he has just said concerning the prophets as not originating prophecy. **The prophecy**—omit 'the'—prophecy in general. **Came not**—or, better, *was never borne*—**in old time. By the will of man.** Not the human will, but the Holy Spirit, was the source of prophecy; yet the Holy Spirit did not impart the spirit of prophecy to men, not even to Christian men, in general; but, as we learn from other Scriptures, to comparatively few, and these were **holy men of God. Were moved**—*borne by.* They were not, strictly speaking, passive, for each prophet showed, in the style of language in which he uttered his prophecies, his own mental peculiarities. 'Holy men of God' (ἅγιοι Θεοῦ ἄνθρωποι), is regarded by textual critics as of inferior authority to *men from God* (ἀπὸ Θεοῦ ἄνθρωποι). Westcott and Hort adopt this text. Assuming this as the correct reading, we should have the translation, *but borne by the Holy Spirit, men spake from God.*

CRITICAL NOTES.—CHAPTER I.

1. The student who has not access to the work may desire to become acquainted with what Cremer says ("Lexicon of New Testament Greek") concerning this much disputed word, δικαιοσύνη (*righteousness*). "The righteousness of God is a state called forth by God's act of justification—namely, by judicial disengagement, or release from all that stands in the way of δίκαιος εἶναι" (*becoming righteous*), "a liberation of which man becomes partaker by means of faith. Hence, δικ. πίστεως" (*righteousness of faith*). "Rom. 4: 11-13, ἐκ πίστεως" (*from faith*); "Rom. 9: 30; 10: 6, to which expressions the others, δικ. Θεοῦ (righteousness of God), ἐκ Θεοῦ (righteousness from God)—correspond. Comp. Heb. 11: 7, τῆς κατὰ πίστιν δικ. κ. τ. λ." (the righteousness which is by faith, etc.). "We see, therefore, that *the Pauline conception of righteousness, which,*

as to form, always expresses a relation to the judgment of God, includes this special feature—namely, it denotes *the state of the believing man called forth by the divine acquittal*, and this is its force in all the passages in question, Rom. 8: 10; Eph. 6: 14; 4: 24; Rom. 5: 21; 6: 16; 2 Cor. 6: 7, 14, etc. This conception is to be recognized also in 2 Pet. 1: 1, . . . where the absence of the article in ἐν δικ." (*in*, or *through*, *righteousness*), "which is more closely qualified by the following genitive, and therefore cannot be taken adverbially, as in Acts 17: 31, makes it more difficult to understand δικ τ. θ., κ. τ. λ." (righteousness of God, etc.) "as the principle on which it is communicated, and thus as the subjective righteousness of God." It will be noticed that *imparted* righteousness is not at all Cremer's conception. *Righteousness*, or, more specifically, *holiness*, *is imparted* to him who accepts God's righteousness as above explained. *Righteousness*, as taught by Paul in his Epistle to the Romans, is "*reckoned*" (Revised Version) to the sinner, or, to use the old word, which really means scarcely anything different, *imputed*. Righteousness *reckoned* is the foundation of righteousness *imparted*. As the life of God is breathed into the soul at the moment when righteousness is reckoned to it, it is unnecessary to suppose any lapse of time between the reckoning of righteousness and the imparting of righteousness. For aught we know, the two acts may be simultaneous, but their natures are different.

1. τοῦ θεοῦ ἡμῶν καὶ σωτῆρος Ἰησοῦ Χριστοῦ (*our God and Saviour Jesus Christ*). It will be noticed that the Greek for *Saviour* has no article. Our God and *the* Saviour would have made it quite certain that two persons are meant, God the Father and also the Saviour Jesus Christ. Does the absence of the article prove that two distinct persons are *not* meant? and may we infer from this absence our Saviour's deity? Reply: The exact reason why Greek writers use the article, or do not use it, cannot always be given. To make, therefore, an important doctrine, like that of the deity of Christ, turn on the presence or the absence of the article is seldom to be justified. Still, as has been affirmed by learned grammarians, it is grammatically possible in the passage under consideration to refer θεοῦ (*God*) as well as σωτῆρος (*Saviour*) to Ἰησοῦ Χριστοῦ (*Jesus Christ*)—that is, there is nothing in the construction of the Greek language to forbid it. On the other hand, it is remarkable that Peter nowhere else, if here, applies θεός (*God*) to Jesus Christ. Expositors differ concerning the question. The weight of critical authority is against the view that but one is referred to. [It seems to me not only "grammatically possible," but grammatically natural to refer θεοῦ as well as σωτῆρος to Ἰησοῦ Χριστοῦ. We need a positive reason for not doing so. The circumstance that Peter does not elsewhere call Jesus Christ *God* is of some weight, but by no means decisive. Yet, as there is this ground for doubt, it is improper to rely on the passage as a proof-text.— A. H.]

5, 7. That ἐπιχορηγήσατε should not be translated *add* but *minister* or *supply*, and that ἐν should be rendered *in* is held by the majority of critical scholars. This is one of the passages used by Trench to illustrate the fact that "our translators do not always seize the precise force of the prepositions." "Tyndale," he says, "had rendered the passage: *In* your faith minister virtue, and *in* your virtue knowledge, etc., and all the translations up to the Authorized had followed him. Henry More (" On Godliness " b. 8; c. 3) has well expressed the objection to 'the present version: 'Grotius would have (*in*) (*ἐν*) to be redundant here; so his suffrage is for the English translation. But, for my own part, I think that ἐν is so far from being redundant that it is essential to the sentence, and interposed that we might understand a greater mystery than the mere adding of so many virtues one to another, which would be all that could be expressly signified if ἐν were left out. But the preposition here signifying causality there is more than a mere enumeration of those divine graces. For there is also implied how naturally they rise one out of another, and that they have a causal dependence one of another.' See this thought beautifully carried out in detail by Bengel."

When the passage is correctly understood, the thought is felt to be one of great richness, and the form of expression one of great beauty. No figurative representation of these eight virtues can do justice to the apostle's thoughts. Links of a golden chain; fruits growing on the same tree; faith the root and

CHAPTER II.

BUT there were false prophets also among the people, even as there shall be false teachers among you, who privily shall bring in damnable heresies, even

1 But there arose false prophets also among the people, as among you also there shall be false teachers, who shall privily bring in ¹destructive heresies,

1 Or, *sects of perdition*.

love the flower; a building with faith for the foundation and love as the crowning glory; rosary and conjugation of Christian virtues; adjoining colors of the rainbow all coalescing into one bright orb of beauty; a garland of virtues; the divine garden of a Christian heart,—all which metaphors have been used by different writers,—add little to Peter's description. The originality, simplicity, naturalness, and easy flow of the inspired words are remarkable. It is divine music. It is an oratorio surpassing all that the great masters have written. But apart from its beauty and power, to what fullness of Christian character does it incite us! Can it be the work of a forger? The writer cannot refrain from saying, that this one passage (5·7) with the verse following should have saved the Epistle from such severity of treatment as it has received from a Christian scholar of England.

9. The Greek tongue has "two orders of negatives," in the one of which is οὐ (*not*), and in the other of which is μή (*not*). The former denies *directly*, the latter *indirectly*—that is, the latter is used in general when the writer wishes to express supposition or condition. See Winer, p. 453, § 55, and Buttmann, p. 344, § 148. Now, in ver. 9 the negative is μή: For he to whom these things are *not* (who lacketh these things), as I am supposing; or to whom these things *may not be;* or, again, in better English, he who *may not* have these things. The use of the conditional *may* brings out with some degree of accuracy the meaning intended to be expressed.

17. *On whom my good pleasure fixed.* The preposition is εἰς (*in*, Common Version and the Revision). whereas in Matthew's own account of the Transfiguration (17:5) it is ἐν (*in*). The variation is worthy of being noticed; for, as it has been well said, it is not the way in which a forger would have acted. He would have kept more closely to his model.

Part II. Section First.

Ch. 2. In this section (1·22) are described the character and overthrow of false teachers.

Nothing so intensely severe is to be found in the Bible, except in Matt. 23, and in the Epistle of Jude. Jude's fiery bolts are hurled against a similar class of persons, and the terrible woes recorded by Matthew fell from the lips of Christ upon hypocrites. Peter's denunciations crash along through the chapter like successive peals of thunder. A moment's pause at the mention of righteous Noah, just Lot, and the forbearing angels, and the thunder peals forth again more terrifically than ever. That in this respect the Epistle differs greatly from the First Epistle is no more evidence that the Epistle was not written by the author of the First, than the great severity of the address in Matt. 23 proves that the address was not uttered by him who delivered the remarkably tender address of John 14.

1. **But . . . also**—in allusion to the true prophets of former times. 'But' (on the other hand), there arose 'also' (in addition to them) very different prophets. **False prophets.** False brethren (2 Cor. 11:26) were persons who pretended to be real brethren (related by regeneration to Christians); false apostles (2 Cor. 11:13) were men who professed to be apostles, but were not; a false Christ (Matt. 24:24) was a Christ only in pretence, not in fact. By 'false prophets' is meant not, primarily, persons who prophesied false things, but those who falsely professed to be prophets. It implies, however, that such pretenders prophesied false things. **The people**—the Jews of ancient times. (Jer. 5:31; 6:13; 29:9; Isa. 30:10; Ezek. 13:3, 6-9.) This historical fact is introduced to prepare the way for speaking of those who will soon arise among even Christians themselves. **False teachers**—persons who falsely affirmed that they were true teachers. It implies that they taught falsehood. **Even as**—'as' among you also. **Who privily**, etc.—who shall bring in stealthily (slyly). **Damnable**—does not express the meaning. The heresies were heresies of *destruction*, and that because they led to destruction. Here the destruction of those

denying the Lord that bought them, and bring upon themselves swift destruction.

2 And many shall follow their pernicious ways; by reason of whom the way of truth shall be evil spoken of.

denying even the Master that bought them, bringing upon themselves swift destruction. And many 2 shall follow their lascivious doings; by reason of whom the way of the truth shall be evil spoken of.

who were taught may be implied, but chiefly, as is clear from the last clause, of those who taught. The word for 'damnable' is the same as the word there used for *destruction*. **Heresies.** This word, now so commonly used to express false doctrine, has, generally, in the Acts, the simple meaning of *sect* (Acts 5: 17; 15: 5; 24: 5, 14; 26: 5; 28: 22); in the Epistles, party divisions, *sect*, but implying factiousness. (1 Cor. 11: 19; Gal. 5: 20.) In Titus 3: 10, a man that is a heretic is literally a *heretical* (factious) man. In the verse before us, the word seems to be working away from the meaning of *sect*, and to be taking on thus early the meaning of *heresy* in the sense of *false doctrine*, but, implying, of course, the existence of a sect or factious set of men. **Even denying the Lord**—(1 John 2: 23), *denying even the Master*. The Greek for *Lord* (*Master*) is stronger than the word usually so rendered. How freely does he who once himself denied that he knew Jesus, now speak of denying the Master; but from *his* eyes fell hot tears of penitence, while the depth and sincerity of his sorrow even now are manifest by the freedom with which he is willing to associate his former sin with an Epistle which is to be sent to the universal Church. **That bought them**—the participle (ἀγοράσαντα) put first for emphasis: *him who bought* them, the Master, denying. Christ bought them with *a price*. (1 Cor. 6: 20.) The price paid was his *blood* (Rev. 5: 9); *precious* blood. (1 Pet. 1: 19.) These men will themselves profess to have been bought with the blood of Christ, for they are evidently to arise among the members of the churches. Compare Acts 20: 30; 1 John 2: 19. 'That bought them.' See here evidence of a *general* atonement in distinction from a particular atonement. President Hovey ("Manual of Theology and Ethics," p. 351), on Heb. 2: 9 (*that he should taste death for every man*), says that 'every man' (παντός) "must here signify every one of our race, or every believer of our race. The former is the natural meaning, and should therefore be preferred. 2 Peter 2: 1; compare Luke 7: 30; 19: 44; Acts 13: 46; 2 Cor. 2: 15." **And bring.** Omit 'and,'

and read *bringing upon*. The clause is connected with the two preceding ones. The *consequence* of smuggling heresies into the churches, and of denying the Lord is, that they bring upon themselves **swift destruction.** In 1: 14 the same word is translated *shortly* (suddenly). Notice the striking twofold use of the word 'destruction': they will stealthily introduce into the churches heresies of destruction; they will bring upon themselves destruction. Their heretical plans may a while have some success, but they themselves will meet the fate they deserve.

2. Pernicious ways—*excesses* (lustful). Their ways will be licentious. It is not easy in every case to separate the origin of error from the origin of immorality. They have a common parentage—opposition to the will of God. In some cases error may seem to be the first born, and in others immorality. The great Church Father, Augustine, said: "To love is to know." **Many.** Compare Matt. 7: 13 ("Many there be which go in thereat"). But there *many* includes all kinds of sinners; here it includes but one kind. And what is saddening, those included are for the most part professing disciples. See 1 Tim. 4: 1; 2 Tim. 2: 17, 18; 3: 1, 6; Tit. 1: 10-14. The early Church suffered from two causes: Ritualism and Gnosticism; the former the outgrowth of deteriorated Judaism, which, overlooking the harmony between the gospel and true Judaism taught by prophets, attempted to engraft Mosaic rites upon Christianity; the latter, the Alexandrian philosophy, which, briefly expressed, was substantially an effort of the human reason to free itself from what it pronounced to be shackles of faith. The germ of these two great errors, more especially of ritualism, was much developed even in the days of the apostles. See Acts 15: 1-32. Hence the frequent allusion to error and errorists. **By reason of whom** —*on account of whom*. 'Whom' may refer both to the false teachers and to those who followed them. **The way of truth**—*of the truth*. Compare John 14: 6 ("I am the way, the truth, and the life"); Acts 13: 10 ("the right ways of the Lord"); 2: 15 ("the right

3 And through covetousness shall they with feigned words make merchandise of you: whose judgment now of a long time lingereth not, and their damnation slumbereth not.
4 For if God spared not the angels that sinned, but

3 And in covetousness shall they with feigned words make merchandise of you: whose sentence now from of old lingereth not, and their destruction
4 slumbereth not. For if God spared not angels

way"). The way of truth is the gospel viewed as leading to a mode of life conformable to its requirements. **Evil spoken of**—sometimes rendered *blasphemed*.

LESSONS. 1. Do not lose heart at the rise and arrogance of error; 2. Be not surprised that even members of churches should follow after error, and fall into dishonesty or licentiousness; 3. Be yourself firm in the ways of the Lord; 4. Resist the errors and immoralities of others, and do so without fear of being called intolerant. 5. *Many;* no proof of rightness.

3. **Through** (*in*) **covetousness**. Covetousness, insatiable desire *to have more*, is viewed as the element *in* which they live. A covetous man lives in his covetousness, as a fish lives *in* the water or a bird *in* the air. **Feigned words**—words plastic, words artfully formed and put together for the purpose of deceiving. **Make merchandise**—*cheat*, say some; *make gain of you* is more probably the sense. The real end of their false words is gain. (Rom. 16: 18.) See 1 Tim. 6: 5; Tit. 1: 11. This is deplorable—under the guise of truth to utter falsehood, and that concerning religious things; and then to plaster over with fair words the real purpose—making gain of their fellow church members, and dragging them down to destruction with themselves.

O cunning enemy, that, to catch a saint,
With saints dost bait thy hook!

Whose judgment—for whom *the* judgment, the *condemnation* (implying punishment). **Now of a long time**—no Greek for *now*, though perhaps necessary to bring out the exact meaning. **Lingereth not**. The contradiction between 'long time' and 'lingereth not' is only apparent. The sense is: Long ago, in anticipation of their errors, excesses, and enticements, God's purpose to punish them had real existence, and that purpose has never been withdrawn. It has hastened on with every revolving period. It has not lingered, and the consummation is as certain as if it had already taken place. **Damnation**—*destruction;* the same word in the original as in ver. 1 (twice). See above on 'damnable heresies.' God's delay in punishing the wicked is a fact which arrested the attention of distinguished pagan writers in ancient times, and is considered at some length in the Book of Job. The actual infliction of punishment is often delayed, but the condemnation, and even the destruction, in so far as it is purposed, *is not delayed* ('lingereth not'). Disapproval, in the strong form of condemnation, flashes instantly upon the committal of the wrong. Much of the Hebrew poetry is characterized by what is called "Parellelism of Members." One form of the peculiarity consists in the repetition of nearly the same thought in equivalent words. This has been called "Synonymous Parallelism." Ps. 144: 6 is an example: "Cast forth lightning, and scatter them; shoot out thine arrows, and destroy them." Instances of Parallelism are found in prose: "There is nothing covered that shall not be revealed; and hid that shall not be known." In like manner the last two clauses of the verse before us give an instance of Parallelism. 'Destruction' corresponds with '*condemnation*,' and '*slumbereth not*' with '*lingereth not*.' The style rises toward the poetic.

4. The apostle fortifies his declaration that the false teachers shall meet with deserved punishment; and this he effects by the case: 1. Of sinning angels; 2. Of the ungodly antediluvians; 3. Of Sodom and Gomorrah. From the fate of these three classes it is certain that punishment will be visited upon those described. **For** connects the illustrations with that which is to be illustrated. I affirm it to be so, *for* facts which occurred under the government of God in past ages prove it.

FIRST ILLUSTRATION. **If**, as so often before, is not expressive of doubt. 'If' (as is the case) **God spared not**, etc. See Rom. 8: 22 ("He that spared not his own Son, but delivered him up" *to death*); the same verbs, but how different the end! The Son was delivered to suffering for our sins; sinning angels were delivered to punishment on account of their own sins: the Son beloved; sinning angels the objects of holy wrath. How tragical the application of the same words, *spared*

cast *them* down to hell, and delivered *them* into chains of darkness, to be reserved unto judgment;
5 And spared not the old world, but saved Noah the eighth *person*, a preacher of righteousness, bringing in the flood upon the world of the ungodly;

when they sinned, but ¹cast them down to ²hell, and committed them to ³pits of darkness, to be re-
5 served unto judgment; and spared not the ancient world, but preserved Noah with seven others, ⁴a preacher of righteousness, when he brought a flood

1 Or, *cast them into dungeons*......2 Gr. *Tartarus*......3 Some ancient authorities read *chains*......4 Gr. *a herald*.

not and delivered, to the Holy Redeemer as are applied to spirits so proud and rebellious! **That sinned**—*when* they sinned, they having already sinned. The sinning was before the sparing not. See Critical Note on 1 Pet. 3: 20: "Who sometime were disobedient." Silence respecting the nature of their sin is a lesson for us. A more groundless view is scarcely possible than that the sin consisted in impurity of conduct with the daughters of men. (Gen. 6: 2.) Nothing more definite can be said than that they kept not their first estate, but left their own habitation (Jude 6), on which see comments. **Cast them down to hell**—one word in the Greek, and that a participle (ταρταρώσας, *having tartarized them*, sent them to Tartarus). It is found nowhere else in the Scriptures. Tartarus is a word of pagan origin. In the earlier writers, it was "a dark abyss, as deep below hades as earth below heaven; prison of Saturn, the Titans, etc. Later, Tartarus was either the *netherworld* generally, like hades, or *the regions of the damned*, as opposed to the Elysian fields." (Liddell and Scott.) No such conceptions are embraced in the word as used by our apostle; and on the other hand, it is not used to express an intermediate state, answering to the supposed intermediate state of the righteous. An intermediate state of either the righteous or the wicked, in any other sense than that of a state in which the spirit is not yet in its resurrection body, and has not yet passed through the ordeal of the general judgment, and may not, therefore, have received that full weight of either bliss or suffering which is probably connected with the repossession of the body, is not taught in the Scriptures. As used by Peter, the word probably means that they were *cast down to hades*, which, as used in the New Testament, is not the place of disembodied spirits, good and bad (the earlier conception of the Hebrews and the Greeks), but the place of *future, endless, punishment*. **Chains**—according to a weightier reading, *caverns* or *pits*. **Of darkness**—a most expressive and solemn metaphor. It shows the utter separation of these fallen spirits from the light of God. Jude (6), speaking of the same beings, says "*chains* (bonds) *under darkness*"; but the original word is not the same as the commonly-received Greek here. **To be reserved**—*reserved* (the more approved reading), *i. e.*, now reserved, or kept; they are *being reserved*. **Unto judgment.** Jude says: "*Judgment of the great day.*" See Matt. 25: 41. In the days of our Lord demons cried out, "Art thou come hither to torment us before the time?" (Matt. 8: 29.) That is, before the general judgment. They seem to know that they are hereafter to be *publicly* judged, and delivered over to a more fearful punishment. All questioning relative to the harmony of the two views—that the fallen angels have already been sent to a place of punishment, and that they are to be judged hereafter—is as useless as similar questioning relative to impenitent men, who are also to be judged publicly after having been consigned to punishment. The question is not one that concerns us. All is known to God.

5. SECOND ILLUSTRATION.—**The old world**—*the ancient world*, the antediluvians, with the exceptions about to be mentioned; all the men of the period immediately preceding the flood. **Saved**—*preserved*, so that he was neither swept away with the others, nor in danger of it. **Noah the eighth**—a peculiar way of saying, *Noah with seven others*. (Buttmann.) See 1 Pet. 3: 20. The keeping of the few is contrasted with the destruction of the many. In every age the majority have been ungodly; whether it will ever be otherwise depends upon the purpose of God; though it should be added that the godly are required to put forth to the utmost their own free powers to bring the ungodly to knowledge of the way in which they may become godly. **A preacher of righteousness**—a *proclaimer* (herald) to the men of his time (1 Pet. 3: 19), not of the righteousness which is distinctively that of the gospel (11: 1; Rom. 1: 17; 3: 22, 25, 26), but of that which consisted of faith in the one God, of reverence for his

6 And turning the cities of Sodom and Gomorrah into ashes condemned *them* with an overthrow, making *them* an ensample unto those that after should live ungodly;
7 And delivered just Lot, vexed with the filthy conversation of the wicked:

6 upon the world of the ungodly; and turning the cities of Sodom and Gomorrah into ashes condemned them with an overthrow, having made them an example unto those that should live ungodly; and delivered righteous Lot, sore distressed by the lascivious life of the wicked (for that righteous man

character, and of readiness to believe all that God might see fit to make known. That was the righteousness which Noah preached, but see Heb. 11 : 7 for the representation of what he himself became. The ungodly were not destroyed till after they had been permitted to listen to faithful preaching. **Bringing in.** There is no Greek for 'in.' The connection may be expressed thus: Saved Noah *when* he brought the flood. Noah's deliverance is not a necessary part of the illustration. His case could have been passed in silence, and the illustration have been equally pertinent; but strength is gained by putting in contrast the antediluvians and the patriarch. This is one of the passages (the other, Matt. 24 : 37-39) which Prof. George Rawlinson regards as teaching with special emphasis the *universality* of the Flood.

6. THIRD ILLUSTRATION.—Overthrow of Sodom and Gomorrah. It is unnecessary to suppose that the Dead Sea was formed at the time of the overthrow of these cities. That supposition, formerly held, is without support. A recent opinion puts the cities at the northern end of the sea, but, unless some further investigation compel the adoption of that view, the opinion that they were at the southern end must stand. It was a matter of no consequence to Peter at which end they stood. The point with him was the illustration which their overthrow gave of the certainty that the false and licentious teachers which were soon to arise would be also destroyed. **Turning ... into ashes**—*having burnt to ashes.* The original is one word, a participle coming from a noun which means *ashes.* The way in which this was done is not given. It might have been done by miraculous or by providential means; the former is probable. It was God's act, by whatever means effected. **With an overthrow**—*to* an overthrow. But the Greek word for overthrow (καταστροφῇ) is rejected by Westcott and Hort; the Revisers retain it. The overthrow is that *to which* the cities were condemned. The punishment, however, was not chiefly the destruction of material structures nor temporal death. The latter might have been followed by eternal life, in which case the burning of the towns and the shortening of life ought to have thrilled heaven with new joy. **An ensample unto**—*an example unto.* See comments on "are set forth for an example" in Jude 7. A different construction may be the correct one: An example *of.* Then the sense would be, that in respect to punishment the people of Sodom and Gomorrah were made a *specimen* of ungodly men, and will continue to be such in all following time.

7. Neither is this deliverance of Lot a necessary part of the third illustration, but, as in the second, it gives force to the view presented. The writer might have said, with less amplification: If sinning angels were cast down to hell, if the ancient world was destroyed by a flood, and if Sodom and Gomorrah were reduced to ashes, how much more will false and dissolute teachers be punished; but, fruitful in thought and intense in feeling, he gives a higher coloring to his description of both classes of sinners by contrasting them respectively with Noah and Lot. He might as well have set off the sin of the angels by contrasting with it the steadfastness of unfallen angels. As he advances, however, he grows warmer and strikes off into contrasts. **Delivered**—*rescued; snatched away* is scarcely too strong. **Just**—*righteous.* The word is akin to that which is rendered righteousness in ver. 5, upon which see comments. **Vexed**—*worn down.* These were a very troublesome, harassing set of sinners. They were far enough from being Pharisees. They sinned openly and audaciously. That Lot lived with them so long is remarkable, and that he lived among them so long with no essential injury, is still more remarkable. The false teachers of apostolic times drew away many from the faith; Lot withstood all the people of four cities. **The filthy conversation**—*the licentious conduct.* The **wicked**—strictly, *the lawless*, men who defied all law, human and divine. See a description of "thy sister Sodom" in Ezek. 16: 49, 50. On

G

8 (For that righteous man dwelling among them, in seeing and hearing, vexed *his* righteous soul from day to day with *their* unlawful deeds:)
9 The Lord knoweth how to deliver the godly out of temptation, and to reserve the unjust unto the day of judgment to be punished:
10 But chiefly them that walk after the flesh in the lust of uncleanness, and despise government. Pre-

dwelling among them, in seeing and hearing,¹ vexed *his* righteous soul from day to day with *their* law-
9 less deeds): the Lord knoweth how to deliver the godly out of temptation, and to keep the unrighteous
10 under punishment unto the day of judgment; but chiefly them that walk after the flesh in the lust of defilement, and despise dominion. Daring, self-

1 Gr. *tormented.*

---

the expression, "full of bread" in Hamlet, a commentator on Shakespeare says: "Shakespeare found this remarkable expression in the Bible: 'Behold this was the iniquity of thy sister Sodom: pride, *fulness of bread*, and abundance of idleness was in her and in her daughter.'"

8. This verse is an expansion of the thought expressed in the second member of verse 7. **In seeing and hearing** stands first in the Greek, and therefore is emphatic. The sinners were so numerous that he could not help seeing them, and so noisy that he could not help hearing them. Not to see and hear was impossible. The impression made, however, by the entire passage is, that he was not wholly silent. He must sometimes have protested against their wickedness. **Dwelling among them**—sad that he continued to do so; yet his righteous life, continually before them, was necessary to give a climax to their guilt. **Vexed**—*tormented*. He was so impressed with the conviction of their lawlessness and impurity, that his righteous soul *was tormented*, and that from day to day. Peter uses the active verb, perhaps to indicate that Lot could not allow himself to sink down into passive indifference to their sin, as if it were so great that all feeling concerning their state was useless. '*Vexed*' (imperfect tense) indicates a continuous state. The good man was continually plagued, and as no other man of that region was.

9. The first clause accounts for Lot's rescue. (Ver. 7.) The Lord *knew how* to do it, yet it is expressed in the general form so as to be applicable to all tempted saints. The Lord knows *how*—sometimes in one way and sometimes in another. **To deliver**—*to rescue;* the same in the Greek as in verse 7. **Godly**—the opposite of *ungodly* in ver. 5, 6; those whose hearts are right toward God (under the control of reverence and love). **Temptation.** An edition of the Bible, 1867, by the American Bible Society, prints in the plural num-

ber; a small New Testament of the same year, by the same Society, prints in the singular number. The latter is correct. **And** (*but*) **to reserve.** Here, at last, the apostle connects the thought, though not even now strictly the words, with the thought in verse 4: For if God spared not sinning angels, antediluvians, and Sodomites, how much less will he spare the false teachers. Yet he expresses his thought not so definitely, but generally—**the unjust.** **To be punished**—not future. They are are even now undergoing punishment. *To keep them under punishment.* (Revised Version.) The Lord *knows how* to keep wicked men for the Day of Judgment and under punishment. From this point onward the writer speaks of the errorists as if they had already come; not, as in verse 1, as if they were to arise in some future time. It is clear, therefore, that the evils against which he is warning the churches have already begun to appear, while it is equally clear that they will continue for a considerable period in the future.

10. A definite description of the overthrow of the false teachers, with a description of their character. The latter extends to the end of the chapter. **But chiefly.** It contrasts the weight of punishment which will fall on the baser kind of sinners with that which will be visited upon the less base kind. (Ver. 9.) **After the flesh**—literally, *behind the flesh*, an original use of the preposition (ὀπίσω). It is commonly used with respect to persons. Jude (ver. 7) uses it as it is used here (going *after, behind,* strange flesh). It is the same word as is used in Matt. 10: 38 (and followeth *after* me), and in 1 Tim. 5: 15 (turned aside *after* Satan). It implies that what is followed after is a leader; that he who follows after is a disciple or partisan. The errorists *are led* by the flesh instead of *leading it;* they follow after it, go behind it, as their leader. **Flesh**—their nature viewed as depraved, and acting through the body. **Lust of unclean-**

II. PETER.

sumptuous *are they*, selfwilled, they are not afraid to speak evil of dignities.
11 Whereas angels, which are greater in power and might, bring not railing accusation against them before the Lord.
12 But these, as natural brute beasts made to be taken and destroyed, speak evil of the things that they understand not; and shall utterly perish in their own corruption;
13 And shall receive the reward of unrighteousness,

11 willed, they tremble not to rail at ¹dignities: whereas angels, though greater in might and power, bring not a railing judgment against them before the Lord.
12 But these, as creatures without reason, born ²mere animals ³to be taken and destroyed, railing in matters whereof they are ignorant, shall in their ⁴destroying surely be destroyed, suffering wrong as the
13 hire of wrong-doing; *men* that count it pleasure to

1 Gr. *glories*........2 Gr. *natural*......3 Or, *to take and to destroy*......4 Or, *corruption*.

ness—*in* which as the element of their life they walk. The *habit* of depravity in the form of lustful excesses is spoken of as a *walk*. Government—*dominion*, probably all kinds of human dominion. They despise all government except that of their own lusts!—not unknown now. That the devil is meant cannot be shown. Compare Jude 8. **Presumptuous**—*audacious, bold*. **Self-willed**. These audacious men are self-willed—a humiliating fact. **Not afraid to speak evil**, etc.—*of dignities they do not fear to speak evil*. At the thought of doing that they never tremble. What is meant by 'dignities' is uncertain. The opinions of expositors greatly differ. The translation of the word in many other places is *glory*. The margin of the Revised Version, *glories*. It is hazardous to speak definitely when there is so little ground even for conjecture. The interpretation of the word has been made by some to turn on the meaning of Jude, ver. 8, 9, which are themselves, especially the latter, too difficult to yield much help. It is upon the ground of those verses that some understand by *dignities* the devil, or at least demons. But that meaning must be rejected. It may possibly refer to the glories of the Father and the Son, but even that has little to support it. It may refer to beings who are high in earthly official glory; possibly, to all glorious religious things.

11. **Whereas** is not to be taken as expressing contrast; it is nearly equivalent to *while:* while the heretics had a given spirit, angels had an opposite spirit. **Angels**—good angels. **Greater**—than the self-willed, audacious heretics. **Railing accusation**—*railing judgment*. **Against them**—*against dignities*. Some say, against the false teachers. **Before the Lord**—in the Lord's presence. The angels, though so superior, have sufficient humility to abstain from such severity of spirit, however wanting in the best elements of character some earthly rulers may be. But the Greek for 'before the Lord' is deemed by some as not belonging to the true text. It is accepted by the Revisers, but Westcott and Hort mark it as an alternative reading, and think it impossible to decide which reading should be adopted.

12. **But these**—the teachers of error in contrast with the good angels. **As natural brute beasts**, etc.—*as irrational creatures, born naturally* (with animal natures) for the very purpose of being captured and destroyed. A marginal reading in the Revised Version: *to take and to destroy*. The comparison, which is striking, implies that these men have lowered themselves to a level with brutes, and have fitted themselves to be destroyed, even as the latter are fitted by nature to be taken. See Crit. Notes. **Speak evil**, etc.—*railing in things of which they are ignorant*. If the interpretation of 'government,' 'dignities,' and 'them' (ver. 11) is correct, it follows that the things of which they are ignorant pertain to earthly rulers. They have not been in the way of knowing much concerning political government and political rulers, and were there no other reason, that is sufficient to show the wickedness of their railing. **Shall utterly perish**—*shall in their destructivenes be destroyed*, is an approximation to the play upon words found in the Greek. According to valuable manuscripts, *even* (καὶ), *surely*, Revised Version, is the correct reading; *shall surely* be destroyed.

13. **And shall receive**—not a new element of punishment so much as the result of the punishment expressed in the closing words of ver. 12. The sense is: shall perish in their own corruption., *thus receiving, as they will, the reward of unrighteousness*. All unrighteousness has reward (reward *for* iniquity), but how different from the reward obtained for righteousness! Compare the case of Abel (Heb. 11:4); Enoch (Heb. 11:5); Moses, (Heb. 11:24-26.) Judas was the cause of a field being pur-

as they that count it pleasure to riot in the daytime. Spots *they are* and blemishes, sporting themselves with their own deceivings while they feast with you;
14 Having eyes full of adultery, and that cannot cease from sin; beguiling unstable souls: a heart

revel in the day-time, spots and blemishes, reveling in their [1] deceivings while they feast with you
14 having eyes full of [2] adultery, and that cannot cease from sin; enticing unstedfast souls; having a heart

---

1 Some ancient authorities read love-*feasts*......2 Gr. *an adulteress.*

---

chased with the "reward of iniquity" (Acts 1:18), with wages obtained by iniquity. A small field; a great price. So these heretics will receive great (terrible) pay for their heresy and vice. **As they that count,** etc., (a participle), *accounting reveling by day a pleasure*. **Day**—may be equivalent to *daily;* it may express *transientness* in contrast with eternal duration; or it may stand in contrast with *night*. If the last is correct, the men are sunk so low, that, unlike those that were drunken in the night (1 Thess. 5:7), they revel in the day. **In the day**—(*ἐν ἡμέρᾳ*) stands between *the* (τὴν) and *riot* (τρυφήν) *the-in-day riot*, and may therefore in Greek usage be adjectival (the *daily* riot). See Buttmann, p. 331. **Spots they are.** The introduction by King James' Revisers of unnecessary words into the intense and vivacious style of this chapter is unfortunate. Says the writer, wrought up to the highest pitch of Christian indignation: *spots and stains, reveling in their own deceivings* (not *sporting themselves with*), while they feast with you. Few connective particles are used, but the writer drives on with a rattling rapidity of words which is like the clashing of battle-axes. **Deceivings.** Jude says (ver. 12), "*feasts of charity*," but in letters and sound the Greek word is remarkably like the word used here. Peter says: *apatais*; Jude, *agapais*. It has been considered either with Peter or with Jude (which ever wrote first) as a play of words. It should be added that, according to some important manuscripts, Peter used the same word as Jude. Westcott and Hort are unable to decide, but have put the word for (ἀπάταις) *deceivings* in the text, and for *love-feasts* (ἀγάπαις) in the margin. **While they feast,** etc. Jude (ver. 12) restricts it to "love-feasts," concerning which see comments; but Peter uses a more general word, which may include the Lord's Supper, love-feasts, and ordinary social festivals. These graceless heretics had a fascinating power of deception. They did not "wear their hearts upon their sleeves." Adroit in address, they were able to smother every spark of suspicion in those whom they purpose to gain to their lustful and avaricious ends. Such gross forms of evil are now so wanting in evangelical churches that it is difficult to see how they could have arisen so early. When the veil is lifted from European Church life in not a few of the ages preceding the Reformation, evils are to be seen which are scarcely if at all less.

14. This verse continues the description. **Eyes full of adultery.** Here, too, the manuscripts differ, but preponderate strongly in favor of the word meaning *adulteress: eyes full of an adulteress.* Not any given woman can be meant, but the singular stands as the representative of a class. So impure are the heretics that their eyes, so to speak, are filled with an adulteress. They can see nothing else. An adulteress is pictured on the retina—that is, their association of ideas and feelings is habitually lustful. The impurity is in the heart, yet the impure do undoubtedly often betray their real character in the eye.

A sin prevailing much in youthful men,
Who give their eyes the liberty of gazing.

That organ which was intended to illustrate so signally the wisdom of the Creator is transformed by the inward power of lust into a tell-tale mirror. **That**—refers to *eyes*. It is the eyes that cannot cease from sin. The writer uses but one word where, perhaps, the English requires three or four, and that one an adjective: eyes *unceasing* from sin. Eyes *soiled, stained,* by sin, would be the rendering of the word found in some of the manuscripts. The student will find the relative value of the two readings considered in Buttmann's "Greek Grammar" p. 65. The sin is that to which the context refers. The eyes retain the picture because the mind retains its impurity. **Beguiling**—*ensnaring,* as a man may snare a bird or bait a fish. **Unstable** (3:16), in that they are not firmly fixed on Christ as the foundation. (1 Pet. 2:6, 8.) The snares and the ensnared—what a meeting must it be at the Day of Judgment! The latter were not necessarily weak in intellect;

they have exercised with covetous practices; cursed children:
15 Which have forsaken the right way, and are gone astray, following the way of Balaam, *the son of Bosor*, who loved the wages of unrighteousness;
16 But was rebuked for his iniquity: the dumb ass

15 exercised in covetousness; children of cursing; forsaking the right way, they went astray, having followed the way of Balaam the *son* of 'Beor, who
16 loved the hire of wrong-doing; but he was rebuked for his own transgression; a dumb ass spake with

1 Many ancient authorities read *Bosor*.

the former were so bad that suspicion and resistance ought to have been awakened. "I was enticed:" that you played the fool is equally true. **A heart . . . exercised with covetous practices**—*having a heart trained in covetousness*. (Isa. 56: 11.) The word for trained (γεγυμνασμένην) is that from which our word *gymnastic* is derived. It came from a word meaning *naked* (gymnos); for those who among the Greeks were *gymnastics* practiced nearly naked. These men were gymnastics in covetousness. The heart was trained to it. A man who is covetous by nature may yet be so unconscious of the sin, as to put himself through a course of training which will make him an athlete in the detestable vice. Most persons who are of penurious disposition are totally unconscious of the fault, and were they charged with it would resent it with great spirit. **Cursed children**—literally, *children of a curse*. See on 1 Pet. 1: 14.

15. Which have forsaken—*forsaking* (the better reading) **the right way.** *They went astray* brings out the relation of the first clause (participial) to the second. And now Peter recalls from the ancient history of the Jews the case of one who was also for the most part a false prophet; for the most part, for the history shows that Balaam was not a mere heathen diviner. Though born and living among idolaters, he had in some way acquired some knowledge of the true God; for in talking with the servants of Balak, he used the peculiar name of the true God, Jehovah (Num. 22: 8, 18, Common Version, *Lord*), in distinction from the name applied also to pagan gods. It is clear that Jehovah made to him for a definite purpose a few isolated revelations (Num. 22: 12, 20; 23: 5-10, 16-24; 24: 2-9, 15-19), but he was never called to the *office* of a prophet. Professionally, he was a diviner or magician after a heathen pattern. For that reason, the comparison between him and the false prophets of Peter's time could be justly made. (Jude 11; Rev. 2: 14.) **The way of Balaam**—his *manner of life* was crooked; the way which the heretics forsook was *the right way* (a straight

way). They followed Balaam's way in that they uttered, as he generally did, falsehood, were impure as he was (Num. 31: 16, compare with Num. 25: 1-3), and were covetous. Balaam's superiority to the love of money was *put on*. He must have been known as receiving pay for his services in the art of divining, or Balak would not have sent him the rewards of divination. (Num. 22: 7.) He *wanted* to go with the messengers, but knew that Jehovah might not permit it. See the history. (Num., chapters 22-24.) Peter knew that, whatever were his pretensions, he **loved wages of unrighteousness**. It is a striking fact that these very words were used by Peter in his address to the "men and brethren" who were assembled in Jerusalem after the ascension. (Acts 1: 18.) So far it is evidence that Peter was the writer of this Epistle. **Son of Bosor**—son *of Beor*. (Num. 22: 5.) The *s* is believed to have arisen from a peculiar way of pronouncing the second consonant of the Hebrew form of the word. The Revisers: *Beor;* in the margin, *Bosor*, the latter having considerable ancient support.

16. But hints that he was not allowed to be his own master in wrong-doing; but **was rebuked.**

And that should teach us,
There's a divinity that shapes our ends,
Rough-hew them how we will.

Yet Balaam's "indiscretion" did not serve him "well"—it served the Lord's purpose well. **His iniquity**—his *own* iniquity; and by this is meant his desire to serve Balak by cursing Israel for pay. Balaam's was a case of informal, conditional contract. There was no direct and positive agreement between him and Balak; yet the course taken was scarcely less criminal than if he had said: "I will go and curse, and you shall pay so much for the work done." Such "indirection" of contract may be specially mean; for, while it shows purpose to effect a given end, it provides, in selfishness, a loop-hole of escape. **The dumb ass speaking.** (Num. 22: 28-30.) The denial of a miracle here would logically lead to the

speaking with man's voice forbade the madness of the prophet.

17 These are wells without water, clouds that are carried with a tempest; to whom the mist of darkness is reserved for ever.

18 For when they speak great swelling *words* of vanity, they allure through the lusts of the flesh, *through much* wantonness, those that were clean escaped from them who live in error.

19 While they promise them liberty, they themselves are springs without water, and mists driven by a storm; for whom the blackness of darkness 18 hath been reserved. For, uttering great swelling *words* of vanity, they entice in the lusts of the flesh, by lasciviousness, those who are just escaping from 19 them that live in error; promising them liberty,

denial of a miracle everywhere else, and thus, in the end, revealed religion would be reduced to natural religion—that is, would be shorn of reality. But does it teach (to use the language of the schools) a *subjective*, or an *objective*, act?—that is, was the miracle performed directly upon the subject, Balaam? or, was it done upon the object, the animal? It is one thing to work a miracle upon Balaam's *ears*, so that he shall seem to hear articulate sounds coming from the animal, and another thing to work a miracle on the *braying powers* of the beast, so that its braying shall become articulate human sounds. If the former is the true view, Peter has taken an odd way to express it, for he says, 'the dumb ass speaking,' *he spoke* **with a man's voice.** In reply to all objections, it is sufficient to say to one who believes at all in miracles, that it was no more difficult for God to utter thought through the mouth of the ass in the words of men, than to stop men, as he once did, from talking in a given language and cause them to talk in another. The ass wastes no words, but—which is more than can be said of some preachers—speaks with directness and force. **Forbade the madness of the prophet**—*repressed* it. His madness was not insanity, but perverseness, downright folly concerning religious things. See another allusion to Balaam in Rev. 2: 14, with Dr. J. A. Smith's notes in his "Commentary on Revelation."

17. The apostle continues the description of the false teachers. **Wells without water.** A well of water in Palestine, and other Oriental lands, was formerly deemed one of the best of earthly things. (Prov. 10: 11; Isa. 58: 11; John 4: 6.) These immoral errorists were dry wells. They had no truth, no grace, and therefore no power of refreshment. Such men, however, in our own day, are believed by their admirers to be wells full of water, sweet and medicinal withal. **Clouds**—according to the true reading, *mists ;* mists **carried** (*driven*) **with** (*by*) **a tempest.** It expresses restlessness, want of stability. (James 1: 8.) One error leads to another, and this to yet another. (Eph. 4: 14.) The errorist has no anchorage. The feverish instability of one who is not grounded on eternal truth is incurable, except by the grace of God. The consequence: **to whom** the **mist (the blackness) of (*the*) darkness.** See 2: 4, 'chains (pits?) of darkness'! There is weighty manuscript authority for rejecting the words **forever** (εἰς αἰῶνα) from the text. Lachmann, Tischendorf, Tregelles, and Westcott and Hort, do not retain it. Nor do the Revisers adopt it.

18. **For.** The apostle illustrates the emptiness of the wells and the unstableness of the clouds. **When they speak**—*speaking*, a participle with which the verb **allure** is connected. **Great swelling words of vanity**—literally, *overswellings of vanity.* Inelegant modern phrase would call them *great swells.* They abounded in high sounding words, but these were as empty of ideas as many of the wells of ancient Palestine were empty of water in the days of our apostle. Their words were even vanity itself. In the utterance of their emptiness, they had as their aim the enticement of others, but this was accomplished **through** (rather *in*) **the lusts of the flesh**—they *lived in* lust. **Through much wantonness**—not put in apposition with 'lusts of the flesh.' Our translators sought to express the plural (ἀσελγείαις) *debaucheries* by means of **much. Clean escaped**—*a little escaping, barely* escaping. He probably refers to persons who had very recently professed conversion. **In error**—of life, the yet unconverted. These converts, when just beginning to escape from the influence of the surrounding depravity, are enticed by these pretended Christians, these impure heretics. 'Clean (*really*) escaped' (ὄντως ἀποφεύγοντας) has much less right in the text than the words for a *little* escaping (ὀλίγως ἀποφεύγοντας), on *the point* of doing so. The latter has been adopted by many well-known scholars.

19. **While they promise**—*promising*, connected, like speaking, with 'allure' (ver. 18):

II. PETER.

selves are the servants of corruption: for of whom a man is overcome, of the same is he brought in bondage.

20 For if after they have escaped the pollutions of the world through the knowledge of the Lord and Saviour Jesus Christ, they are again entangled therein, and overcome, the latter end is worse with them than the beginning.

21 For it had been better for them not to have known the way of righteousness, than, after they have known ¹it, to turn from the holy commandment delivered unto them.

while they themselves are bondservants of corruption; for of ¹ whom a man is overcome, of the same 20 is he also brought into bondage. For if, after they have escaped the defilements of the world through the knowledge of ²the Lord and Saviour Jesus Christ, they are again entangled therein and overcome, the last state is become worse with them 21 than the first. For it were better for them not to have known the way of righteousness, than, after knowing it, to turn back from the holy com- 22 mandment delivered unto them. It has happened

---

1 Or, *what*......2 Many ancient authorities read *our*.

---

they allure, promising liberty. The dry well! the pompous but empty words! The liberty promised was liberty to yield to unbridled indulgence of passion. Contrast the words of Christ. (John 8: 32, 36.) This wretched working of evil, beginning in the times of the apostles, has often been repeated. In the history of a body, which, for the most part, has been only a politico-priestly organization, are some saddening illustrations: and in our own country are individuals and communities of whom the description in this verse is too true. The servants—*bond-servants*. The original is the word used by the Greeks for *slave;* and were *slave* used here, it would scarcely overmatch in strength the other terms of the description. For of whom. *By what* is grammatically possible. It is the expression of a general fact, and has often been verified in war. (1 Sam. 17: 9.) It is here applied to the heretical teachers. That in their case *corruption* may be held as the overcoming power is a consideration in favor of *by what*. They are overcome by their own corruption. Hence it is said they are the 'servants' of corruption.

20. For. The point is contained in the last clause, and, corresponding with the final clause of ver. 19, is intended to explain it, but it is a step in advance. The bondage is such that the false teachers are in a worse state than at first. If. As Huther has neatly expressed it, the reality, as often, is expressed hypothetically. The pollutions. *Miasms* is the Greek transferred into English; yet it must not be supposed that the writer used the term with figurative reference to that foulness of the air which the word is now used to express. Its original meaning is *a coloring, staining;* hence, *moral defilement.* The world—those who live in wickedness (*error*, ver. 18). Through (*in*) the knowledge of the Lord and Saviour Jesus Christ. See 1: 2, 8. In the knowledge of whom else is

escape possible? 'Lord and Saviour' are both connected with 'Jesus Christ,' for there is but one article for both words. The Greek for 'our' (our Lord) is found in some manuscripts. Therein stands first in the original for emphasis: *but* (omitted in the Common Version, and even in the Revision) *by these* (pollutions) *having been again entangled*, are overcome. 'Entangled' is highly descriptive. (2 Tim. 2: 4.) A spider's web is not more entangling for the luckless fly than the world's pollutions for unstable souls. The latter end—literally, *the last things;* the beginning—*the first things.* That is, the state into which they have come is worse than even their state before supposed conversion. (Matt. 12: 45; Luke 11: 26; Heb. 10: 26, 27.) That in relapsing from the Christian profession the soul becomes harder, even more bitter, than it was, is a fact often observed. Great scoffers are born of re-entanglement in evil.

21. For. The startling statement just made is confirmed, though not by formal proof. It had been better—*it were better.* It is a positive, unconditional declaration; there is not the least reason to doubt that it were better. Not to have known—and so by implication to be *now* ignorant of. The way of righteousness is the way of righteousness which comes by faith in Christ. Compare 'the way of truth' (ver. 2), and 'the right way.' (Ver. 15.) See on 1: 1, especially the Critical Note. Than (*it is*), after they have known (*it*). It implies that they know it yet. The *knowledge* of the way has not been lost: they have not relapsed into that state of ignorance in which they once were; that is impossible, however fearfully they have relapsed in profession of interest in the way. The holy commandment—essentially equivalent to *the way of righteousness,* but representing the way from a different point—that is, as a way which they were commanded to enter. It

22 But it is happened unto them according to the true proverb, The dog is turned to his own vomit again; and, The sow that was washed to her wallowing in the mire.

unto them according to the true proverb, The dog turning to his own vomit again, and the sow that had washed to wallowing in the mire.

CHAPTER III.

THIS second epistle, beloved, I now write unto you; in *both* which I stir up your pure minds by way of remembrance:

1 This is now, beloved, the second epistle that I write unto you; and in both of them I stir up your

---

was *holy* in nature and end. **Delivered**—Compare "faith once delivered to the saints." (Jude 3.)

22. But—not a genuine reading. **It is happened**—*it has come to pass*. Literally, *that of* (that contained in) *the true proverb has happened unto them: A dog turning to his own vomit; and, a sow washed, into a wallowing place of mire.* In proverbs brevity and sententiousness were secured by using no verbs. It is almost as if the apostle pointed his finger at them, and exclaimed: "A dog, turning to his own vomit! a washed sow, rushing into and wallowing in the mire!" It is possible that the first was derived from Prov. 26: 11. Both must have been current among the people. "Throughout the whole East 'dog' is a term of reproach for impure and profane persons, and in this sense is used by the Jews respecting the Gentiles (Rev. 22: 15), and by all Mohammedans respecting Christians. . . . We still use the name of one of the noblest creatures in the world as a term of contempt." (Smith's "Bib. Dict.," p. 612.) Compare Matt. 7: 6; Phil. 3: 2.

QUERY: In applying these proverbs to the false teachers, what is the point which the apostle intended to make? The dog *returns* to his vomit and the sow *returns* to the mire. That, clearly, is the chief point; but can no reference to the *nature* of the animals have been intended? and to that, in their common use of them, could the people among whom the proverbs were current have had no reference? On the supposition that the writer believed such impure and deceitful men to have been begotten into spiritual sonship (1 Pet. 1: 3), would he have applied to them such terms as 'dog' and 'sow'? 1 John 2: 19 should be noted. The descriptions of ver. 20 (*escaped*, etc.) and of ver. 21 (*known the* way, etc.), are indeed just such terms as might have been applied to regenerated persons, but there is nothing unreasonable in the supposition that

the application was made on the ground of their *appearance*. They once appeared to be renewed persons; they had professed to be such. That would be sufficient to justify such phraseology. The question should be answered, not in support of a theological system, be the system either this or that, but in view of what the word of God teaches. It may seem to be *possible* that regenerated men, falling from grace, may never be restored, and may therefore be forever lost; but a thorough examination of all the passages bearing on the question makes it quite certain that God has made provision for preventing the possibility from ever becoming a fact. Praise to his grace!

CRITICAL NOTE.—CHAPTER II.

12. The Common Version makes **natural** (φυσικὰ) an adjective belonging like **brute** (ἄλογα) to **beasts** (ζῷα), but the four oldest manuscripts have the adjective after the participle **made** (γεγενημένα), and this reading is adopted by most of the ablest critics. On that ground the above rendering is admissible.

PART II. SECTION SECOND.

Ch. 3. This section warns the readers against the mockers of the final coming of Christ, exhorts to constant expectation of that coming, and, after referring to Paul, urges them to grow in the grace and knowledge of Christ. It is both stimulating and strengthening.

1. This second—a reference to his First Epistle. It aids in confirming the belief that this is not a forgery, but was written by Peter himself. **Beloved**—a touch of affection all the more tender after the resounding of the blows laid upon the heretics. He employs the same loving address in 1 Pet. 2: 11; 4: 12. **Now write. Now** qualifies **second.** This *now second* Epistle; or, this Epistle I write as already the second. **In both which.** Though

2 That ye may be mindful of the words which were spoken before by the holy prophets, and of the commandment of us the apostles of the Lord and Saviour:
3 Knowing this first, that there shall come in the last days scoffers, walking after their own lusts,
4 And saying, Where is the promise of his coming? for since the fathers fell asleep, all things continue as *they were* from the beginning of the creation.

2 sincere mind by putting you in remembrance; that ye should remember the words which were spoken before by the holy prophets, and the commandment of the Lord and Saviour through your apostles:
3 knowing this first, that [1] in the last days mockers shall come with mockery, walking after their own
4 lusts, and saying, Where is the promise of his [2] coming? for, from the day that the fathers fell asleep, all things continue as they were from the beginning of the creation. For this they wilfully

1 Gr. *in the last of the days*......2 Gr. *presence.*

---

the English supplies *both*, it was unnecessary to print it in italics, for *which* being in the plural number, 'both' is necessary to a clear rendering. **Stir up,** etc. See on 1: 13. How the anxiety of the aged apostle repeats itself! His longing heart could not rest till it had poured itself out once more, this time embracing the elect of all lands. (1:1.) **Pure.** The Greek, a beautiful compound word, literally means, *judged in sunlight.*

2. Here is mentioned that which he desires them to keep in remembrance: **the words spoken before**—in former ages, before the birth of the Saviour. **The holy prophets** were therefore those of the former dispensation. (1: 19-21; 1 Pet. 1: 10-12.) **Us**—rather, *your,* the authority for which is strong. The idea may be expressed thus: and *of your apostles' commandment of the Lord and Saviour*—that is, of the commandment which your apostles received from the Lord. It is a general expression, including himself as well as other apostles. **Commandment.** See on *holy commandment* in 2: 21. **Lord and Saviour** —the same being. (2: 20.) Peter had not, like some in later times, lost his interest in the Old Testament. We learn here also that in authority the writings of the apostles are equal to the gospels. See on 1 Pet. 2: 6.

3. Knowing this first. See on the same phrase in 1: 20. **Last days.** See on 1 Pet. 1: 5. The margin of the Revision says: "Gr. *in the last of the days.*" **Scoffers, mockers** —so rendered, Jude 18. According to the Greek now authorized, *mockers in mockery*— that is, when they mock they are in their element, and the converse is true, that when they are in their element they mock. **Walking after**—(*according to*) **their own lusts**— their customary mode of life. 'Their own'; in the original a strong expression and seldom found in the Greek of the New Testament. It is also used in ver. 16. The persons here mentioned seem to be different from those described in chap. 2, for their characteristic is denial of the second advent of Christ; yet like them they have no piety and indulge in the lowest kind of immorality. Compare 1 Tim. 4: 1; 2 Tim. 3: 1-4.

4. Saying. The spirit of mockery will not restrain itself; it will flash out in taunting words. **Where?**—a more contemptuous form of denying than a direct affirmation. See Mal. 2: 17; Ps. 42: 3. The affirmative, the promise of his coming has failed, would have been too weak to express the spirit of the mockers. Infidelity is a system of stubborn negation; skepticism of contemptuous interrogation. Interrogation often leads to negation. **Of his coming**—Christ's second coming, with special reference to the judgment of the wicked. **For.** Even skepticism can use the language of inspired reasoners, but its reasoning is neither logical nor Scriptural. **The fathers**—the ancestors of the human race, or the founders of the Jewish nation, or the first generation of Christians. The first is the least probable; strong considerations lie against the second; and even the last supposition is not free from difficulty. On the whole is to be preferred those to whom the promise of the second coming was made—that is, the prophets (1: 19 compared with 1: 16; Heb. 1: 1; 1 Pet. 1: 10, 11) of ancient times, to whom may be added all who were in hearty sympathy with them. The connection between **since the fathers fell asleep** and **from the beginning of creation** is not clear. "From the time when the fathers fell asleep" gives one point of departure, and "from the beginning of the creation" gives, apparently, a different point. Perhaps the idea is this: since the fathers fell asleep all things so continue, and indeed all things so continue from the beginning of creation. The argument of the mockers is this: "From the time when the universe was made, nature has swept on its way with great uniformity"; and,

5 For this they willingly are ignorant of, that by the word of God the heavens were of old, and the earth standing out of the water and in the water:
6 Whereby the world that then was, being overflowed with water, perished:
7 But the heavens and the earth, which are now, by

forget, that there were heavens from of old, and an earth compacted out of water, and ¹ amidst water,
6 by the word of God; by which means the world that then was, being overflowed with water, perished:
7 but the heavens that now are, and the earth, by the

1 Or, *through*.

---

applying this general thought to the case in hand, their argument more specially expressed is, that the uniformity has not been broken since the time when, as Christians affirmed, a promise was made that Christ would come a second time. The question 'Where is the promise of his coming?' is still heard, and, under the broader generalizations of modern discovery, is not less persistently and contemptuously asked than in early Christian times. Even ministers and churches are giving little attention to that blessed event which so fired the heart of our apostle. See on 1 Pet. 4: 7.

5. For. The apostle accounts for their skepticism, and at the same time opposes it. **This**—what follows—**that by the word of God,** etc. **Ignorant** they are, *hidden from* them it is; but their ignorance is voluntary, and voluntary in the largest sense of the word —that is, it implies both an act of the will and a depraved state of the affections. Willing ignorance is conscious ignorance; and this is more nearly universal than most apologizers for human sinfulness are disposed to admit. **That,** etc. The point which Peter makes is this: The creation of the earth, and the attendant material heavens, was effected *by God;* and it was God who, after a long period of apparent sameness in the operations of nature, made a sudden and miraculous change in the condition of the earth and its inhabitants; yet it was unexpected by most of the people then living—nay, they scoffed at it. That change was effected by means of water. However great the disposition to mock, God can, and will, effect another change on the same heavens and earth; and that can be effected by fire. It is at the time of such a change that Christ will come. *The word of God*—not the second person of the Trinity, as in John 1: 1. See Gen. 1: 3, 6, 9, 11, 14, etc. ("And God said.") Speaking was equivalent to acting. Even if it should be conceded that the method in which creation came into being was exclusively by "development," that method would have been an expression of the will of an Intelligent and Almighty Being. **Of old** is to be referred to the beginning of things. (Gen. 1: 1.) **Standing**—*constituted.* "'The earth,' says Peter, 'was *constituted out of* water,' out of the material contained in the water—not, ' rose up out of water.'" **In the water**—*by means of water.* The earth was formed by means of water (Gen. 1: 6, 7, 9, 10)— "*i. e.,* through the action of water, which partly retired to the low places, and partly formed the clouds in the sky." (Winer.) Another view is possible—that water yielded its solid particles for the formation of the earth. The account given by most heathen nations respecting the origin of water and land is very absurd compared with the representation given in the Scriptures.

6. Whereby—*by which* (means). The reference is doubtful, and is the more so because the pronoun is in the plural. It is referred by some to *heavens* and *earth*—by the heavens pouring down their waters, and the earth pouring them forth. But *world* here means *heaven* and *earth.* It is the destruction of the material world, involving, indeed, the destruction of men and animals, to which the writer is referring; and, therefore, he could not have meant to say, by which heavens and earth the heavens and earth were made to perish. Some say: *In consequence of which arrangement of things.* Others refer it to *water,* and account for the plural by making a double reference to water "as the material out of which water was formed, and to water as the means by which the earthy part of the globe was made," or, as Huther adds, "which is more natural, to the word of God as well as to water, so that *whereby* (δια ὧν) is to be translated, *by which things.*" **Overflowed . . . perished**—not annihilated, but changed. The change was miraculous. It did not occur as a mere development of natural law. It was effected by the direct touch of the hand of God, breaking up the natural order of things. See Crit. Notes.

7. But contrasts destruction by water and destruction by fire. **The heavens,** etc. 'The

the same word are kept in store, reserved unto fire against the day of judgment and perdition of ungodly men.

8 But, beloved, be not ignorant of this one thing, that one day *is* with the Lord as a thousand years, and a thousand years as one day.

same word have been ¹ stored up for fire, being reserved against the day of judgment and destruction of ungodly men.

8 But forget not this one thing, beloved, that one day is with the Lord as a thousand years, and a
9 thousand years as one day. The Lord is not slack

1 Or, *stored with fire.*

---

heavens' which are now is contrasted with *the world that then was.* **Kept in store ... fire.** The Greek allows 'fire' to be brought in earlier; thus, as in the Revised Version, *stored up for fire,* or stored up *with* fire. **Reserved**—or, *being* reserved (while they are reserved). See upon ver. 10. This, with the related statements in ver. 10, 12, 13, is an instance of Peter's originality, though remote allusions to the destruction of the earth even by fire, as connected with God's coming to punish, are numerous. (Ps. 50: 3; 97: 3; 102: 26; Isa. 34: 4; 51: 6; 66: 15.) Such allusion is made in the words of Christ: "Heaven and earth shall pass away" (Matt. 24: 35), by the writer of Hebrews (12: 26, 27), and by Paul. (2 Thess. 1: 8.) Very striking is the implication in Isa. 66: 22.

This representation of the certainty of the world's destruction appears to be confirmed by recent scientific conclusions. "Our earth is approaching a finality through various causes of change. Its surface is wearing out, and its lands becoming sea-sediments. Its progressive refrigeration will result in the complete absorption of atmosphere and water. Tidal action will slacken the rate of rotation until each side is turned alternately two weeks toward the scorching sun, and two weeks toward the cold regions of space. If this is not enough, the sun is destined to be extinguished, and the earth to be precipitated upon the central funeral pile of our system. Any one of these contingencies demonstrates that the duration of the habitable globe is limited." (Alexander Winchell, LL. D., Professor, University of Michigan, "Journal of Christian Philosophy," Vol. I, No. 3.) "We can see distinctly many causes in operation which must finally result in an entire change of conditions for the earth, and ultimately, unless the course of affairs is somehow arrested in a way we cannot even guess at now, must terminate in its lifelessness or destruction." (C. A. Young, LL. D., Professor, Princeton College, *idem,* Vol. I, No. 2.) Says the same distinguished astronomer, when speaking of the one solar problem, "which excites the deepest and most general interest "—" that relating to the solar heat "—" I perceive no reason to doubt the final cessation of the sun's activity, and the consequent death of the system." ("Christian Thought.") The gradual shrinking of the earth's orbit, and *the falling of the earth upon the sun,* millions of millions of years from the present, seems to be a necessary result of certain existing conditions. It is added that "almost certainly one thing, of great and decisive importance to the planetary system, will happen before the earth has approached the sun a single mile under this meteoric action."

But the reason why the heavens and the earth are reserved is yet to be stated: they are reserved with reference to the day of judgment, and of the destruction of godless men. The day of judgment will indeed be the day of perdition (destruction, not annihilation) for the godless.

8. The apostle proves from the nature of the divine mind in relation to time, that the objection of the scoffers (ver. 4) is groundless. They say: *All things so continue from the beginning of creation;* there has been delay in Christ's coming, and the delay has been so great that we have the right to believe that Christ will never come at all. But, says the apostle, the Lord's conception of duration is such that the argument from long delay is without force. To his infinite mind a thousand years are as one day: not that even the Lord sees no more duration in a thousand years than he sees in one day, but so far as respects the accomplishment of his purposes, a thousand years' delay is no more to him than one hour's delay. The first part of the reply, one **day as a thousand years,** was doubtless suggested to the apostle by Ps. 90: 4 (perhaps he intended it as a quotation); but not seeming to be a pertinent reply to the skeptics, he adds, as his own conception, **a thousand years as one day.** Peter's estimate of this view is such that he gives it much prominence in the words, **this one thing,** and also in the emphatic position which he gives them. In

9 The Lord is not slack concerning his promise, as some men count slackness; but is longsuffering to us-ward, not willing that any should perish, but that all should come to repentance.

10 But the day of the Lord will come as a thief in the night; in the which the heavens shall pass away with

the Greek, thus: *But this one thing permit not to be hidden from you* (do not lose sight of it).

9. That there has been delay in the fulfillment of the promise is clear; but has this delay been of the nature of dilatoriness? Has the Lord shown slackness? Slackness is the result of indifference or of inability; has the delay resulted from either? **Not slack**, says our apostle with characteristic positiveness. Man has not the "*standard*" time. **As some men count slackness**—not *as some think it* (the delay) *to be slackness*, but as some *judge what slackness is*. Some think delay to be slackness; not by such a "standard" is God to be judged. Is the delay, then, the result of arbitrariness? May not the Lord have some benevolent end in view? **Long-suffering.** God's tender forbearance toward men is the true explanation. (1 Pet. 3: 20; Luke 18: 7.) **To us-ward**—toward *you*, according to the better reading, 'you' referring to the readers; but as the remainder of the verse refers to men in general, it is most natural to suppose that these also are included. **Not willing.** *Purposing* that none shall perish would be neither a fair expression of the meaning, nor a justifiable inference. The original expresses inclination, disposition. God's disposition is such that he has no desire in itself that men perish; and hence, to affirm, as does the theological system of Dr. Emmons, that God creates sinful volitions in men (in Pharaoh, for example) for the purpose of "damning" them, is untrue, and in the highest degree derogatory to the character of God. Peter here has nothing to say concerning that eternal and loving purpose by which the sufferings of the Son are prevented from being borne in vain; but he is accounting for the delay of Christ's coming to judge the world. The judgment is delayed, in order that, if possible, all men may be saved. If men are lost before Christ comes, it is not because no opportunity to be saved is given them. **Should come**—to repentance; should *enter into* repentance. And by 're-pentance' is meant a change of mind, and

concerning his promise, as some count slackness; but is longsuffering to you-ward, not wishing that any should perish, but that all should come to re-
10 pentance. But the day of the Lord will come as a thief; in the which the heavens shall pass away

also a corresponding change of conduct, and in relation to God not less than in relation to men. The attempt has been made to apply the last clause to the elect, thus: not willing that any of the elect should perish, but that all of them should enter into repentance. Theology must not attempt to overmaster interpretation; nor will Scriptural theology make the attempt. The words cannot be restricted to the elect. Compare Mark 16: 15; 1 Tim. 2: 4; Ezek. 18: 23; 33: 11. The reference to men in general is so much more natural that it is to be preferred. Disharmony between the view which the apostle gives here and that in 1 Pet. 1: 2 cannot be shown. The lesson from this verse is twofold: encouragement to Christians—for the delay does not spring from dilatoriness; and to all men—for it gives opportunity for repentance.

10. **But the day of the Lord will come** warns against the presumption that in consequence of the long-suffering of God the coming of Christ may never occur. The emphasis is remarkable: *But come will* the day of the Lord. It is possible that *but* was intended to direct back to ver. 4. The scoffers say: '*Where?*' '*But*,' says the apostle, 'that day will come.' 'The day of the Lord'; a striking expression, since all days are days of the Lord In ver. 12 it is called 'the day of *God*,' yet God's day is the day of the coming of Christ. (ver. 4.) See James 5: 7; 2 Thess. 2: 2. ("The day of *Christ*.") The phrase was used in the times of the prophets. (Joel 1: 15; Ezek. 13: 5; Isa. 2: 12.) To the elect the day of the Lord will be resplendent with joy; to scoffers and sleepers a day of dismay and despair. **As a thief**—unexpectedly and suddenly. Our apostle's Divine Teacher used the same comparison (Matt. 24: 43, 44); and Paul. (1 Thess. 5: 2.) To those who live in continual expectation of the coming of Christ, that coming cannot be sudden (1 Thess. 5: 4); and in that state of expectancy it is most precious to be. A name to live while one is dead will make Christ's coming like the coming of a thief. (Rev. 3: 3.) See the letter to the Church in Sardis. **In the night**—the Greek not found

a great noise, and the elements shall melt with fervent heat, the earth also and the works that are therein shall be burned up.
11 Seeing then *that* all these things shall be dissolved, what manner *of persons* ought ye to be in *all* holy conversation and godliness,

with a great noise, and the [1] elements shall be dissolved with fervent heat, and the earth and the
11 works that are therein shall be [2] burned up. Seeing that these things are thus all to be dissolved, what manner of persons ought ye to be in *all* holy
12 living and godliness, looking for and [3] earnestly

1 Or, *heavenly bodies*......2 The most ancient manuscripts read *discovered*......3 Or, *hastening*.

in the best manuscripts. **In the which**—in the which *day*. **The heavens**—the visible heavens surrounding the earth. **Will pass away**—compare comments on ver. 13. **With a great noise**—the rendering of but one word (an adverb), and used in the New Testament by Peter only (ῥοιζηδόν). Farrar ("Early Days of Christianity") gives it the remarkable rendering, *hurtlingly!* The Revised Version adheres to the more simple rendering of the Common Version. Like *rasp, rattling*, and many other words, the sound of the Greek word, in pronunciation, corresponds with the sound of the act intended to be expressed. The English seems to have no word which is like it in both sense and sound. "The crackling of destructive fire," "the noise of falling houses," "crashing roar," have all been suggested as expressive of the sense. **The elements**—"the component parts of the physical world" (Robinson); perhaps, as some say, *the stars, sun, and moon*. Revision, in the margin, "Or, *heavenly bodies.*" **Shall melt**, etc.—literally, *the elements being burnt, shall be dissolved;* that is, they shall be destroyed by being burnt. **The works that are therein**—both the works of man, and the natural material found upon and within the earth. "This grand epoch in the physical world, represented by the burning of the earth and the melting of the elements, preparatory to a new cycle of the divine manifestations, which the glorified will see, but which it is not permitted us to understand, is connected with the coming of Christ, the resurrection of the dead, and the final judgment." Professor Samuel Harris, D. D., LL. D. ("Bib. Sac.," Jan., 1873). There is in the text no intimation that these great events are to be followed by a millennium. Compare 2 Tim. 4: 1. The wide prevalence of Christianity, with the consequent prevalence of holiness and peace, is to precede the dissolution of the earth, the resurrection, and the general judgment. One of the theories of the premillenial advent of Christ is "that the righteous dead will be raised, living believers changed, and yet the race be continued by natural generation; all, or nearly all, who are born, being converted in early life. In the millennium, therefore, Christ will reign with his saints in their glorified bodies over the race of mankind in their natural bodies. It" [the above view] "is inconsistent with the language of Peter. (2 Pet. 3: 10-13.) For this language predicts such a dissolving of the earth by fire as will make it a new earth, if the new earth be not rather wholly distinct from it." (President Hovey.)

11. **Seeing**, etc.—literally, *all these things dissolving*, in view of the fact that they *are dissolving*, the apostle conceives the change as even now in the process of accomplishment; either, 1. Because dissolution is inherent in the nature of things (Winer), or, 2. Because God, having willed it, it is certain to occur. Winer gives the participle (λυομένων) the sense of the present. Buttmann would justify the Revisers; for he says that present participles are frequently used in a future sense, and adduces this very case. (§ 137, p. 206.) The word here translated 'dissolved' is the same as is rendered in ver. 10 'shall melt.' The researches of modern science afford a striking confirmation of those inspired representations. See the citations in the comments on ver. 7. **What manner**—possibly a question, perhaps an exclamation. Assuming the former, some make the question end at **be**, and consider all that follows to the end of ver. 12 as the answer; but others extend the question to **godliness**. 'What manner' refers to quality of Christian character. **Ought**—here the obligation seems to be put only on the ground of the dissolution of the earth; but the context shows that with this are connected the other great final events, including (ver. 14) even their own entrance into the peace and purity of heaven. **Holy conversation and godliness**. The Greek words are in the plural: all *forms* of holy deportment and piety. Query: How much are the people of God to-day incited by such a motive to seek such a character?

12 Looking for and hasting unto the coming of the day of God, wherein the heavens being on fire shall be dissolved, and the elements shall melt with fervent heat?
13 Nevertheless we, according to his promise, look for new heavens and a new earth, wherein dwelleth righteousness.
14 Wherefore, beloved, seeing that ye look for such things, be diligent that ye may be found of him in peace, without spot, and blameless.
15 And account *that* the longsuffering of our Lord *is* salvation; even as our beloved brother Paul also ac-

desiring the ¹coming of the day of God, by reason of which the heavens being on fire shall be dissolved, and the ²elements shall melt with fervent
13 heat? But, according to his promise, we look for new heavens and a new earth, wherein dwelleth righteousness.
14 Wherefore, beloved, seeing that ye look for these things, give diligence that ye may be found in peace,
15 without spot and blameless in his sight. And account that the longsuffering of our Lord is salvation; even as our beloved brother Paul also, accord-

1 Gr. *presence*......2 Or. *heavenly bodies.*

12. Looking for—expecting it. **Hasting unto**—*hastening*. The Greek has no word for 'unto.' See Matt. 22 : 42, 44; 1 Thess. 1: 10. The readers are exhorted *to hasten the coming*, etc. The day was fixed in the purpose of God; yet, by constant growth in holiness (ver. 18), and by effort, in accordance with God's longsuffering (ver. 9), to turn men to Christ, they are to hasten its coming. Compare Phil. 3: 20; Tit. 2: 13. As always, so here, the point of harmony between God's purpose and man's activity eludes us. **Wherein**—on account of which day, or, perhaps, on account of the coming of which day. The meaning is, that the coming of the day will be *the occasion of* the destruction of the heavens and the earth. As to the remainder, see on ver. 10.

13. Nevertheless expresses the contrast too strongly; *but* is preferable **New heavens and a new earth** is put first in the Greek for emphasis; but new heavens and earth new, according to his promise, we look for. **Promise.** (Isa. 65: 17; 66: 22.) **Righteousness** —to the exclusion forever of all unrighteousness is certainly implied. It cannot, therefore, refer to the condition of human society on earth, after the supposed second advent of Christ, during what some regard as the Millennium; for Premillenarianism teaches that toward the end of the period unrighteousness will again arise. 'New heavens and a new earth'—a figurative representation of the resurrection bliss of that heaven to which Christ ascended, where he now is, and will be forever. There is, neither here nor elsewhere in the Epistles of Peter, evidence that the earth, after its destruction, will be refitted as a dwelling-place for the elect. Innumerable passages show that heaven has already an actual existence, and the supposition that that will be deserted for another, or that there will be at length two heavens, the one there and the other here, is groundless. That heaven, strictly so called, is now elsewhere. See, among many other passages, Matt. 6: 9; John 14: 2, 3; 16: 28; 17: 24; Acts 7: 56; Phil. 1: 23; 1 Tim. 6: 7.

14. Wherefore—a sign of inference. *In view* of what is said in the preceding verse as the object of their expectation. **Seeing that** ye **look**—*looking for, expecting*—the same form as in ver. 12. **Be diligent** (*earnest*), as in 1: 10, 15; translated in Hebrews, "let us labor." **That ye may be found of him.** What Peter meant to express by the pronoun is not clear. The meaning will depend on the connection supposed to exist. Does he mean to say, *blameless by him?* or, *may be found by him?* The former, probably. But possibly the rendering should be, *for him.* Consult Winer § 31, 10, p. 219, and Buttmann § 133, p. 179, and § 134, p. 187. It is rendered in the Revised Version, "*in his sight,*" and is connected with *blameless.* Notice the doubleness of the motive: 1. The dissolution of the earth (ver. 11); 2. The possession of a new earth. (Ver. 13.) **In peace.** Compare John 14: 27. How different with the wicked, first in this life (Isa. 57: 20, 21), and then in the next! (Rev. 14: 11.) Sorrow over the immoralities and errors of men, and even indignation at the more Satanic forms of sin, are possible in connection with habitual desire to be found by Christ in peace.

15. The long-suffering—already referred to in ver. 9. **Is salvation**—equivalent to salvation, for it gives them time to make their calling and election sure. (1: 10.) Such delay for such a purpose is not, however, absolutely necessary; otherwise the converted robber (Luke 23: 40-43) needed more evidence that he would be saved than his brief period of repentance gave him. Very beautiful and magnanimous is the reference to Paul, and the more so inasmuch as Peter was once the object of Paul's rebuke. (Gal. 2: 11, 12.) Peter's

cording to the wisdom given unto him hath written unto you;

16 As also in all *his* epistles, speaking in them of these things; in which are some things hard to be understood, which they that are unlearned and unstable wrest, as *they do* also the other Scriptures, unto their own destruction.

17 Ye therefore, beloved, seeing ye know *these things* before, beware lest ye also, being led away with the error of the wicked, fall from your own steadfastness.

16 ing to the wisdom given to him, wrote unto you; as also in all *his* epistles, speaking in them of these things; wherein are some things hard to be understood, which the ignorant and unstedfast wrest, as *they do* also the other scriptures, unto their own destruction.

17 Ye therefore, beloved, knowing *these things* beforehand, beware lest, being carried away with the error of the wicked, ye fall from your own

18 stedfastness. But grow in the grace and knowledge

fault was serious, and had not God already raised up a man having broad views and a decided will, and had Peter been willful and stubborn, it is impossible to say what harm the infant religion might not have suffered. A note in the Douay Version calls Peter's act "only a certain imprudence"; which is intended to save the reputation of "the founder" of the Romish Church, but, as it detracts proportionally from the value of Peter's allusion to Paul, little is gained for "the founder." **Wisdom given him**—partly natural, chiefly supernatural. **Hath written**—*wrote*. **Unto you.** See 1: 1. What epistle or epistles Peter means cannot be determined. It has been assumed by too many that he must refer to an epistle sent to Christians of Asia Minor; but the present Epistle was not sent to them alone, but to all who had obtained like precious faith. The epistle or epistles intended may have been written to the Ephesians or to the Colossians, but they must be presumed to have come into circulation among those to whom Peter's Second Epistle was sent. This supposition will explain the 'you.'

16. **All his epistles.** Probably all Paul's epistles were written before this time, and most of them must have attained circulation among other churches besides those to which they were sent. Nearly all of them touch some of the subjects which Peter presents, and some make extended allusion to them. **In which**—either among *which things*, or, with another form of the Greek pronoun (more probably correct), *in which epistles*. **Hard to be understood**—not only some things which are common to Paul and Peter, but some things which only Paul has presented. See for example, the 9th chapter of Romans; 1 Cor. 15; 2 Cor. 12: 1-7; Gal. 3: 24-28; 4: 21-31; 1 Thess. 4: 13-17; 2 Thess. 2: 1-12; and, assuming that Paul wrote it, many things in Hebrews. A book professing to come from a Being of infinite wisdom, yet with nothing in it which needs to be *studied*, nothing which, even with hard study, could not be understood in this life, might be presumed to be more human than divine. The Scriptures, as a whole, are easy to be understood—much easier to most men than books originated with men themselves upon philosophy and law. **Unlearned**—not learned in spiritual truth. **Unstable.** See on 2: 14. The adjectives have but one article; they apply, therefore, to the same class of persons. Ignorance and instability—a well-matched pair, but bad for good service. Knowledge of divine things the best foundation. **Wrest** —by perverting the meaning, which is often done. **The other scriptures.** The article points, apparently, to all the current sacred writings in addition to Paul's—that is, to the Old Testament, the Gospels, the Acts, and perhaps Peter's First Epistle. **Unto** indicates result. **Their own destruction.** Eternal punishment (Matt. 25: 46), is *the result* to which their perversion of the Scriptures leads. In attempting to destroy the Bible men destroy themselves.

17, 18. These verses condense the exhortation which runs through the Epistle. In the beginning the apostle desires that *grace* may be multiplied unto them through the *knowledge* of God, and here, at the end, he exhorts them *to grow* in grace and knowledge. **Therefore**—in view of all that I have said. **Seeing ye know**—*knowing;* the same form of expression as in ver. 11, 14. 'Know.' What? For no object is expressed in the original. Know that lustful mockers are to come. (Ver. 3.) They know it *beforehand*, before they come; for they learn it through this very Epistle. Peter's prophecy will not fail, for it is Christ who speaks through him. Ye also. 'Also' has no corresponding word in the original, and it makes the contrast between the readers and others too great. **Error.** See on the same word. (2: 18.) **The wicked**— *the lawless*, as in 2: 7. **Fall from**—a warning against apostasy. See Query, at the close of comments on 2: 22. **Your own stedfast-**

18 But grow in grace, and *in* the knowledge of our Lord and Saviour Jesus Christ. To him *be* glory both now and for ever. Amen.

of our Lord and Saviour Jesus Christ. To him *be* the glory both now and [1] for ever. Amen.

---

[1] Gr. *unto the day of eternity.*

ness—not originating with them, for that general virtue is not less the fruit of the Holy Spirit than particular virtue. (Gal. 5: 22, 23,) A quiet contrast between their own steadfastness and the instability of those mentioned in ver. 16 may be intended. Steadfastness is not merely continued adherence to the Church, its creeds and rites; but, while including that, adherence to Christ in spiritual life. **But grow**—not *fall from* (ver. 17), but on the contrary, *grow*. Satisfaction with present attainments may prove the beginning of a fall; growth is the only security. **Grace**—holiness, but with reference to its origin as a gift of unmerited mercy, and here called the grace of Christ. **Knowledge.** *Grow in grace and in the knowledge.* The repetition of *in* before knowledge, and the use of the article in the one case, and not in the other, has the effect to separate growing in grace too widely from growing in knowledge: *in the grace and knowledge* is better. Growth in the knowledge of Christ is indispensable to growth in the grace of Christ. Ignorance cuts the sinews of spiritual growth. INFERENCE: The more knowledge ministers have the better for their people, as well as for themselves; the more they have, the more, in that respect, are they like God. The church which cares little whether its religious teacher be well furnished with knowledge, dishonors the all-knowing Saviour more than words can express. Preaching which is not instructive, but "saws the air too much," "tearing a passion to tatters," and "o'ersteps the modesty of nature"; preaching which is "overdone or come tardy off," "making the unskillful laugh and the judicious grieve"—"pray you avoid it."

The doxology. See on 1 Peter 1: 3; 4: 11. The form here employed varies from that found in 1 Pet. 4: 11. It is, literally: *To whom the glory both now and unto the day of eternity.* The remarkable combination of *day* and *eternity* may have been unconsciously suggested to the writer by what he had already said in ver. 8. Bengel: "Eternity is a *day*, without night, unmixed and perpetual." Hutter: "The day in which eternity begins as contrasted with time, but which day is also eternity itself." **Amen.** See on 1 Pet. 4: 11.

CRITICAL NOTE.—CHAPTER III.

Says Winer: "In 2 Pet. 3: 6, ὕδατι [*water*] would not be superfluous, even if ὑδάτων were supplied with δἰ ὧν [whereby]; it would designate water as an element, whereas ὕδατα (comp. Gen. 7: 11) would signify the concrete (separate) bodies of water. Comp. further Jude 4."

www.ingramcontent.com/pod-product-compliance
Lightning Source LLC
Chambersburg PA
CBHW020141170426
43199CB00010B/836